Five in a Row

Volume Six

Inspired learning through great books.

Ages 10-12

Second Edition

By Becky Jane Lambert

Introduction by Jane Claire Lambert

Five in a Row Volume Six

ISBN 978-1-888659-28-3

Published by:
Five in a Row Publishing
312 SW Greenwich Dr.
Suite 220
Lee's Summit, MO 64082
816-866-8500

Send all requests for information to the above address.

Units for *Thomas A. Edison: Young Inventor* and *Homer Price* were originally published in *Beyond Five in a Row, Volume 1*; the unit for *Sarah, Plain and Tall* was originally published in *Beyond Five in a Row, Volume 2*; and the unit for *The Saturdays* was originally published in *Beyond Five in a Row, Volume 3*. All of these units have been revised for inclusion in Volume 6.

Many Five in a Row units contain go-along titles that complement the FIAR book selection. Since every family and every child is different, it's important to preview these additional titles before reading aloud or giving to your child to read.

For my father, mother and sister—
You believed in me when I didn't believe in myself.
Always remember and never forget, I love you!

And for Matt and Megan—
Two of my favorites.

Contents

Introduction

Good books have always been the doorway to learning. That doorway leads to growth and an appreciation for the wonders around us. The *Five in a Row* curriculum was created to bring excitement and fun to learning and to enrich children's lives through wonderful children's literature. This foundation is evident in every volume, beginning with *Before Five in a Row*.

Continuing this unique and effective way of learning, **Five in a Row Volume 6** contains **complete units for four chapter books and accompanying lessons** (selections that were formerly published in *Beyond Five in a Row Volumes 1, 2,* and *3*). These units are designed for students aged 10 through 12; many of these students will have used earlier *Five in a Row* volumes and both teacher and student will be familiar with the very similar approach to learning in Volume 6.

Just as in previous FIAR volumes, the chapter book units in Volume 6 are intended to be extremely flexible, allowing you the option to do any combination of the lessons for each chapter. You may elect to skip over certain lessons which do not fit the needs of your student and you may place additional emphasis on certain ones which seem appropriate. You will find more exercises than you can use, so enjoy choosing just the right lesson elements for your students.

You can adjust school time to fit your needs as well. By using only one lesson element each day, you can work through *Five in a Row* in as little as 30-60 minutes daily, including the time to read the chapter. If you choose to use all or most of the lesson elements, field trips and follow-up exercises, you could easily spend several hours daily. Use *Five in a Row* however it best suits your needs and the needs of your students. The more lessons you do together, or that your student does independently, the more skills that will be acquired—skills which will benefit them through high school, college and throughout life!

Five in a Row chapter book units are complete studies that cover Social Studies (including History, Geography, and Career Paths), Science, Language Arts (including Writing and Discussion Questions and Vocabulary), Fine Arts, and Life Skills. You'll also find Teacher's Notes pages for every title, providing a place to record lessons, go-along resources, favorite memories, and more; and Activity Sheets for every chapter that support and add to the lessons.

As with all volumes of *Five in a Row*, the purpose and mission remain the same: to provide students with "inspired learning through great books." You are the leader for this adventure, so gather the children around you and have a great time!

Jane Claire Lambert, author and creator of *Five in a Row*
February 2022

Tips and Advice for Five in a Row Chapter Book Studies

• There is **no right or wrong order** for covering the material or ordering the books. You will find that throughout the Five in a Row curriculum, some subjects are revisited once, and some several times! This repetition is intentional to remind your student of other books' lessons that have a similar theme or lesson topic. Covering the same topic in new ways or in greater depth at an older age is of great benefit to students.

• Following the individual units in this manual, you'll find **Sample Lesson Planning Sheets** (and a blank sheet for your use). These sample sheets demonstrate how you might organize your studies for two weeks of a sample unit. You can also make your own planning sheets or simply work directly from the manual.

• Keep in mind that there are **more lessons in the manual than you can use**. For each chapter, you'll be choosing the lessons that are especially suited to your student. You might choose topics you've never covered, topics you want to cover again, topics of particular interest to your student, etc.

• You'll occasionally be using **other resources such as your library or the internet** for further information or research. You may want "go-along" titles that match up with a particular lesson, a video that explains or illustrates a certain principle, or a website or book where your student can research additional information. Many times you'll find suggestions for other resources right in the lessons, but you may also desire additional resources depending on the needs of your particular student.

• These chapter book units do not include math; therefore, **you'll need to provide a separate math curriculum** for your child (this is true of all levels of Five in a Row). You'll also want to **add in the narrower language arts subjects** of grammar, spelling, and possibly continue with handwriting (printing and/or cursive) at some point (the timing on language arts may be different for different students). These subjects don't lend themselves to a unit study approach and you'll want to be sure to include them each week.

• Five in a Row was created to be gender-neutral and you'll find a wide variety of **fascinating lessons that appeal to both boys and girls**. Don't assume that a boy may not enjoy a book that has a girl as the main character, or vice versa! And, please note that we've referred to "teacher and student" in the singular. Many of you will have more than one student.

How to Use Five in a Row Volume 6

In Five in a Row chapter book units, you'll no longer be studying certain **academic subjects** on particular days of the week, as you did in early volumes of the FIAR curriculum. Instead, you'll be guiding your student into **a variety of areas each week**; some weeks will have a heavier emphasis on science while others may have a greater emphasis on fine arts, for example. What you study each week derives directly from what chapter you have just read at the time. Overall, your student will receive a comprehensive education in five principal areas:

- **Social Studies** (includes history, geography, and career paths)
- **Science**
- **Language Arts** (includes writing and discussion questions and vocabulary, among other topics)
- **Fine Arts**
- **Life Skills** (includes human relationships, problem solving, and personal development, among other topics)

If you have previously studied picture books in Five in a Row, you're already familiar with many of these subject areas. The following are areas that are new or unique to the chapter book units:

Career Paths are lessons that allow your student to explore and learn about various professions that tie in to the chapter. Use these in a way that fits the needs of your student. You may choose to skip some career paths, while others you may choose to investigate in depth, including a field trip to meet and interview someone in the profession.

Writing and Discussion Questions are found in every chapter, and can be used in different ways. You may choose to simply discuss the question together, or you may assign it as a writing topic. The length is dependent upon your student's age and ability; it may range from a few sentences to several paragraphs or a couple of pages. You can adjust the assignment length depending on your academic goals and what works best for your student.

Fine Arts lessons include such diverse topics as cooking, visual and performing arts, fabric arts and needlework, design and architecture, drama, and other creative arts.

Life Skills lessons cover a wide variety of topics and can be used as springboards for discussion or as writing assignments. The topics are especially appropriate for students ages 10 and up who are growing in maturity and learning to navigate human relationships, develop critical thinking skills, and practice problem solving for upcoming teen and adult years.

With chapter book units, you'll likely vary in the **number of chapters you read each week and the amount of time you spend each day**. Some chapters are brief and you might finish the chapter and activities in one day, but some are longer or more complex and could take up to a week to explore thoroughly. Many families find that they average about two chapters per week, but again, this is a generalization and some weeks may not follow this pattern. In addition, you'll find that amount of time varies per day with your chapter book activities. Some lessons may take only 30 minutes to complete, while some could take an hour or two, or extend to a long-term study or project.

Because chapter books vary in length and number of lessons, the **amount of time it will take you to complete a chapter book study will vary**, as well (two families could easily spend different amounts of time on the same book, even!). Each Five in a Row chapter book could take you as little as 4 to 5 weeks to finish, or as many as 8 to 9 weeks—it's up to your daily and weekly lesson plans, your student's needs, and your academic calendar. The flexibility of Five in a Row is great in all areas, including length of time spent on each unit!

Should you be reading the chapters to your student or should the student read silently? Either way works! Your student may want to read alone, or may want you to read aloud, and that's a decision you can work out together, depending on your child's reading ability and personal preference. Many children who are perfectly capable of reading to themselves still wish to be *read to*, and this could be a perfect opportunity for you to share that time together. Or, you may have a student who is more than willing to read alone—this is also just fine. A **Teacher Summary** has been provided at the beginning of every chapter for your convenience. You can take turns reading, listen while your student reads, read it aloud, let your student read alone ... there's no right or wrong way to do it. You might employ a combination of all these approaches.

Whatever method of reading you choose, you and/or your student will only **read each chapter only once**. Unlike the Five in a Row picture book units, no repetitive reading is necessary with the chapter books unless you are simply rereading a small section for a particular lesson, etc. This means that on some days, you'll read a chapter and also do a lesson; on other days, you will only do a lesson (from the same chapter) and not start a new chapter. Be sure to see the **Sample Lesson Planning Sheets** following the unit studies in this manual for a clear picture of how this works.

In each chapter's list of "What we will cover in this chapter," you'll see that one lesson is **marked with an asterisk** (there is an asterisk on the actual lesson, as well). This indicates that there is an **activity sheet** for this lesson at the end of the chapter book unit.

Thomas A. Edison:
Young Inventor

Title: *Thomas A. Edison: Young Inventor*
Author: Sue Guthridge
Copyright: 1947

Chapter 1—An Idea That Didn't Work

Teacher Summary

We are introduced to six-year-old Tom Edison. The Edison family resides in Milan, Ohio and the year is 1853. One morning, Tom has a great idea. Since warmth is what causes baby goslings to hatch and Tom is much larger and warmer than his goose Lulu, Tom concludes that if he sits on the eggs they will hatch quickly! Grabbing some ham and biscuits to sustain himself, Tom runs out to the hen house to test his idea. After Tom has been sitting carefully on the eggs for most of the afternoon, his mother, Nancy, comes out to find him. Finding him sitting atop the eggs, Nancy Edison laughs and laughs. Realizing his experiment isn't working, Tom heads back to the house to help with the chores.

What we will cover in this chapter:

Social Studies: Geography - The Great Lakes
Social Studies: History - The Erie Canal: How It Came to Be
Social Studies: Geography - Making a Map of Edison's Life*
Science: Incubating Eggs

Science: The Scientific Method*
Language Arts: Descriptive Word Choices
Language Arts: Creative Writing - Living on a Canal
Language Arts: Classic Literature Connection
Language Arts: Writing and Discussion Question
Fine Arts: Music - Folk Song: "The Erie Canal"

Social Studies: Geography - The Great Lakes

On page 12 we learn about Lake Erie and the barges. Take this opportunity to explore the Great Lakes with your student.

The Great Lakes are the five largest freshwater lakes in the world. The names of the lakes going from west to east are: **Lake Superior**, **Lake Michigan**, **Lake Huron**, **Lake Erie**, and **Lake Ontario**. Of the five, only Lake Michigan is entirely in the United States.

The other four share a common border between Canada and the U.S. The depth of the Great Lakes differs greatly. Lake Superior (its name comes from being the biggest) is over 1,300 feet deep. Lake Erie, the smallest lake and the one cited in our story, is only 210 feet deep.

Your student might have heard of many Great Lakes locations including Niagara Falls (the falls are caused by level differences between Lake Erie and Lake Ontario), Straits of Mackinac (MACK i naw, between Lake Michigan and Lake Huron) and Lake St. Clair (mentioned in our story in chapter 2). If you live near the Great Lakes, by all means take a day trip and visit! Such a massive body of water is always an awesome sight. If you do not, look for information, pictures, and videos online or at your library on the Great Lakes. Using the map of the Great Lakes that follows the Teacher's Notes at the end of this unit, have your student label each of the lakes.

Social Studies: History - The Erie Canal: How It Came to Be

On page 12 Lake Erie is mentioned. Take some time to talk with your student about the famous Erie Canal. The man behind this huge project was named De Witt Clinton. Mr. Clinton became governor of New York in 1817 and on the Fourth of July, 1817, men broke ground in Rome, New York for the canal. It took eight years to build and was completed in 1825. The first ship to traverse the canal's full length was the *Seneca Chief* on October 26, 1825. The canal cost over $7 million and was paid for entirely by the state of New York. Interestingly, during the 60 years while tolls were collected (tolls were abolished in 1882) over $121 million was collected by the state!

A classic book about the Erie Canal published by Landmark Books in 1953, is *The Erie Canal* by Samuel Hopkins Adams. Another excellent title is *The Amazing Impossible Erie Canal* by Cheryl Harness. Other books will likely be available at your library, or you can find photos online.

You and your student also might want to delve into the study of other important canals. The Panama and Suez are two of the more famous. Look online or go to your local library and find some books on each. One such resource you should look for is entitled *Locks, Crocs & Skeeters: The Story of the Panama Canal* by Nancy Winslow Parker. Including excellent maps, description and interesting details, this book makes the Panama Canal come to life! (Also, you may want to consider comparing the dates of the building of the Erie, Panama and Suez Canals as well as their locations.)

Social Studies: Geography - Making a Map of Edison's Life*

Throughout this story you will read about many towns, regions, lakes and sites which were a part of Thomas Alva Edison's life. Using the map of the Great Lakes that follows the Teacher's Notes at the end of this unit (you may already have the Great Lakes labeled, from the previous lesson), mark each site on the map as you read about it. By looking at a real map of the state or region you can then visually locate it on your map.

For this first chapter your student might want to map out several of the locations mentioned, including Milan (Ohio), Huron River, Lake Erie, Detroit, and New York City. As our study of Edison's life continues, you will be reminded to continue to identify additional landmarks on your map.

Science: Incubating Eggs

Tom Edison thought he could hatch an egg! He knew warmth was necessary (page 18) but he thought he could speed up the process! What is involved in hatching an egg?

The story of Tom's experience with the eggs centers on unhatched goslings—baby geese. The usual incubation period (time the mother has to sit on the eggs) for geese is 28-32 days. Chicken eggs, a more common variety for most of us, have an incubation period of approximately 21 days. A hen will lay one egg a day until she has a full nest (generally 6-10 eggs, but never more than one a day). If the eggs become cold, even for a few hours, the chicks will die. The hen only leaves the nest for a moment at a time to feed. As the mother hen sits on the nest, she will routinely turn the eggs over.

If you have the opportunity, try incubating chicks for yourself. Many state conservation offices rent or loan incubators and fertilized eggs in return for the chickens. Watching this miracle take place is absolutely amazing and your student will never forget it!

If you don't have this opportunity, look for a video online or detailed book on the subject at your library. The important thing to remind your student is that store-bought eggs are not fertilized. No chick will ever hatch from an unfertilized egg.

Teacher's Note: You can take the discussion of "fertilized" versus "unfertilized" eggs to whatever level of reproductive knowledge you wish with your student.

Tom Edison was not able to hatch eggs himself—that job was better left to Lulu, the mother goose!

Science: The Scientific Method*

Edison had a specific thought process regarding those goose eggs. He knew it took warmth to hatch them (observation and reasoning). He thought that perhaps his body would be warm enough to speed up the hatching process (hypothesis). He tried sitting on the eggs for an entire afternoon (tested the hypothesis). He finally concluded it wouldn't work (evaluated and expressed his findings).

As young as age six, Edison was already thinking in logical terms. These four simple steps make up a critical skill used in science called the **scientific method**. Every discovery Edison will make throughout our story will follow these four steps. Encourage your student to make lists of each discovery/invention of Edison's as he reads about it, and then record the steps of the scientific method he can see Tom using. Every experiment includes these four phases. Challenge your student to point out the scientific method whenever he sees it applied! Use the activity sheet at the end of this unit for Tom's discoveries, as well as whenever your student would like to make a record of times when he is thinking like a scientist!

You and your student might discuss how you use the scientific method in your own lives. You might share with your student, for example, that you recently *observed and reasoned* that bread rises when warmth activates the yeast. You *formed a hypothesis* that perhaps bread might rise more quickly in a bowl suspended in warm water. You *tested your theory* and discovered it worked, reducing the rising time for bread by more than 50% and you *evaluated and expressed your findings* (told) to your next-door neighbor.

Ask your student if he can think of any recent examples when he has used the scientific method. Encourage him to look for opportunities to use Tom Edison's method in the future.

Language Arts: Descriptive Word Choices

Draw your student's attention to page 17. At the bottom of the page, it says Mrs. Edison "opened the door with a quick jerk." Instead of simply saying "opened the door," this author chose a descriptive phrase. Using descriptive adjectives (quick) and interesting action words (jerk) adds life to our stories.

As an exercise in using descriptive language, have your student make a list of all the phrases he can think of to describe the way a person can open a door. Answers might include: slowly drew the door open, gingerly pried the door open, slammed the door back, etc.

If your student is having trouble thinking of ways, have him walk over to a door and try opening it in different ways. Then, help him find words to describe what he did. This last idea may be a better plan for students who struggle with abstract thinking.

Language Arts: Creative Writing - Living on a Canal

Have your student imagine (based on his research of the topic) what it would be like to live and/or work on a canal. Let him write his imaginings into an essay or a story.

Language Arts: Classic Literature Connection

Do you remember the incident when Mr. Toad was disguised as a washerwoman in *The Wind in the Willows*? Your student might enjoy this "canal life" portion of the famous story by Kenneth Grahame.

Language Arts: Writing and Discussion Question

Can your student remember a time when he acted like Tom? Has he ever believed he could "improve" something and found out his idea was rather silly? What happened?

Fine Arts: Music - Folk Song: "The Erie Canal"

When you study about the Erie Canal, be sure to listen to the song with the same name. One enjoyable way to learn this song is to find a copy of *The Erie Canal* by Peter Spier. This book follows the lyrics to the famous American folksong "The Erie Canal." There are many fascinating pictures of this canal done in Spier's inimitable style. There is also a valuable history page in the back which covers family life on the canal, travel costs, barge speed limits and much more!

Chapter 2—Tom Visits the Shipyards

Teacher Summary

We discover in this second chapter of our story that Tom is full of questions! He visits his friend, Mr. Anderson, at the barge landings and peppers him with questions. Tom discovers, after watching Mr. Anderson pound nails with a hammer, that he doesn't hear the hammer strike for several seconds. This leads to a discussion of the speed of light versus the speed of sound. Tom is enthralled! He is just beginning to understand what Mr. Anderson is saying when his brother Pitt arrives at the dock. Pitt is beaming and shares with Tom some very important news. The Edison family is moving away from Milan, Ohio. The new railroad being built is bypassing their town and business will be lost. Tom is so excited to be moving! After the boys arrive back at home, we learn Tom's birthday is coming. He will be seven and it will be his last birthday in Milan.

What we will cover in this chapter:

Social Studies: History - Parlors: A Room of the Past
Social Studies: Geography - Your Map of Tom Edison's Life
Science: Pitch - What It Is and What It's For
Science: Speed of Light and Sound
Language Arts: A List of Travel Options
Language Arts: The Day You Were Born - Autobiographical Writing
Language Arts: Writing and Discussion Question
Language Arts: Vocabulary*
Fine Arts: Cooking - A Birthday Cake for Tom
Life Skills: Listening to People Who Are Younger

Social Studies: History - Parlors: A Room of the Past

On page 26, Pitt and Tom find their parents talking in the parlor. The word **parlor** is an old-fashioned term and it means a formal room set aside for guests. Parlors were generally decorated elaborately compared to the rest of the house, and the family generally reserved it for company or special occasions. Today, some people have rooms like this in their homes, but it is unusual.

Here is a detailed description of a parlor in the book *Farmer Boy*, by Laura Ingalls Wilder.

"They tiptoed in, without making a sound. The light was dim because the blinds were down, but the parlor was beautiful. The wallpaper was white and gold and the carpet was of Mother's best weaving, almost too fine to step on. The center-table was marble topped, and it held the tall parlor lamp, all white-and-gold china and pink painted roses. Beside it lay the photograph album, with covers of red velvet and mother-of-pearl. All around the walls stood solemn horsehair chairs, and George Washington's picture looked sternly from its frame between the windows... When company came, they had to sit in the parlor... then they looked at the shells and the coral and the little china figures on the what-not."

It is not as practical in today's world to have an entire room set aside just for guests, but it is a luxurious concept. If your student wishes, have him draw a picture or build a simple model (perhaps inside a shoebox) of what he thinks the Edison's parlor looked like. Parlors are a beautiful part of the past.

Social Studies: Geography - Your Map of Tom Edison's Life

On the map your student started in Chapter 1, continue to mark rivers and cities the Edisons discuss. In this chapter we can add Detroit, Lake St. Clair, St. Clair River, Michigan, and Port Huron.

Science: Pitch - What It Is and What It's Used For

Sandy spread pitch on the underside of a little barge (page 22). Does your student know what **pitch** is? Tom doesn't know what it is (page 24). Pitch is actually the substance created when coal tar is distilled (heating the coal tar to separate its parts and then cooling it and condensing the vapor, leaving a pure substance). The result is a sticky, water-repellent, gum-like paste that can be used for roofing a house, patching a boat, paving a road and much more. Pitch is black, gooey and unattractive. However, until the 20th century pitch was the only effective method of waterproofing or patching objects. Today, there are many synthetic, high-tech products of urethane and polymers used on boats, houses, etc.

Remind your student of the *scientific method* and discuss his *observations* about the effect of sun and rain on wood. Form a *hypothesis* about what would happen to two pieces of wood if one was protected from weather, and the other piece was exposed to the sun and rain. Now *test your hypothesis* by sealing a small piece of wood (a 6" piece of lumber is sufficient) using any sealant convenient, such as paint, varnish, etc. (If you have several different sealants and several different wood blocks you might try more than one variety. Be sure to label each block as to which type of sealant was used.) Now set one piece of unprotected wood and your freshly-sealed sample outside and continue to observe your experiment's results during the next few weeks. Have your student write a report evaluating and expressing his findings at the end of the semester.

Science: Speed of Light and Sound

In this chapter, Edison's observations lead him to a discussion about the speed of light versus the speed of sound (page 20). Mr. Anderson talks to Tom about lightning and thunder. Has your student ever noticed he can see the lightning first? That is because light travels faster than sound. To understand this phenomenon, begin by explaining the basics to your student. Both light and sound travel in waves. The speed of the waves depends on the material the waves are passing through. Did you know that sound travels faster through water than through air? Even more interesting, sound will travel faster through sea water (salty water) than through fresh water. No matter what the material is, a light wave will always be faster than a sound wave—almost *one million* times faster, in fact!

In 1926 an American physicist named Albert A. Michelson measured the speed of light as 186,282 miles per second. Scientists today believe Michelson's figure was so accurate it is probably less than 2 miles per second off. How far is 186,282 miles?

(As you discuss this question, you might want to remember that the United States is approximately 3,000 miles across, and the earth is approximately 24,000 miles in diameter. You may also want to discuss with your student the fact that the moon is approximately 238,000 miles away from Earth. How many times could light cross the United States in one second? How many times could it circle the world? How long does it take for the reflected sunlight from the moon to travel to Earth?)

Sound travels at approximately 1,100 feet per second. (Light travels nearly one million times faster than sound!) No wonder we see the lightning before we hear it! The next time you have a good thunderstorm, have your student count the seconds between seeing the flash of lightning and hearing the sound of thunder. Now, divide the number of seconds by 5 and you'll know approximately how many miles away the lightning struck. (Sound travels approximately one mile every five seconds!)

If your student is interested in science, you might take this discussion further by talking about a light year (the distance light travels in a year—5.88 trillion miles), supersonic speeds (jets traveling faster than the speed of sound—approximately 768 miles per hour), sonic booms (shock waves on the ground from supersonic jets), and much more. Check online or go to the library and find additional books on these fascinating topics.

Language Arts: A List of Travel Options

On page 28 Tom is so excited about traveling by both train and boat. Have your student list all the means of transportation he has used thus far in his life. The list might include car, bus, train, airplane, bicycle, tricycle, etc. Encourage him to keep adding to this list every time he travels by a new mode.

Begin an interesting list of every way your student can think of to move from one point to another. For example, walking, running, skipping, jumping, roller skating, skate boarding, go-carting, surf boarding, or riding a dune buggy, motorcycle, jeep, tank, etc. Place this list on the refrigerator and have the whole family keep adding to it. You will amaze yourselves! Can you think of 100 ways to move? Can you think of 500 or 1000? List making is a beneficial skill in many areas of life and exercises like these are good practice as well as fun.

Language Arts: The Day You Were Born - Autobiographical Writing

Tom's father recalled what the weather was like and the time of day when Tom was born (page 27). It is exciting and interesting to learn about the events surrounding our birth. If possible, have your student find out about the events surrounding his birth. The hospital or location, time, weather, name of doctor, etc., are all interesting facts. If you want to get even more information to add to the story, see if you can access online a newspaper that came out on your student's birthday. In this way, your student can learn what events took place in the world on the day of his birth.

When all the information is gathered, have your student write an autobiographical paragraph (or even several pages, depending on his age) describing his birthday. Talk to your student about **biographies** versus **autobiographies**. The book we are reading now is a biography of Thomas Edison. It is the story of his life. An autobiography would mean he wrote it himself. Autobiographies generally are written in first person (using the word "I ").

Teacher's Note: This assignment for younger students can be a quick discussion about the day they were born and a 10-sentence paragraph. For older students it can become a major assignment lasting a week or more and including interviews of several relatives and additional research. If your student lives near his birthplace, he may even want to take a picture of the hospital and include that along with pictures of himself as a newborn in his report.

Learning about our first day in the world can be a satisfying project as we learn more about ourselves while we develop our research and writing skills!

Language Arts: Writing and Discussion Question

Have you ever seen a big thunderstorm? What was it like? Were you unafraid like Tom? This is a great opportunity for your student to use descriptive language (adjectives and adverbs) as he describes the storm and his feelings.

Language Arts: Vocabulary*

pitch A black, sticky substance made of coal tar and used for waterproofing.

parlor A room set aside for entertaining guests.

light year The distance light travels in one year; 5.88 trillion miles.

biography The story of a specific person's life.

autobiography The story of your own life, written by you.

Fine Arts: Cooking - A Birthday Cake for Tom

Cooking is a delightful and delicious art. Preparing great meals for loved ones is a wonderful way to nourish both body and soul. Tom's birthday is coming up (page 27) and he wants a "hickory-nut cake with burnt sugar icing." While hickory nuts are not commonly available, the following recipe is a type of nut cake with burnt sugar icing that is delicious and easy to prepare. Supervise your student as you talk together about Tom's adventures so far and bake and enjoy the birthday cake!

Tom's Birthday Nut-Apple Cake with Burnt Sugar Icing

2 cups flour
2 cups sugar
4 eggs
3 cups peeled, grated apple
1/2 cup raisins

1 cup chopped nuts (pecans or walnuts work best)
1 tsp. vanilla
3/4 cup corn or vegetable oil
2 tsp. cinnamon
1/2 tsp. salt
1 tsp. baking powder
2 tsp. baking soda

Preheat oven to 350° F. Grease a bundt pan with butter and sprinkle liberally with granulated sugar; set aside. Mix the dry ingredients (flour, sugar, salt, soda, baking powder and cinnamon) together well. In a separate bowl combine the apples, raisins, nuts, vanilla, eggs, and oil. Now, stir this mixture into the dry ingredients. Don't overblend. Pour batter into prepared bundt pan and bake for approximately 50 minutes or until toothpick comes out clean. Turn cake out onto a plate. This cake is best when it is cooled and then stored in an airtight container overnight. Ice the following day.

Burnt-Sugar Icing

2 egg whites
1 1/2 cups sugar
2 Tbs. burnt-sugar syrup*
1/3 cup cold water
dash of salt
1 tsp. vanilla

Place all ingredients, except vanilla, in double boiler. Cooking over boiling water, beat constantly with portable mixer or very fast with wire whisk till soft peaks form, about 7 minutes. Remove from heat; add vanilla. Beat until spreadable consistency is reached.

*Burnt-sugar syrup
Melt 1/2 cup white sugar in heavy skillet over low heat till dark brown and smooth. Remove from heat and add 1/2 cup boiling water. Return to heat and stir till it looks like molasses syrup.

Life Skills: Listening to People Who Are Younger

Mr. Anderson and Sandy were extremely patient with all of Tom's questions. Sometimes older people can be uncaring and ignore children just because they don't feel their questions and comments are important. Encourage your student, even at his young age, to listen and care for younger children and siblings. He probably knows what it is like to be ignored by someone older. It makes us feel unvalued.

Chapter 3—A Birthday to Remember

Teacher Summary

Tom's birthday finally arrives and he awakens to frost-covered windowpanes. At breakfast he opens his gifts and finds new ice skates, colored pencils and a sketchpad. Excited, Tom finishes eating, does his chores and then grabs his skates and heads for the frozen canal. After greeting his friend Sandy and receiving some words of warning about thin patches of ice, Tom sets off. Enjoying himself immensely, he begins to skate in broader figure eights. Before he knows what's happening, the ice breaks and Tom plunges into the icy water below. Sandy soon sees him and with his help Tom is able to get out of the canal. Frightened but still smiling, Tom heads back home in Sandy's arms to get in bed for the rest of his birthday.

What we will cover in this chapter:

Social Studies: History - Ice Skating*
Science: Ice Skating - How it Works

Science: Dew Points and Frost
Science: Health and Safety - Hypothermia and Frostbite
Science: Non-Homogenized Milk
Language Arts: Literature - *Hans Brinker and The Silver Skates*
Language Arts: Writing and Discussion Question
Language Arts: Vocabulary
Fine Arts: Colored Pencils - Creating Color by Blending
Life Skills: Obedience

Social Studies: History - Ice Skating*

Until he fell in, Tom certainly had a wonderful time ice skating on the canal (page 40). Has your student ever been ice skating? Take this opportunity to explore with him the rich variety of ice skating sports. Begin by sharing a brief history of the sport.

Ice skating isn't a new idea! We know that crude ice skates made from wood and using animal bone for blades have been recovered in Roman ruins more than 2,000 years old. Ice skating didn't become a recreational (just for enjoyment) form until the 12th century in Britain. Before that, many Scandinavian countries used ice skating as a common source of transportation down the frozen canals. Skates had wooden blades until the 15th century when the Dutch began forming steel blades. In 1850, E.W. Bushnell of Philadelphia created the first pair of all-steel skates. And another American, ballet dancer Jackson Haines, began to create a new, modern form of skating that came to be called "figure skating" by combining dance movement with ice skating in 1870.

Now, there are many forms of ice skating in addition to traditional figure skating. Done by both single skaters and pairs, this sport is known for its beauty, grace, spectacular jumps, lifts (one partner lifts the other) and spins. Your student may have seen figure skating competitions on television or at an area ice rink. Take some time to search online for famous Olympic figure skaters of the past and present. Watch videos of their performances and note both the ways that figure skating has changed and how it has remained the same over the years.

There are more sports using skates. Speed skating is very popular in the United States, as well as world-wide. In this sport, the blades on the skates are much longer than figure skates and the sport consists of race competition. The object of the race is to be the first to cross the finish line. Unlike figure skating, where

part of the score is always subjective (a decision based on personal preference or feeling), speed skating is purely objective. Men and women always compete separately in speed skating and the races vary from 500 meters to 3,000 meters in length. This sport requires excellent balance, rhythm and powerful leg muscles.

Discuss other sports involving ice skates with your student. Hockey is an extremely popular sport in the northern United States and throughout Canada. Ice dancing (similar to figure skating) is also popular.

Broaden your student's awareness to include the exciting world of skating! Watch some televised competition—or go to a rink and skate yourself!

Science: Ice Skating - How It Works

Does your student know how ice skates work? It seems simple. The blade somehow glides across the surface. But how does it actually happen? Ice is a liquid (water) that has been changed into a solid by freezing. However, when a solid is compressed (having high pressure focused on it), heat is created. This is a scientific principle—compression produces heat.

As you glide along on that thin metal blade, your entire body's weight is pressing down on the blade. The pressure created by your body's weight momentarily melts the frozen (solid) ice back into a liquid (water). The water quickly refreezes once more as soon as you have passed by. This principle—ice melting under pressure and then refreezing when the pressure is lifted—is called **regelation** (REE juh LAY shun).

Teacher's Note: If your student is older and very interested in math, you can have him calculate the pounds of pressure per square inch on his ice blades. For example, if his skates were 1/8 inch wide and 11 inches long, that is 1 3/8 square inches. If your student weighs 80 lbs., that is more than 58 pounds of pressure per square inch—assuming you are skating on one foot at a time.

To demonstrate how ice skates actually work at home, create a block of ice by freezing approximately one inch of water in the bottom of an empty ice cream carton so you can peel away the paper. Now set it on a tall coffee can or pedestal. Then cut a piece of dental floss long enough to lay across the block of ice with several inches hanging down on either side. Attach weights (ball fishing weights, small magnets off the refrigerator, or even two spoons) on each end of the floss. Lay the floss across the surface of the ice and leave it alone. Ask your student what he thinks will happen?

This is going to be his **hypothesis**. In actuality, the compression of the weighted floss will slowly melt through the ice (much faster than the entire piece of ice will melt—due to the regelation factor). Before you know it, the ice block will be cut in half. This is just the kind of experiment Tom would have loved!

Science: Dew Points and Frost

Tom woke up to frosty windowpanes. What is frost? Many people think frost is frozen dew. This is not correct. Since this is common error, begin by explaining what dew is and then explore frost together.

Dew is the little droplet of water we see on the grass in the morning. Dew is formed by the condensation of water vapor (humid air) near the ground. During the day, the ground absorbs heat from the sun. When the sun goes down at night, the surface of the earth cools down quickly. As it cools, the humid air right next to the ground chills as well. When the temperature of this air decreases to a certain point (known as the dew point) the air can no longer contain all of its humidity (vapor) and moisture condenses, forming dew. Therefore, a scientific definition of dew point is the lowest temperature at which the air can still contain all its vapor.

This temperature, unlike the boiling point (212° F.) or freezing point (32° F.) of water, is variable. It depends on the amount of humidity in the air. There are two main conditions that must be met for dew to form: clear skies and no winds. Cloudy skies prevent dew because they form a barrier. When the sun goes down and the earth's surface begins to give off heat, it is trapped by the clouds and returns to the earth, preventing the surface from ever reaching the dew point. Wind prevents the water molecules from staying in close enough contact to form droplets.

There is an old weather-watcher's poem your student can memorize which, although not foolproof, gives good indications of weather patterns:

When dew is on the grass
Rain will never come to pass.
When grass is dry in the morning light
Look for rain before the night.

Even though the temperature of the dew point is variable, there is a way to average a week's dew point temperature in your area at home.

Take a fairly thin, glass container (drinking glass, vase or beaker) and fill it with ice cubes. Then fill it with water. Using a good science thermometer, record the temperature reading at the point when you first see condensation (dew) form on the outside of the glass. Because the humidity in the air changes every day, do this experiment every day at the same time for a week. At the end of the week, average the results to determine the average temperature for the dew point that week.

In their weather reports, meteorologists sometimes tell the average dew point each day.

Now that your student understands the general principles of dew, explain that if frost were frozen dew, it would form perfectly round frozen drops on the blades of grass and our windows. But we know this isn't true.

What Tom Edison saw on his window is what we see on a frosty morning. Feathery, flat patterns of frozen water vapor. Frost is formed when the air near the ground's surface drops in temperature so rapidly the humid air bypasses the stage of condensation (liquid) and turns directly to solid.

The next time your student notices frost or dew, talk about what you learned in this lesson and remember Tom's birthday morning windowpane!

Science: Health and Safety - Hypothermia and Frostbite

Tom was extremely lucky that Sandy was able to retrieve him from those icy depths quickly (page 44). Has your student ever heard the terms **frostbite** or **hypothermia**? These are both dangerous physical conditions that can arise when the body is exposed to very cold temperatures. Learning to protect ourselves from harm and how to treat ourselves in case of emergency is another sign of maturity. Share with your student some simple first aid steps to care for frostbite.

Frostbite actually occurs when ice crystals form in your skin. In more severe cases, the crystals form deep in the tissue below your skin. The signs of frostbite are tingling and numbness. The skin may appear reddish in color or even bluish-white. An old-fashioned remedy was to rub the tingling area of skin with snow. This is dangerous! The affected skin might be further injured. Instead, begin to bathe the finger, toe, foot, etc., in fairly warm, but not hot, water (approximately 100° F.). This may cause severe pain in the affected limb, but it will subside. Then keeping the frostbitten area elevated, have the person rest, lying down.

Hypothermia is caused by accidental (Tom's falling in the canal) exposure to cold temperatures for an extended period of time. The body's temperature gauge falls below the normal level of 98.6° F. As the body loses heat, the internal organs begin to slow down. In severe cases, the person may die. Elderly people or people who are thin and frail are especially susceptible. To treat hypothermia, allow the victim to soak in a warm bath and then wrap the person in several layers of warm blankets.

Teacher's Note: If you have completed FIAR Vol. 5, you may wish to refer back to the lesson on fevers and temperature in *The Boxcar Children*, chapter 11 lesson.

Both frostbite and hypothermia can be prevented under normal circumstances. Remind your student that wearing warm winter clothing is not just something our mothers bother us with. It is an important part of keeping our bodies safe. Health experts now say instead of just wearing one extremely thick wool sweater, wearing several layers of natural fibers (cotton, silk or a blend) is better for our bodies. It allows the air to circulate and keeps us warm. Mittens are warmer than gloves because our fingers touch one another and the body heat is transferred from one to the other. Hats which cover the ears are important, and two layers of warm socks and a pair of boots finish off our winter wear. These tips can keep you safe and warm, especially if you are sledding, shoveling snow or hiking in the winter!

Science: Non-Homogenized Milk

On page 36 we are told Tom's glass of milk was flecked with golden dots of cream. If you have completed FIAR Vol. 5 and chose to do the science lesson on dairy product preservation in *The Boxcar Children* (chapter 5), remind your student that Tom's milk is *non*-homogenized. The milk is whole and has not been shaken so the cream droplets are combined.

Language Arts: Literature - *Hans Brinker, or The Silver Skates*

Part of enriching your student's knowledge of the world is introducing him to well-known literature and literary vernacular. Perhaps one of the most famous tales worldwide is the story of Hans Brinker and his silver skates. *Hans Brinker, or The Silver Skates*, written in 1865 by Mary Mapes Dodge, is filled with adventure and vivid details. The story centers around a young boy, Hans, and his sister, Gretel. Their father is sick, and to help raise money for their family the children enter Hans in a skating race. The outcome is exciting and good, strong family values are portrayed throughout. Take some time and read this wonderful story with your student. There are many good abridged versions available, if you don't want to read the somewhat lengthy original.

Language Arts: Writing and Discussion Question

When Tom returns home, the author tells us very little about the conversation Tom must have had with his parents about his accident. What do you think the conversation was like? Use written dialogue to write what you think Tom's parents might have said and what Tom might have said in reply.

Language Arts: Vocabulary

regelation The term for ice melting under pressure and refreezing when the pressure is lifted.

dew point The lowest temperature at which the air can contain all of its vapors.

hypothermia Dangerous condition occurring when the body's temperature falls below the normal range of 98.6° F.

frostbite Numbness and possible loss of affected area which occurs when skin is exposed to severe cold.

Fine Arts: Colored Pencils - Creating Colors by Blending

One of Tom's beautiful birthday presents is a set of colored pencils. Colored pencils are excellent art tools because by shading one color over another you create different hues and textures. It helps to have a quality set of colored pencils.

Teacher's Note: Cheap colored pencils from the discount store aren't the best for this project. Go to an art supply store or hobby store and ask for an inexpensive, but good quality set for a student. Another versatile medium, similar to colored pencils, is watercolor pencils. Used dry they work just like ordinary colored pencils, but when you add water you can paint with them. A good brand is called Aquarell and is available at most art stores.

Once your student has experimented with different colors, encourage him to try drawing a picture of the canal where Tom was skating. The areas where Sandy warned Tom the ice was thin should be lighter in shade. Challenge your student to explore creating depth and shadow in the canal by using different layers of colored pencil drawing.

Life Skills: Obedience

Ask your student how Tom might have prevented his accident in the canal? He could have listened to Sandy's advice. When adults or those older than us offer advice, it is often for our own good. Ignoring what our parents say and trying things on our own is foolish at best and can be dangerous as well. Encourage your student to look at obedience in a new light. Instead of thinking of obedience as a subservient role, have him consider it as wisdom from people who care. When we were little and our mother said not to touch the stove, she was trying to protect us. Even when we don't understand why our parents or teachers are telling us something, we must give them the benefit of the doubt. It is usually easier to swallow our pride and trust their good judgment, than to fall in the canal like Tom did.

Chapter 4—Off For a New Home

Teacher Summary

Moving day has finally arrived! The Edisons are busy at work, packing everything they own into crates. Bustling around the house, Mrs. Edison shouts out last-minute orders about coats and hats. As they are about to leave, Tannie, Tom's sister, finds a suspicious looking box in the attic. The top of the box is covered in holes. Tom begs his mother to let him take the box, and before discovering what is inside, Tom's mother is distracted by the wagon arriving and goes outside. In the box is Tom's special goose Lulu!

Much to Tom's relief, Tannie agrees to keep Lulu under her lap robe and they all climb in the wagon. With a final look and wave, Tom says goodbye to the little red brick house in Milan.

What we will cover in this chapter:

Science: Inventing Packing for Breakables - Modified Egg Toss
Language Arts: Writing and Discussion Question
Fine Arts: Drawing Illustrations - The Edisons' Home*

Science: Inventing Packing for Breakables - Modified Egg Toss

Tom's family had to pack everything they owned very

carefully into boxes and crates. It took a lot of time, but think of the waste if they arrived in Port Huron and their possessions were broken! Has your student's family ever packed boxes and moved? Sometimes it takes inventiveness to think of how to pack something securely for shipment or transit. That's what this activity is all about. This project can be absolutely hilarious, as well as practical.

Take approximately one dozen raw eggs (hard-boiled eggs defeat the purpose of this exercise!) and go outside with your student. Your student will think you're crazy, but ask him to toss the egg across the yard. Of course, it will break upon impact. Now, give him the assignment to try to invent "packing" that will allow the uncooked egg to be thrown without breaking. The packing might include a shoe box filled with cotton balls and taped shut, a balloon (the egg tucked inside) filled with water, kitchen towels wrapped around the egg a "zillion times," etc. Have your student vary the distance he tosses his wrapped egg. If you have more than one student, organize a competition to see whose egg can be thrown the greatest distance without breaking. (Alternate experiment: you can also toss the packaged egg from a height such as off a deck, balcony, staircase landing, or another high place you have easy access to.)

This experiment could take the better part of an afternoon and the entire dozen eggs, but it will be unforgettable and a great way to spark your student's creativity. Encourage your student to record his findings and come to a conclusion regarding the best way to wrap a breakable egg! Have fun!

Language Arts: Writing and Discussion Question

How do you think Tom is planning to care for Lulu on the train and boat? What would you do if you had a goose on a trip?

Fine Arts: Drawing Illustrations - The Edisons' Home*

Your student should be familiar with what an illustrator does for a book. An illustrator takes passages from the author's text and illuminates it through art. Draw your student's attention to the charmingly descriptive paragraph at the end of this chapter.

Pay particularly close attention to the following details: "...little red brick house on the hillside. Behind it he could see the silver thread that was the canal which led out to Lake Erie." Encourage your student to be the "illustrator" for this chapter. By drawing this scene and following the author's description, he can make a beautiful scene—adding his own embellishments, of course!

Chapter 5—Tom's First Train Ride

Teacher Summary

The Edisons arrive at the train station. Unable to contain his excitement, Tom races ahead and begins to ask the engineer, Mr. Benjamin, many questions. Mr. Benjamin likes the young boy's energy, and says Tom may ride in the engine with him for a few miles. Mr. and Mrs. Edison agree and Tom is joyous. His ride with the engineer goes quickly, and Tom learns all about how a steam engine works. When he is back with his family, Tom relates his experiences to them and the rest of the trip to Detroit goes by quickly.

What we will cover in this chapter:

Social Studies: People's Signature Trademarks
Social Studies: History - American Rail History: Harvey and Pullman
Science: Pollution - Air, Water and Ground
Science: Speed - How Fast Is Fast?
Language Arts: Famous Sayings*
Language Arts: Writing and Discussion Question
Life Skills: A First Time for Everything
Life Skills: Observation - Keeping Your Eyes Open

Social Studies: People's Signature Trademarks

On page 55, Tom is pulling his right eyebrow in excitement. Draw your student's attention to page 13 and page 21 in the book. Thomas Edison always pulled at his right eyebrow when he was thinking or excited. This type of unusual movement is known as a signature trademark. Most of us do something when we think: chew our lower lip, twirl a piece of hair with our fingers, drum our fingers, etc. Most of the time these habits are performed subconsciously.

Tom's habit of tugging on his right eyebrow stayed with him through his lifetime and became well-known. Talk with your student about little movements and nuances he sees people doing. Sometimes famous entertainers and personalities choose something as their signature trademark. Your student will not remember, but you might tell him about Carol Burnett (pulling on her right ear lobe meant "I love you" to her mom), Minnie Pearl (who always said "Hoooowdee!" and wore a price tag on her hat), and Johnny Carson (famous for subconsciously tapping his pencil). There are many, many more. Becoming aware of people's signature trademarks is both interesting and great fun!

Social Studies: History - American Rail History: Harvey and Pullman

Tom's family was amazed at the power and performance of the railroad! They were able to travel at much faster speeds than before and in considerably more comfort. In comparison to horse-pulled wagons, rail service offered comfortable benches to sit on, candy and beverages for refreshment, and you weren't blown around by the wind or dust. For the Edisons, this method of travel was a vast improvement! But rail service would eventually offer even more comfort and luxury!

Take this opportunity to share with your student the changes which occurred during the next forty years (1860-1900) in both the types of amenities passengers could enjoy and the jobs available on the railroads.

Two important names in the late 19th and early 20th century world of railroads were George Pullman and Fred Harvey. George Mortimer Pullman was chiefly a businessman. He was born in New York in 1831, but moved to Chicago when he was 23 years old. It was then that he saw a need for improving the sleeping quarters on trains. At that time, people were forced to sleep sitting up in their seats, with no privacy or comfort. Ask your student if he would like to sleep on a wooden bench next to a lot of other strangers?

Mr. Pullman and a friend introduced a new kind of sleeping car they called the **Pioneer**. It featured bunkbed-like berths, which pulled out from the wall. In this way they could be folded up during the day, allowing for more room, and pulled out at night. The beds were made up with soft sheets and blankets. It was an amazing invention! Before George Pullman was 34 years old (1865), his new discovery, the comfortable berth, was standard on the Chicago & Alton Railroad. Also, the name for his invention, the **Pioneer**, was soon changed to the **Pullman**.

To this day, sleeping cars on railroads are known as Pullman cars. By 1899, Mr. Pullman had a monopoly on the sleeping-car business. His cars were used on every railroad in the country. Imagine what Tom would have thought of sleeping in his own little bed on the train! If your student seems interested in this topic, you might continue the discussion by looking online or getting books at the library on George Pullman and railroad service.

Another major name in railroad service was Fred Harvey. During the time Tom's family rode the railroad, people had to pack their own food or eat at the food stops along the way. At that time the food service offered at the stops was really awful! Bad meat was often served, and stale, soured breads and beverages were customary. For this reason, most travelers opted for the "pack your own lunch" choice. But, this terrible food service was about to change! In 1876 a man named Fred Harvey went to the Santa Fe railroad with a proposal. Harvey suggested he hire employees, operate food service stops and serve decent food at a fair price along the route of the Santa Fe. He only needed the railroad to buy the restaurant spaces for him and charge him no rent. He said he could pay his employees and then would split his earnings with the railroad 50/50!

Santa Fe took Harvey up on his offer and soon railroad food stops were changed forever! Mr. Harvey insisted on his lunchrooms being impeccably clean, his food of the highest quality and his workers (all women) of the utmost moral character. Becoming known as Harvey Houses, his restaurants became the standard by which all other restaurants were judged within the railroad industry. Offering fresh fruits, vegetables, seafood and even ice cream, and serving them on china and fine linens, made the Harvey House extremely popular.

The servers, known as Harvey Girls, had to have at least an eighth-grade education, be able to speak clearly, have a pleasant manner and a clean appearance. Some of these young women worked for Harvey House restaurants for years! They were paid well and were highly respected. Besides the staff of Harvey Girls, the Harvey House staff also included bakers, butchers, managers, housemaids, and many others! What would Tom have thought to sit down at a beautifully set table and eat ice cream!

If it is possible, have your student ask his grandparents or even great-grandparents if they have ever eaten at a Harvey House restaurant. If your student is able to interview a grandparent, older friend or neighbor, perhaps he could write a paper summarizing his conversation.

Isn't it interesting how creative men like Pullman and Harvey saw a need and found a way to fill it? Both the names Pullman and Harvey have become a part of the American vernacular for the benefits they gave to society.

Science: Pollution - Air, Water and Ground

On page 56, Mrs. Edison makes a comment about the railroad's smoke and its effect on nearby homes. Tom thinks the puffing, black smoke is exciting, but his mother is also right. The soot and smoke of the railroads created a new type of air pollution. Before the railroads, not much interrupted the clean air of the country other than the smoke from fireplaces.

In today's world, pollution has become a significant problem in most cities and urban areas. Talk with your student about the pollution problems your area faces. Also, you may want to take this opportunity to discuss several current pollution problems facing many areas of the world—plastic in oceans, landfills and smog. All three of these dilemmas are in the news quite often and your student may have heard of them already. Talk about each briefly.

Plastic in oceans is a serious problem in all of the world's oceans. About 8 million tons of plastic enters our oceans every year and ends up floating, sinking, or landing on beaches. This pollution greatly endangers marine wildlife, who may eat it, get entangled in it, or become suffocated by it. Hundreds of marine species are affected by this growing problem.

Landfills are massive "dumping" grounds for garbage and waste. In many cities, landfills are overflowing with plastics and glass, items that could be recycled but instead are thrown away. Most of these items are not biodegradable (capable of decomposing naturally) and will continue to be in landfills for many centuries to come. Cities are struggling with decisions on how to eliminate such massive amounts of waste in their communities. It is a significant problem.

Finally, **smog** is a type of air pollution created by excessive amounts of exhaust fumes and chemical compounds released into the air and trapped by warm air or mountain ranges. Smog is particularly serious in major cities. Smog poses a serious health threat to people and greatly diminishes the beauty of the skylines in our cities.

Other pollution topics your student may be interested in include ground water contamination from pesticides, medicines, or other toxic liquids, and oil spills in oceans, caused by tankers, refineries, or drilling rigs. Have your student research recent articles about pollution control projects that may be underway in your community, state or region. Have him write a report about his findings. Learning about our environment and how to protect it is vital to preventing future problems. Tom's mother thought the smoke from the steam engine was bad. What would she think of plastic in oceans, air pollution and overflowing landfills?

Science: Speed—How Fast Is Fast?

On page 63, Tom thinks the train is going very fast. He asks Mr. Benjamin and finds out it is going 15 miles per hour. Ask your student if he thinks that is fast? If he can't relate the number to actual speed, take him out in a car and drive 15 miles per hour. Does he think it is fast now? What speed does your student consider fast? Remind him of the lesson on the speed of light in chapter 2. Now, *that* is fast!

Some exotic airplanes can travel in excess of 2,100 miles per hour and commercial airliners routinely go approximately 500 miles per hour. Why did Tom think the train was going so fast? Compared to walking, running, riding a horse or boat, it was fast! If your student is interested in this topic, go to the library and find additional books on trains, airplanes, attempts at world speed records, etc. Speeds continue to increase as technology has progressed. (Also consider comparing the speed of light, sound, etc.)

Language Arts: Famous Sayings*

Part of mastering a language includes becoming familiar with the "sayings" of that language. For example, someone unfamiliar with English would not understand the saying, "this meal is *on the house*." They might imagine that dinner was going to be served on the roof!

Show your student the opening line of this chapter. Tom assumes there must be a fire because he sees smoke. A famous saying is, "where there's smoke there's fire." Explain to your student what that means. It generally means that when we see certain symptoms, it's usually wise to assume the obvious conclusion about their cause. Hence the statement, "wherever you see smoke, there's undoubtedly a fire nearby that is causing it."

Be on the lookout for more common sayings as they present themselves. Share them with your student and encourage him to listen for unique sayings himself. Learning about these special language devices will enrich your student's cultural literacy and increase his understanding of conversations around him.

Language Arts: Writing and Discussion Question

Tom's first train ride was exciting! Write about something you remember doing for the first time. What were the sounds, sights, feelings, smells or tastes of your experience?

Life Skills: A First Time for Everything

Tom was very excited about his first trip on a train! Imagine what he must have thought about riding with the engineer on his very first trip! Ask your student about things he's done for the first time. Has he ever flown on an airplane, gone sailing, fishing or camped in a tent? There is a first time for everything. If your student is interested, have him make a list of all the things he wants to try, but hasn't yet done. For an extension of this lesson, refer to the Writing and Discussion Question above.

Life Skills: Observation - Keeping Your Eyes Open

The book tells us Tom wanted to be sure to see everything (page 57). Being observant helped Thomas Edison be the great inventor that he was! Noticing people, places and activities are all a part of being observant. Keeping your eyes open is a major part of learning all about the world around you. Encourage your student to record interesting things he notices around him, using a journal or notebook. He might observe a baby bird, a diesel truck, an old woman with long braided hair, etc. Sometimes the best inventions are born from careful observation.

Making lists of details we notice can also help us in our writing. Have your student take one or more of the items on his list of observations and write a paragraph about them. His paragraph might describe the old woman with the braided hair in greater detail and describe what she's doing, who she's talking with or what she's saying, etc. Challenge your student to become more observant, just like Tom!

Chapter 6—The House in the Grove

Teacher Summary

The Edisons complete the final chapter of their journey to Port Huron. They pass the area schoolhouse on their way to their new home. His parents tell him he must go to the school soon. Finally, they turn onto a narrow road and see a large white house straight ahead. Mrs. Edison is shocked by how big their new house is and Tom runs off to explore the grounds. Soon they begin to move things into their new home, and Tom and Pitt spend the better part of the day helping their mother insulate the floors with straw. After the family eats supper, they decide to name their new home "The House in the Grove." The next afternoon, Mr. Edison takes Tannie back to the train station and sends her back to Milan. That evening, the family sits and listens to Mr. Edison read from *The Detroit Free Press* about current events. Tom listens closely to stories about President Fillmore and Commodore Perry. He is interested in the concept of trade and commerce. Learning things from his father's reading becomes a useful tool for Tom!

What we will cover in this chapter:

Social Studies: History - President Fillmore
Social Studies: History - Commodore Perry*
Science: Tree Identification
Language Arts: Names for Houses
Language Arts: Writing and Discussion Question
Life Skills: Being Neighborly

Social Studies: History - President Fillmore

Tom listens to stories about President Fillmore as his father reads to him from the paper (page 78). Discuss some facts about the 13th president of the United States with your student.

Millard Fillmore (1800-1874) was the second president to assume the position during someone else's term. President Zachary Taylor died in 1850 and Vice-President Fillmore served the balance of Taylor's term. President Fillmore was in office for almost three years, and during that time two things of major significance occurred. First was the signing of an important trade agreement between the United States and Japan (discussed in the next lesson). Second was the Compromise of 1850. The 1850 compromise abolished the slave trade in the District of Columbia, admitted California to the Union as the 31st state and established stricter slave trade laws across the Union. If your student is interested in this period of presidential history, find a biography on President Fillmore and continue your research.

Social Studies: History - Commodore Perry*

Tom was interested in Commodore Perry and the concept of trade. Ask your student if he has ever heard of Commodore Perry. Matthew Calbraith Perry (1794-1858) first opened world trade ports in Japan after more than two centuries of Japanese isolation. With a signed letter and an appeal from President Fillmore in hand, Perry headed to Tokyo in 1854. Perry refused to speak with anyone other than the highest Japanese leaders. The Japanese eventually agreed to allow trade, and signed the now-famous treaty in Yokohama.

This agreement is considered one of our most significant acts of diplomacy. Talk with your student about what *diplomacy* means. It usually is defined as "the management of relations between two countries." Because of Commodore Perry's diplomacy, Japan and the United States discussed the situation and came to a common understanding. Commodore Perry, under the order of President Fillmore, was practicing what is known as "foreign diplomacy." Is your student interested in this concept? Do more research on your own and continue to talk about the importance of foreign diplomacy in an ever-shrinking world.

Science: Tree Identification

Doesn't Tom's new house sound beautiful? Draw your student's attention to the vivid description of the yard and trees on page 70. What types of trees are in your student's yard or neighborhood? Are they native to the region? Have your student collect leaves from each different species and document the types of trees he finds. Are there any oaks, like in Tom's yard? Find a good tree identification reference online or at your library and help your student learn to use it.

Language Arts: Names for Houses

Tom decides his new home needs a name. He chooses The House in the Grove. Share with your student some other famous names for homes. Thomas Jefferson's beautiful mansion was named Monticello. George Washington's home was known as Mount Vernon. Many Southern homes in the U.S. have names, such as Tara and Twelve Oaks in the film *Gone with the Wind.* Most western ranches have names. Often these ranch names are associated with a cattle brand, such as the Circle C, the Rocking K, the T Bar J, etc. Does your student think naming a house is an interesting idea? Have him come up with a list of creative names for his own home. Perhaps your student could sit down with his family and decide on a name for his house! Naming an inanimate object, like a house or car, gives it extra character! (If you've used FIAR Vol. 3, second edition, your student will probably make the connection to *The Old Woman Who Named Things.*)

Language Arts: Writing and Discussion Question

On page 71, Tom is excited about the size of his new home's hallway. He says it is "so wide he can play games up there." What kind of games would you want to play in a large, upstairs hall?

Life Skills: Being Neighborly

Mrs. Edison didn't have to work as hard when she arrived at her house because her neighbors had already cleaned out the rooms for her (page 72). Being a good neighbor is an important part of being a good citizen. Encourage your student to think of things he can do for his neighbors. Raking leaves for an older neighbor, baking cookies for a new family or helping someone carry in groceries are thoughtful ways to be a good neighbor. Challenge your student to be on the lookout for neighborly acts he can do to serve others!

Chapter 7—First Day of School

Teacher Summary

Tom's first day of school arrives. With Pitt and his mother by his side, Tom sets out for the one-half mile walk to his new schoolhouse. Tom has heard bad stories about his new schoolmaster, Mr. Crawford, but he tries to be optimistic. When Tom arrives, Mr. Crawford tells him that even though he is seven, Tom must be in the first grade since he has had no formal schooling. The rest of Tom's day doesn't go much better. He is sent to the corner for drawing pictures instead of doing his penmanship, and his lunch is stolen by the biggest boy in class. That boy, Michael Oates, however, decides to befriend Tom and the lunch hour becomes the best part of the day.

What we will cover in this chapter:

Social Studies: History - One-Room Schoolhouses
Science: One-Half Mile - How Far Is That?
Language Arts: Penmanship Review*
Language Arts: Writing and Discussion Question
Life Skills: Focusing Our Attention

Social Studies: History - One-Room Schoolhouses

Tom's school was a one-room schoolhouse. All the grades from kindergarten on up were in the same classroom. Ask your student if he has ever seen such a school. This convention of education was popular in the past, primarily in small towns where the community couldn't afford to pay more than one teacher. This type of school is still found in a few very small towns in the United States, but for the most part is now extinct.

One-room schoolhouses are still alive today in homes where parents homeschool their children. In this setting, several siblings in different grades may all be taught by the same teacher. Discuss with your student the many other types of schools: private, public, parochial, boarding, military, etc. Broadening our horizons and learning how other schools operate allows us to appreciate the world! Have your student pick one type of school and research his subject before writing a paper explaining the advantages and disadvantages.

Science: One-Half Mile - How Far Is That?

On page 80 we see Tom walking one-half mile to school. Does your student think that is far? If you wish, it might be fun to go outside and walk one-half mile with your student. What would your student think of walking to school? Tom was fortunate to live less than a mile from school. In years past, many children walked five miles or more to get to school each day. If this is of interest to your student, continue your discussion by talking about how many feet are in a mile (5,280). How many inches? How many yards? Now challenge your student by calculating the distance in metric units. (Hint: 1 meter equals approximately 39 inches.)

Language Arts: Penmanship Review*

Tom was supposed to be working on his penmanship, instead of drawing a picture of the House in the Grove. Review with your student the importance of good penmanship. In Tom's day, penmanship was considered a very important subject of study. Both the quality of the handwriting and the discipline it required reflected on the person's character. Encourage your student to continue refining his penmanship. Perhaps your student would enjoy trying something more elaborate. Calligraphy is the beautiful art of embellished penmanship. If your student is interested, find a good book on calligraphy at the library and buy an inexpensive calligraphy marker. Have fun and focus on the discipline of fine penmanship!

Language Arts: Writing and Discussion Question

On page 81 Tom overhears the children saying Mr. Crawford "isn't fair." Do you agree with this statement about Mr. Crawford? Why or why not? What is involved in being a "fair" person? What does the word "fair" mean to you?

Life Skills: Focusing Our Attention

On page 86 Tom is drawing on his slate instead of listening to Mr. Crawford and participating in the penmanmanship lesson with the other students. Talk with your student about Tom's lack of attention and non-participation in class. Why didn't Tom pay attention? Drawing is a wonderful, creative outlet, but all things have a proper time and place. Sometimes, with the teacher's permission, drawing may be acceptable in school (such as when listening to a story or to music), but sometimes it's a distraction (such as when a student is supposed to be doing something else, like penmanship or another activity). When we are in class, our focus should be on the topic and we should respect someone by listening when they speak. We owe our elders and teachers our full attention, even if they're less than kind like Mr. Crawford. Talk with your student about times when it may be appropriate to draw while listening, and times when it would not be appropriate (include situations outside of school, such as church, extended family activities, etc.).

Chapter 8—The Basement Laboratory

Teacher Summary

Tom's schooling continues to be a trial. Tom makes friends easily, but Mr. Crawford becomes increasingly negative toward Tom. One day, after Tom asks a question, the schoolmaster yells at Tom and calls him "addled." Tom runs home weeping, and his mother promises he does not have to return to school again. Mrs. Edison understands that questions and curiosity are the way children learn. She decides to teach Tom at home.

Michael Oates, the boy who had stolen Tom's lunch box, comes to work for the Edison family. He and Tom become good friends. Michael and the other children wish they could be taught by Mrs. Edison, too. Tom always seems to be having a good time.

One day Mrs. Edison teaches Tom about a branch of science called chemistry. Tom is fascinated by this and studies a book in which he sees a picture of a "laboratory." Tom decides he wants his own laboratory so he and Michael Oates set out to collect various bottles. Then Tom makes labels for them and fills them with a variety of items (feathers, dried corn, flour, etc.). It's just pretend, but Tom thinks his laboratory is perfect! Mrs. Edison lets Tom set his bottles on a table in the basement and Tom is thrilled!

What we will cover in this chapter:

Science: The Different Branches of Science
Science: Warning Symbols
Science: Setting Up Your Own Laboratory*
Life Skills: Differences and Assumptions

Science: The Different Branches of Science

Tom was learning about an area of physical science called chemistry. Discuss with your student the other branches of science. If your student is younger, discuss this lesson briefly, concentrating on becoming familiar with the concepts only. If your student is more advanced or older, challenge him to define each section more extensively. To begin with, there are four main divisions of science: **Mathematics and Logic, Physical Science, Life Science** and **Social Science**. It might be helpful in this discussion to have your student chart or outline each section as you talk about it.

The first branch, *Mathematics and Logic*, is made up of six different areas:

Arithmetic is the study of numbers and simple calculations like addition, subtraction, multiplication and division.

Algebra is the study of equations and unknown quantities represented by letters.

Geometry is the study of the mathematical relationship of solid shapes, angles, line and points.

Calculus is similar to algebra but deals with changing quantities.

Probability is the study of events and the likelihood of their occurrence.

Statistics is the study of analyzing trends or similarities in large mathematical calculations.

The second branch of science is called *Physical Science*. There are five primary areas that make up Physical Science:

Chemistry is the study of the composition, structure and reaction of elements and compounds, both natural and artificial.

Geology is the study of the earth and its makeup.

Meteorology is the study of the earth's atmosphere and weather.

Astronomy is the study of outer space, planets and stars.

Physics is the study of all matter and energy.

The third branch of science is called *Life Science* or *Biology*, and is organized into two separate sections:

Botany is the study of plants.

Zoology is the study of humans and animals.

Finally, there is the section of science called *Social Science*. This area of science deals with humans and society. It is made up of five subdivisions:

Anthropology is the study of origin and development of humans and society.

Economics is the study of production, distribution and uses of goods produced by a society.

Political Science is the study of a society's government and laws.

Psychology is the study of human beings' thought processes and behaviors.

Sociology is the study of human communities and the relationships among various individuals and groups in societies.

Encourage your student to begin identifying the different sections of science when he notices them. It is important to remember science is a comprehensive and expanding subject. Ask your student what areas he enjoys studying. There are so many occupations and jobs in each area of science (zoologist, geologist, statistician, psychologist, etc.). Challenge your student to research one or more of those occupations and discuss them. Science is an exciting subject—filled with fascinating and eye-opening wonders! (It might be fun to use the list above and apply it to lessons in *Beyond Five in a Row*. For instance, the lesson on Dew Point would be Meteorology, Eggs would be Zoology, a lesson on Budgeting would be Economics, etc. This is an advanced concept, so keep it fun.)

Science: Warning Symbols

Tom carefully makes little labels for his "chemicals" which bear the symbol of a skull and crossbones (page 98). This symbol is the universal (internationally recognized) picture representing a *poisonous* substance. If you have one, show your student an example of this picture on a household cleaning bottle or medicine bottle. Explain the importance of this symbol to your student. It is there for our safety and protection. There are several other important universal symbols to learn as well. Talk about where you find them and remind your student to leave substances with these markings alone.

Science: Setting Up Your Own Laboratory*

Wasn't Tom's idea for his own laboratory delightful? Would your student enjoy having his own little laboratory? Feed your student's interest by letting him set up his own lab, using baby food jars or other bottles he finds. Here is a list of common household compounds and their chemical names that can be collected for your student's chemistry set: white vinegar (acetic acid), household ammonia (ammonium hydroxide), Epsom salts (magnesium sulfate), baking soda (sodium bicarbonate), washing soda (sodium carbonate), table salt (sodium chloride), instant tea (tannic acid), borax (sodium borate), fruit juice (ascorbic acid), and soda water (carbonic acid).

Before filling the bottles, your student can create labels just like Tom (with or without the sign for poison) and paste them on the front of each bottle. Then, encourage your student to label each chemical with the scientific name in large print and the common name below it.

There are many excellent resources available for home science experiments. Search online or at your library for experiments using common chemicals you're likely to already have, such as books on "kitchen science," etc. In the meantime, here are a couple of simple, yet fun experiments your student can conduct with his new "chemistry" set and laboratory.

Invisible Writing—The Salt Water Script

Gather the following items:
- sheet of white paper
- drinking glass
- small paint brush
- sodium chloride (table salt)
- soft lead pencil

Fill the drinking glass with 1/4 cup warm water. Add 4 tablespoons sodium chloride (salt) and dissolve by stirring. Dip the paintbrush into the solution. Paint a design or your name on the piece of paper. Let it dry. Then, with the pencil, rub the lead across the design/name lightly. The painted areas will suddenly appear in black.

Dancing Rice—Perpetual Motion

Gather the following items:
- tall glass or jar
- 1/4 cup rice (instant works best)
- sodium bicarbonate (baking soda)
- acetic acid (white vinegar)

Fill the glass 3/4 full of water. Add 1 tablespoon sodium bicarbonate and stir. Add the rice, and then 1-2 tablespoons of acetic acid. Soon bubbles of carbon dioxide from the sodium bicarbonate and acetic acid will collect on the rice and bring them up to the surface. As they float on the surface, some of the carbon dioxide will escape into the air, and the rice will sink again. See how long the rice continues to "dance!"

Tom would have loved these experiments! Encourage your student to view science as exciting, understandable and applicable. It can be all of those things and more!

Life Skills: Differences and Assumptions

Why did Mr. Crawford call Tom "addled"? (page 93) **Addled** means confused or muddled. Ask your student why he thinks Mr. Crawford would assume Tom was confused. Maybe Mr. Crawford thought Tom's questions weren't intelligent. Perhaps Mr. Crawford thought that because Tom was different from the other students he wasn't smart. Or maybe Mr. Crawford didn't want to take the time to answer Tom's questions and so he tried to eliminate the problem by calling Tom addled.

Unfortunately, people sometimes assume when someone is different they aren't as intelligent. When we **assume** something, it means we are pretending to understand something without gathering the facts. Assumptions lead to misunderstandings and often mean we lose out on really knowing someone. Discuss with your student examples of assumptions. Ask your student what he thinks about Mr. Crawford's assumptions about Tom.

Just because someone is different from us, does not mean they are less intelligent or capable. For example, someone from a different country might just nod and smile when we speak to them. If someone assumed they were not intelligent, they would be wrong! It's more likely that the person doesn't understand a word you're saying because of the language barrier! Always give people the benefit of the doubt! In that way, we increase our respect of others and at the same time we grow in personal character. Next time you find yourself assuming something about someone, take some time to get to know them. There's an excellent chance you'll be quite surprised by the person you meet.

Chapter 9—Tom Tries an Experiment

Teacher Summary

Michael and Tom have worked all summer long on a garden. They harvest the vegetables and fruits and sell them in Port Huron. Tom has saved nearly all his earnings to spend on chemicals for his laboratory. September arrives and after Tom and Michael sell their last load of apples, Tom goes to the chemist's shop and buys a bottle of mercury. It is the final addition he has been needing for his set of chemicals. On the way back to the House in the Grove, Michael notices some birds flying in the sky. Tom suggests that if the human body were filled with gas (making it lighter than air) we could fly as well! Tom is excited by his hypothesis and convinces Michael to drink a gaseous liquid he mixes together when they arrive home. Michael drinks it and promptly gets sick. Mrs. Edison is very angry with Tom's foolish experiment and threatens to make Tom destroy his laboratory. Tom offers an alternative suggestion (a lock on his chemicals and a promise not to ever experiment on people again) and so his mother relents, simply punishing Tom by sending him to bed without dinner.

What we will cover in this chapter:

Science: Periodic Table of Elements
Science: Mercury
Science: Economics - Two Ways to Make Money
Science: Economics - Savings, Budgets and Compound Interest
Language Arts: Writing and Discussion Question
Language Arts: Vocabulary*
Fine Arts: Advertising - Creating a "Look" For Your Business
Life Skills: How We Respond to Discipline

Science: Periodic Table of Elements

If your student has progressed through the FIAR curriculum, especially *Betsy Ross* in Vol. 5, he might already be familiar with this important scientific tool. Have him take a look at the complete table, which you can find in a library book or print a copy online. Ask your student what he notices? To scale the topic down to a more manageable size, draw your student's attention to the specific square showing sulphur (on the right-hand side, under oxygen). Talk a little about what each of the notations signify. You will find the following basic information symbolized on each square: the chemical symbol (S), atomic number (16), element name, and the atomic weight (32). If your student is interested, you may want to check out a book on the periodic table from the library or find videos or more information online.

Science: Mercury

Tom bought some mercury for his laboratory from Mr. Stevenson (page 107). Ask your student if he knows what mercury is? Begin the discussion with a simple explanation. Mercury is a shiny, silver metal element. It is the only metal in the world that is a liquid when it is at room temperature. Other metals—iron, for example—can be liquid when heated to a very high temperature but are always solid at room temperature. Mercury is liquid without this additional heat added. Share with your student the many important properties of mercury. It expands and contracts evenly when heated or cooled, remaining in liquid form over a wide range of temperatures. For this reason, mercury was used in household thermometers for many years.

Mercury is found in the earth as an ore (a natural combination of mineral deposits from which a metal can be extracted) called **cinnabar**. Cinnabar deposits are found in China, Slovenia, Slovakia, Ukraine, Kyrgyzstan, Egypt and Mexico. California and Nevada have the largest deposits of cinnabar in the United States.

Be sure to warn your student that mercury is highly poisonous! You should never play with a ball of mercury. The metal can actually seep into your skin and carry with it toxins which can damage brain cells. Mercury is also potentially dangerous to the environment, poisoning our fish and waterways. Industrial wastes have been dumped into rivers, lakes, oceans and bays all over the world. In many regions native fish now carry dangerous levels of mercury. The United States has made substantial progress in reducing mercury contamination during the past few decades, although a few areas are still dangerously affected—a dramatic reminder of our continuing need to research and respect, the dangers of our industrial waste.

While mercury is dangerous to touch, it's fascinating to observe—do this safely by watching a video online!

Science: Economics - Two Ways to Make Money

Tom and Michael were financially successful in their truck farming business. On page 104, Tom convinced Michael they could make more from truck farming than by working at odd jobs in town. Take this opportunity to talk with your student about beginning economics.

There are two ways that most people make money. One is to provide labor for another person. For example, Tom could have cleaned stables for the neighbors or run errands for a shopkeeper in town. We can also make money by being an owner. This is what Tom did! He and Michael ran their own business and sold their own goods. Remind your student of this classic economic saying—the greater the risk, the greater the potential reward. This is an important principle of economics. If Tom had chosen to run errands for a shopkeeper in town he would have been guaranteed a certain wage for a certain amount of labor. But instead, he chose to take some risks (crop damage, weather variabilities, no demand for product, etc.) by starting his own truck farming business and reaped greater rewards by doing so.

A person who starts his own business is called an **entrepreneur**. Tom was an entrepreneur. Choosing to work for wages is never wrong. Make sure your student understands the relative risks and potentials of being an employee or owning your own business. Being an entrepreneur always carries greater risks but offers greater potential rewards.

Would your student like to own his own business someday? Why not start the creative ideas flowing now? To come up with a realistic business plan, your student will need to examine several issues. Use the example of a lemonade stand to explain the questions he'll need to answer.

First, what will he produce or sell? (Lemonade.) Second, who will he sell his product to? (Neighbors.) Third, what raw materials (ingredients) will he need to produce his product? (Lemons, sugar, water and ice.) Fourth, what other equipment will be necessary for production and marketing? (Table, sign, spoon, pitcher, cups, chair and money box.) Fifth, how much will his product cost? (50 cents a glass.) Finally, how will he obtain each of these items and what will each cost? Perhaps the table, spoon, pitcher, chair, cups, water and ice can be borrowed from Mom and Dad. He'll have to spend several dollars on lemons and sugar. Then he'll have to buy some poster board and draw his sign.

Once you've finished the "business plan" you can begin the production and distribution of your product. If your student seems interested in this ownership and business venture discussion, have him come up with three viable business ideas he could operate right now. (Possible ideas might include: lemonade stand, snow shoveling, window washing, lawn care business, walking neighbors' dogs, etc.) This project might last for weeks. For more information on this subject, look at the Fine Arts lesson in this chapter.

Science: Economics - Savings, Budgets and Compound Interest

Tom and Michael made a great deal of money in their truck garden business. Tom, we know (page 106), saved most of his earnings. Using Tom as an example, talk with your student about the importance of saving money and living within a budget. Even young children with small amounts of income can learn to budget their resources and save some of their money. By choosing a specific amount or percentage of their allowance/earnings, begin to set up some guidelines for savings. Allow your student to come up with his own suggestions and guidelines too.

The decision to put off purchases and save our money instead is often difficult. Perhaps sharing the power of **compound interest** may help motivate your student to begin saving.

When we save money in a bank or savings account we earn interest on our investment. The interest we earn continues to generate additional income as the money "compounds." One interesting way to calculate how quickly our money will grow is by using the "rule of 72's." We can determine how many years it will take our investment to double in value by dividing the rate of return into 72. For example, if we put our money in a savings account paying 6% annual interest, we know our money will double in 12 years. (72 divided by 6 equals 12.)

Likewise, we can determine what rate of return (or interest) our investment needs to return in a given period by dividing the number of years into 72. For example, if we set aside money for our child's college education and we need for it to double in 10 years, we know we'll need to earn at least 7.2% interest on our investment. (72 divided by 10 equals 7.2)

Here's a fun experiment for your student. Ask him whether he would rather receive $1,000,000 or have you give him a penny and then double it every day for a month. Sit down together and do the math, either by hand or with a calculator. You'll discover that the penny grows to two cents on the second day of the month, four cents on the third day, eight cents on day four, etc. By day ten you only have $5.12. By day 20 your compounded investment will have grown to more than $5,000, but still far less than one million dollars. Now look at the 30th day—you have more than $5,000,000 in your savings account. And imagine if it was a 31-day month—wow!

Language Arts: Writing and Discussion Question

Tom's punishment for making Michael sick might have ended differently. If Mrs. Edison had stuck by her decision to have Tom destroy his laboratory, what might have been the long-term effects on Tom's life?

Language Arts: Vocabulary*

cinnabar A heavy, bright-red mineral and the principal source of mercury.

entrepreneur A person who manages his own business, assuming the risk for the sake of the potential profit.

Fine Arts: Advertising—Creating a "Look" For Your Business

Whether your student came up with a real or fantasy idea for his own business, now he can begin designing his advertising. Explain to your student that an advertisement's purpose is to make the public want his service or product. It must appeal to the audience he is selling to and describe what he is selling. If he is interested, perhaps your student would like to create his own business card, making sure to include the name of his business, a phone number where he can be reached, etc. He might also enjoy creating a billboard design. Be sure to use strong colors or pictures to show his product or service. He might want to try thinking up a catchy slogan. Encourage your student to try several different designs before deciding on the final choice.

If your student is older and interested in film or television, he might even want to write a script and make a video commercial for his product. For example, he could take some exterior shots of the lemonade stand and a person smiling after drinking a glass of lemonade. Then he could direct the person to turn to the camera, lift their glass and say something like, "Mmmm! Leo's Lemonade is the best in town! And at 50 cents a glass you can't beat it. Come on by and try some. It's cold and refreshing!"

Have fun with this project. And if your student decides on a real summer job, he may even be able to use the business cards and signs he has designed!

Life Skills: How We Respond to Discipline

Tom should never have conducted an experiment on another human being. Tom's mother told him that as punishment for his actions, he would have to destroy his laboratory (page 113). What would have happened if Tom had responded by screaming and complaining? His mother would probably have stuck by her original punishment. Instead, Tom respectfully offers an alternative. Discuss with your student that how we respond to consequences can sometimes affect the situation. Mrs. Edison did not have to relent and allow Tom to keep his lab. However, she was more apt to consider this option when Tom responded respectfully. Encourage your student to examine his reactions to authority. Does he respond with anger, whining or begging or does he remain calm, respectful and considerate? Continue talking about this topic when it seems appropriate and remind your student of Tom's situation.

Chapter 10—Tom's First Telegraph

Teacher Summary

The year is now 1859. Four years have passed and Tom's studies with his mother have continued to serve him well. Port Huron has grown and the House in the Grove has truly become a home. Mr. Edison decides to build a 100-foot tower on their property and charge people 25 cents to see the view. The attraction becomes quite popular and people come from all over.

When no one is around, Mrs. Edison and Tom enjoy sitting on the tower and doing their lessons. Standing at the top and looking out, Tom pretends he is Christopher Columbus and the St. Clair River is the great Atlantic. Other things are changing around the Edisons besides the new tower. Fort Gratiot, located across the road from the Edisons' home, has been inactive since the French and Indian war. But with increased worry that the nation might be facing a civil war, soldiers have again taken over the fort. So, people come to see the restored Fort Gratiot and climb Mr. Edison's tower!

Tom, now twelve, makes a new friend, James Clancy. He and James become very interested in a new form of communication they have heard about called a telegraph. Inspired by the thought of wired, coded discussions, Tom decides to rig up a telegraph between the boys' houses. By collecting bottles, wire and nails they build a simple telegraph. Now the boys can "talk" anytime they want from their own homes. Learning the Morse Code is fun and soon Tom and James are tapping away. Even Mr. Edison is interested in the new system and learns the code, too! Tom is having a lot of fun!

What we will cover in this chapter:

Social Studies: History - Samuel Morse and the Telegraph*
Social Studies: History - Marconi and Wireless Communication
Language Arts: Writing and Discussion Questions
Fine Arts: Drama and Memory Enhancement

Social Studies: History - Samuel Morse and the Telegraph*

Tom and James loved using Morse code. Introduce your student to a brief background of the man behind this famous "language." Born in 1791, Samuel Morse was the son of a minister and began studying art at a very young age. By the time he graduated from Yale College in 1810, he wanted to pursue art full time. Morse attended the Royal Academy of Arts in London the following year, receiving several important honors during his three years there.

Within ten years, Samuel Morse had established himself as a leading American painter of historical portraits. One of his best known works, a portrait of Marquis de Lafayette, still hangs in New York's City Hall. It was not until 1832, while aboard the ship *Sully* on his way back from Europe, that Morse became interested in the electric telegraph. Overhearing a dinner conversation about electric currents through wire, Morse set out to create what would eventually be known as the telegraph. After completing dozens of sketches during his voyage back to America, Morse began to work on the project as soon as he arrived on shore. Morse lived with his brothers in New York City and worked as an art teacher at an area university in order to make money and continue his work on his new invention.

Teacher's Note: Morse was not alone in his dual giftings of science and art. Another example of such giftedness is the great Leonardo da Vinci. If your student has been interested in this aspect of Samuel Morse's talent, take some time to research da Vinci as well.

Eleven years and many thousands of dollars later, Samuel Morse strung his wire from the Supreme Court in Washington, D.C. to Baltimore, and on May 24, 1844 tapped out on the telegraph his famous line, "What hath God wrought!" Within a few years, Morse became internationally known as the inventor of the telegraph and Morse code. Today, people have nearly forgotten his artistic achievements and know him as the father of telegraphy. Samuel Morse died in 1872.

If your student is interested in Morse code, examine a simple chart of the Morse code alphabet. With practice, anyone can learn the system of dots and dashes. Have fun experimenting with the codes and look for more books and information on Samuel Morse and his amazing invention!

Teacher's Note: For students who continue to show an unusual interest in Morse code and telegraphy, encourage them to investigate becoming a ham radio operator. Amateur radio, as it is known, has a long and rich history and has been credited by many of this century's great inventors as being the source of a life-long interest in science. There are no age restrictions on becoming a licensed radio amateur.

Social Studies: History - Marconi and Wireless Communication

To further spark your student's interest, spend some time discussing the next great historical step in the world of communication—radio. Guglielmo (goo LYEL moh) Marconi (mahr KOH nee) became fascinated by the accomplishments of Samuel Morse. Marconi set out to improve on the system by creating a way to communicate *without wires*. People would be able to communicate across the ocean! It was a daunting and seemingly impossible goal, but Marconi was determined!

Working in the area of electromagnetic waves, Marconi began his journey. Unsupported by his own country, Italy, Marconi moved to Great Britain and gained financial backing for his experiments. After many failed attempts and frustrations, on December 12, 1901, Marconi sent the world's first wireless transatlantic communication! He sent the Morse code for "S" from England to St. John's, Canada.

Coming only fifty-seven years after Samuel Morse's first telegraph message, it was an incredible feat that changed the face of communication forever! Today, radio and television are direct descendants of Marconi's brilliant invention. It is worth taking some extra time to study Marconi's inventions and life in greater detail, too.

Language Arts: Writing and Discussion Questions

1. If Tom and James had lived today, they would have called one another on the telephone (or emailed, texted, messaged online, etc.) instead of using a telegraph. Write a short essay on what your life would be like without today's primary means of communication. What would be different?

2. Tom's father builds an incredible tower. Tom likes to imagine he is Columbus, high on a mast. What would you pretend to be if you could be high up on the tower?

Fine Arts: Drama and Memory Enhancement

Tom liked to pretend he was Christopher Columbus or Commodore Perry (page 118). It helped him remember his lessons. Encourage your student to use drama as a memory tool. Acting out historic scenes and speeches helps us remember things more easily—and it's fun! Perhaps your student would like to act out Marconi's first wireless transmission or Samuel Morse's first telegram. Your student can either write a short "script" of an historical event or make a speech. Consider taking a video of your student's presentation, or better yet, invite other homeschoolers or family to see the presentation! There are many ways dramatic arts can make history come alive! Explore this area with your student— maybe you could even "get in on the act"!

Chapter 11—A Job on a Train

Teacher Summary

Mr. Edison comes home with important news one day: the Grand Trunk Railway has finally completed the track from Port Huron to Detroit. Tom is elated! After dinner, Tom reads an article about the new railroad completion in *The Detroit Free Press*. The next day there is to be a celebration and unveiling of the new locomotive and coach cars. The Edisons decide to attend.

Wearing their best finery, they arrive and the crowd is already swarming. Tom runs to the front so he can see the shiny new locomotive and coaches. Suddenly, Tom overhears a conversation beside him. An older man is saying to another man that they will need to find "a boy to sell newspapers and candy on the train each day" as it travels from Port Huron to Detroit and back. Tom thinks quickly. He needs a real job to buy more chemicals for his laboratory and he loves trains! He walks bravely over to the men and asks if he can have the job. They ask to see his parents, and Mr. and Mrs. Edison give their permission. Tom can't believe it! He is going to work on that beautiful new train and he will be able to expand his laboratory!

What we will cover in this chapter:

Social Studies: History - Steam Locomotives: Wood, Coal and Oil*
Language Arts: Similes and Metaphors
Language Arts: Writing and Discussion Question
Life Skills: Being Helpful
Life Skills: Observation and Opportunities
Life Skills: Your First Job

Social Studies: History - Steam Locomotives: Wood, Coal and Oil*

Tom was fascinated by the powerful steam engine. Encourage your student to do some research on this important part of American history. Steam engines produced energy by boiling water (carried in the tender) until it produced steam. The steam was used to push simple pistons with large steel rods connected that in turn rotated the locomotive's wheels. The fire that heated the water was created by wood, coal or oil. Some locomotives burned cut, split firewood while others burned coal. Still another group of locomotives injected oil into the burner area to produce heat. Regardless of fuel, locomotives carried their source of heat in the tender, along with the water. Steam engines were eventually replaced by modern diesel locomotives, but they remain popular today in many railroad museums and millions of tourists travel behind old-fashioned steam locomotives every year on railfan excursions. A learning diversion on steam engines can be an enjoyable way to learn a great deal about science, history and Americana.

Language Arts: Similes and Metaphors

Draw your student's attention to page 131. Tom describes the smokestack on the train as a "tall silk hat." If your student isn't sure what a "tall silk hat" looks like, show him the illustration at left. Does he think Tom's comparison is a good one? Review the language arts devices known as **similes** and **metaphors**. A simile is the term we use for a comparison using the words "like" or "as." For example, Tom used a simile in his conversation with the man at the train station. He said, "The smokestack looks exactly *like* a tall silk hat."

A metaphor is the term for a direct comparison, omitting the word "like" or "as." For example, Tom might have said, "The smokestack *is* a tall silk hat." This device is much more poetic in nature. Both the simile and metaphor add to our writing and give interesting texture to our description. Encourage your student to try to think of similes and metaphors for some everyday objects around your home. Examples might be: "That garden rake is like a bear's claw" (simile), or "My fingers are thin string beans" (metaphor). If your student enjoys this exercise, make up a list of five objects and have him try to think up at least one simile and one metaphor for each item.

Challenge your student to use these literary devices in his writing and to notice similes and metaphors when he hears others use them.

Language Arts: Writing and Discussion Question

What do you think Tom was thinking when he saw the beautiful new locomotive and coaches? Describe what he might have been feeling as he stood there. Try writing in first person (using words like I, me and my) as you write from Tom's viewpoint.

Life Skills: Being Helpful

At the very beginning of our chapter, Tom is helping his mother with dinner (page 125). Here is yet another example of Tom's helpful spirit. Ask your student what he does to help around the house. Perhaps helping with the meal preparations, assisting younger siblings get dressed in the morning, or mowing the lawn are things he can do. What we do to help is not as important as our willingness to be of service. When we contribute to our family, we reap the benefit of feeling like we're part of a team and the self-confidence that we can help makes a difference! Encourage your student to help out when he can—just like Tom!

Life Skills: Observation and Opportunities

We have discussed in previous lessons the amazing **curiosity** and observation skills Tom has demonstrated. Once again, in this chapter (page 131), Tom is paying strict attention to all that is going on around him. He "pricks up his ears" and hears the man saying they will need a boy to help on the train. By being **observant**, Tom learns of an exciting opportunity! Then, by being **brave**, Tom seizes the opportunity and inquires about the job. Discuss with your student the importance of being observant in his own life. Encourage him to begin watching all that goes on around him. It is in this way we learn about life and discover opportunities along the way!

Life Skills: Your First Job

Tom's first real job has come! Spend some time imagining with your student what he would want to do for a first job. Often, working in a restaurant or a supermarket is a young person's first job. Share with your student what your first job was and what it was like. Everyone in the world at some point begins their first job, but in the United States today, few of us begin as young as Tom! If your student already has specific ideas about what he wants to do for his first job, perhaps researching that industry or position is in order. Have fun dreaming with your student about the future and imagining his first real job!

Chapter 12—The Underground Railway

Teacher Summary

The spring of 1860 is passing quickly. Tom gets up early every morning and eats a good breakfast before setting out for his job on the train. After a hurried time of selling candy, newspapers and ham sandwiches, Tom's train arrives in Detroit at ten o'clock. The train that brings him back to Port Huron doesn't leave until four-thirty in the afternoon, so Tom has a lot of spare time in Detroit. He decides to read all the books in the Detroit Library—twelve inches of books off the shelf each week. Then he goes and spends time watching the men work at the Detroit Locomotive Works. Tom is always interested in how things are made!

For lunch, Tom finds a great hotel. There, Tom meets many interesting men. The men seem to like Tom too, even though he is young. They like Tom's intelligent, mature attitude and how he is always learning. During the lunch period at Finney's, Tom eats his lunch and watches the people around him. He notices there are many African-Americans eating in a back room. Tom knows about the Underground Railroad from listening to conversations and reading the newspaper. He guesses that most of these people are escaping slavery and Finney's is a stop on their Underground Railroad. Tom is glad they are finding a way out of slavery. The days pass quickly and Tom invests more earnings into his laboratory—he now has 200 bottles of chemicals!

What we will cover in this chapter:

Social Studies: Geography - Canada: The Provinces and Territories*
Social Studies: History - Canada: A Brief History of Its Beginning
Social Studies: History - The Underground Railroad
Social Studies: History - The President *Before* Lincoln: Buchanan
Language Arts: Creative Writing
Life Skills: Organizing Your Personal Study

Social Studies: Geography - Canada: The Provinces and Territories*

Every morning at 6:15, Tom's train blows its whistle on the Canadian side of the river (page 134). Use the activity sheet for this chapter to introduce your student to the fascinating geography of the United States' northern neighbor, Canada.

Canada is divided into ten regions called provinces and three regions known as territories. The provinces are, from west to east: British Columbia (capital: Victoria), Alberta (capital: Edmonton), Saskatchewan (capital: Regina), Manitoba (capital: Winnipeg), Ontario (capital: Toronto, as well as the capital city of Canada: Ottawa), Quebec (capital: Quebec City), New Brunswick, (capital: Fredricton), Prince Edward Island (capital: Charlottetown), Nova Scotia (capital: Halifax) and Newfoundland and Labrador (capital: St. John's).

Teacher's Note: Remind your student of the term Maritime Provinces which you learned in FIAR Vol. 5, *The Boxcar Children* lesson (chapter 4). New Brunswick, Nova Scotia and Prince Edward Island as a group are considered the Maritime Provinces. With Newfoundland and Labrador they form the Atlantic Provinces.

Besides the Canadian provinces, there are three more regions known as "territories." These are the Yukon Territory (capital: Whitehorse), the Northwest Territories (capital: Yellowknife), and Nunavut (capital: Iqaluit). Although these last three regions make up more than one-third of Canada's land mass, they represent only 1% of the total population of Canada. This is because much of the terrain in the territories is frozen year-round.

By no means should your student be expected to fully understand the economic and cultural differences of each region in Canada, but do encourage him to do further research into this fascinating geographic area if the interest is present.

Social Studies: History - Canada: A Brief History of Its Beginning

In conjunction with your lesson on Canada's geography, continue your studies by sharing with your student a brief introduction to the history of Canada. Canada's name comes from an Iroquois Indian word **kanata**, meaning village or community. This country has been forced to live up to its name— fighting for unity and community ties has been a constant goal for Canada since its inception.

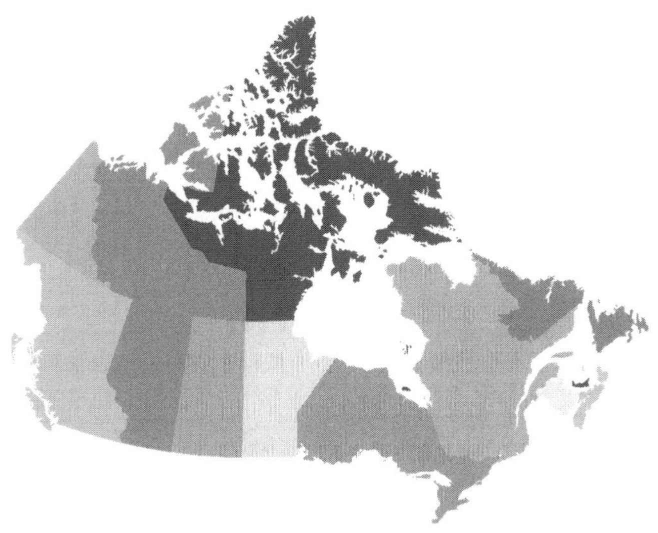

In approximately A.D. 1000, the Vikings, led by Leif Erikson, were the first known Europeans to land on North America. Erikson settled a region called Vinland, on what is believed to be Newfoundland. By the early 1500s French traders began to set up fishing ports and fur trading posts on the eastern coast of Canada. Their region became known as New France, and this influx of culture became the backbone of the now-established French-Canadian heritage.

By 1690, many British colonists were immigrating to Canada and from this time to 1763, the struggle for dominance between the British and French resulted in four separate wars which Great Britain eventually won, conquering New France. Following the war of 1812, Canada's population soared and the immigration of colonists caused an ever-increasing demand for more democratic-like governments. This struggle between the French-Canadian segment of the population and the British/Nouveau Canadians is still an issue of importance today.

If your student is interested, it is highly recommended that you do additional research and topical study on your own regarding Canada's history and culture, so that your student has a beginning understanding of this northern U.S. neighbor and ally. If you have friends or relatives who live, or have lived in Canada, encourage your student to interview them. If you live in a northern state, perhaps a field trip to Canada is appropriate. Even a day trip can be greatly beneficial. Broadening our horizons is part of the learning process!

Social Studies: History - The Underground Railroad

On page 139, Tom is thinking about the Underground Railroad and slavery. Your student may be familiar with this important part of United States history from previous studies in Five in a Row, such as *Follow the Drinking Gourd* (Vol. 2).

The "Underground Railroad" was the secret code name for the way in which slaves made their trek across the country from south to north—away from slavery, toward freedom. Many people helped the slaves escape from their masters' ownership. Other people, known as "slave catchers" worked to capture the runaway slaves and bring them back to the South. One anonymous writer described the Underground Railroad saying, "It was a network of people, from all walks of life, who worked, often illegally, for the freedom of slaves in pre-Civil War America."

Branching off from this subject, explore with your student other related topics of importance including: the abolitionist movement, *Uncle Tom's Cabin* by Harriet Beecher Stowe, and the important historical figures Harriet Tubman and Sojourner Truth.

Teacher's Note: Two excellent sources are *If You Lived at the Time of the Civil War* by Kay Moore and the biography *Sojourner Truth: Ain't I a Woman?* by Patricia C. and Fredrick McKissack.

Social Studies: History - The President *Before* Lincoln—Buchanan

President Buchanan

Point out to your student the following sentence on page 140: "They hoped Abraham Lincoln would be the next President of the United States." Tom is anxious for Mr. Lincoln to step into the role of president, but who is president at this time? Remember, the year is 1860. The current leader is the United States' 15th president, James Buchanan. Share with your student an introduction to this leader of our country.

President James Buchanan was born on April 23, 1791 at Cove Gap, Pennsylvania. He was affiliated with the Democratic Party and was the only U.S. president never to marry. Buchanan was appointed Secretary of State in 1844 by President James Polk. During Polk's administration, war broke out between the United States and Mexico. It was under Secretary Buchanan's leadership that the Treaty of Guadalupe Hidalgo (a peace treaty) was signed in 1848. In this treaty, the United States purchased from Mexico the region extending west from Texas to the Pacific Ocean.

Following Polk's presidency, Buchanan left politics. Retreating to his famous mansion, "Wheatland," in Pennsylvania, he lived the life of a country gentleman. However, the attraction to political life remained. In 1852 he was nominated for president. He was defeated by Franklin Pierce, a little-known candidate from New Hampshire. Under Pierce's administration, Buchanan was appointed Minister to Great Britain. He served in this position for four more years, and in 1856 when the Democrats sought a new candidate for president, they nominated James Buchanan once more. At last, Buchanan was elected president!

It has been said that Buchanan was "**a president sitting atop a volcano**," for during the four years he served as president, the United States was edging closer and closer to the War Between the States. Buchanan was influential in stemming the tide of war for a season, but perhaps no one could have prevented the war entirely. By December of 1860, during the final days of Buchanan's presidency, several states began seceding from the Union, setting the stage for the Civil War.

Draw your student's attention to several of the interesting occurrences that happened during Buchanan's presidency. First, it was during these four years the Pony Express was inaugurated. Also, the watershed decision of Dredd Scott occurred in 1857. If there is time and interest, encourage your student to do further research on this landmark event. Finally, in 1859 John Brown was seized at Harper's Ferry and hanged for his attempt to start a slave revolt. In light of the volatile circumstances in the United States at the time, it is perhaps understandable that Buchanan did not seek renomination. Buchanan supported his vice-president John C. Breckinridge's nomination for president, but Breckinridge was defeated by the tall man from Illinois, Abraham Lincoln.

As you continue to discuss this chapter of Edison's life, encourage your student to locate additional information on our 15th president.

Language Arts: Creative Writing

Your student may want to write an essay on a particular aspect of the large topic of slavery. It can be based on his research of the Underground Railroad, or it may expand on knowledge that he's gained from previous Five in a Row studies or books that he's read. Another idea is to write a short fictitious story utilizing an interesting plot and good characterization that includes the subject of slavery.

Life Skills: Organizing Your Personal Study

Wasn't Tom organized? He looked at the library and decided to read a foot of books per week (page 136). Then he modified his plan to read only the science books. In this way, Tom could keep track of what he was learning and follow a specific goal (to read every book in the library). Encourage your student to begin organizing his study time like Tom did. By setting goals for ourselves, we can better focus on what we're studying at the moment.

Remember, not all students are as gifted in this area as others. The point of this lesson is not to create "organized little robots." Instead, gently share with your student new ways to learn and structure his studies. Good organization skills and study habits are essential to academic success.

Check your library's online catalog to see what they offer on the topic of study skills for students. Many books give an age-appropriate overview of reading comprehension, taking notes, writing essays, and much more.

Chapter 13—The Laboratory on Wheels

Teacher Summary

Tom now has a business partner! James Clancy, Tom's good friend, rides with Tom, helping sell newspapers on the train. Recently, the Grand Trunk Railway has added two new cars onto Tom's train—a new coach and a baggage/mail car. Tom decides, since there is never much mail and because he doesn't have enough time to work on his experiments at home, to ask permission to move his laboratory into the second new car. Tom and James quickly move the laboratory onto the train. Now Tom will have more time to work on his experiments and a friend to help pass the time in Detroit. Tom shows James the library and the Detroit Locomotive Works, and they eat lunch at Finney's Hotel. Tom is happy about all of it!

What we will cover in this chapter:

Social Studies: History - The Railway Post Office System
Science: A New Element: Phosphorus
Language Arts: Sherlock Holmes and *The Hound of the Baskervilles**
Language Arts: Writing and Discussion Question
Life Skills: Problem Solving

Social Studies: History - The Railway Post Office System

On page 143 we read the Grand Trunk Railway adds a mail car to Tom's train. Why did trains have mail cars? Who was the mail for? When did the recipients get their mail? Take this opportunity to share with your student the story of the Railway Post Office.

Trains were used in the mail service to speed up delivery. The train would stop at towns and pick up the bags of outgoing mail. Then, while the train moved across the country, workers sorted the mail by town and date. In smaller towns where the train didn't stop, a device called a "catching arm" was employed. The town postmaster would put their bag of outbound mail on a tall pole. When the train rolled by, the catching arm would snag the bag of mail and pull it back to the train. Likewise, for those same towns, the train postmaster would throw the sorted mail in bags onto the platforms while the train sped down the track.

This method of mail delivery was by far the fastest and most reliable known at this point. By 1869, when the Golden Spike was driven (connecting the Pacific and Atlantic coasts), mail could be delivered from the west coast to New York in only five days! (If your student did the lesson on the Golden Spike in FIAR Vol. 5, *The Boxcar Children*, chapter 3, remind him of what an exciting time that was for the nation to have a transcontinental railroad.)

In today's world, how fast can a letter be delivered in the United States? The Postal Service, as well as many other delivery services, can now deliver letters and packages in as little as one day by using planes instead of trains for delivery. The Post Office first began experimenting with the use of airplanes in the delivery process in 1918. By 1927, airplane carriers had contract routes as delivery operators for the Post Office.

If your student is interested, take a field trip to your local post office. You can point out the different stamps and packaging materials. He can also see the mailbags and sorting bins. Ask if tours are available.

Another related topic of interest is stamps. Ask your student if he would be willing to take a letter from his house across the country and personally deliver it for less than a dollar—probably not. Even today, with increased stamp prices, the cost still seems like a bargain considering the magnitude of the task!

Science: A New Element: Phosphorus

Tom's laboratory is getting huge! Tom has to be particularly careful with his chemical called phosphorus (page 147). Ask your student if he can remember why? Phosphorus is highly flammable (catches on fire easily) and Tom has to keep it wet. Take this opportunity to introduce your student to this new chemical.

Teacher's Note: If you already covered the periodic table of elements in chapter 9, continue this discussion with your student by introducing phosphorus. If you did not do that lesson, go back and use the pictures and explanations listed in chapter 9 to assist you at this time.

Phosphorus was discovered in 1669 by a German scientist, Hennig Brand. The chemical symbol for phosphorus is P. Show your student the atomic weight and number located on the element square.

Phosphorus is essential for healthy bodies! A small amount of phosphorous is found in egg yolks, milk, fish and peas. Phosphorus helps build strong bones and strengthens our brain and nervous system.

Tom was right about phosphorus being dangerous! Because it burns so easily, match tips (the part that strikes the strip) are covered in phosphorus.

Tell your student to watch and see if phosphorus is mentioned again in our story (chapter 15).

Language Arts: Sherlock Holmes and *The Hound of the Baskervilles**

Enriching your student's literary awareness is essential to providing him with a complete education! If you covered the previous lesson on phosphorus, an interesting literary note on this chemical is found in the classic tale, *The Hound of the Baskervilles* by Sir Arthur Conan Doyle.

Teacher's Note: If your student is older and interested in mysteries, all the stories by Sir Arthur Conan Doyle are great reads and will stretch your student's reading comprehension and vocabulary. If your student is younger, these stories also make excellent read-alouds, or you can find good adapted editions such as Great Illustrated Classics.

In *The Hound of the Baskervilles*, phosphorus is the chemical used to create the glowing, fiery eyes of the hound, which frightens the people. The inimitable Holmes, of course, discovers this and solves the mystery of the mysterious hound.

Language Arts: Writing and Discussion Question

What could Tom have done to prevent the fire on the train?

Life Skills: Problem Solving

In this chapter, we see another excellent example of Tom Edison's problem solving skills. Tom doesn't have enough time to work in his laboratory at home. Instead of quitting his job or giving up his laboratory, he comes up with a plan (page 143). Why not move his laboratory onto the train? What a creative thought process!

Teacher's Note: In the end, as you will see in chapter 15, this plan was perhaps not the wisest decision. But, the end result does not negate Tom's creative thinking!

Draw your student's attention to this incident as another way Tom solved a problem. This skill of looking at difficult situations and coming up with solutions is a tremendous life skill. Problem solving takes creativity, intelligence and hard work. The next time your student faces a difficult situation, encourage him to look for creative solutions to his problem, rather than giving up or growing frustrated.

Chapter 14—Tom's Own Newspaper

Teacher Summary

It is now the fall of 1861. The Civil War is underway and people are hungry for the news. The papers Tom and James are selling on the train are more popular than ever! But Tom notices a problem. The telegraph operators get the latest news, but by the time the printers of *The Detroit Free Press* and other papers get the information and print it, the news is already old. Tom decides to solve the problem. He finds an old secondhand printing press for sale and buys it, along with some ink and metal type. Then, he buys some paper from his friend at the *Free Press* office. Now he is ready to print his *own* newspaper!

Tom decides he can stop by the telegraph office in Port Huron each morning, gather the latest news reports on the war and then print his paper on the way to Detroit. Tom decides to call his paper *The Weekly Herald* and sell it for three cents a copy. Tom knows what the people want to read. He includes the latest news of the war, names of the fathers and sons who have joined the Union Army, the market prices of things like eggs and chickens each week, and much more. Tom's *Weekly Herald* is a success! Some people even want to buy a year's subscription!

One day, Tom is so busy selling his papers with the latest news of the Battle of Shiloh, that he doesn't hear the train pulling out. The conductor reaches down to pull Tom up onto the train, and grabs Tom by his ears. Tom hears a popping sound but doesn't stop to notice. From then on, however, Tom Edison was always partially deaf. The popping sound he'd heard was something being injured in his ear canal.

What we will cover in this chapter:

Social Studies: History - Gutenberg and the Printing Press
Social Studies: Market Prices Today
Science: Human Anatomy - The Ear
Language Arts: Different Styles of Writing
Language Arts: Subscriptions
Language Arts: Writing and Discussion Questions
Fine Arts: Making Your Own Newspaper Printing Block
Life Skills: Learning to Communicate with the Deaf*

Social Studies: History - Gutenberg and the Printing Press

Tom buys an old printing press to use for his newspaper (page 150). The press was antiquated, but still functional. Does your student know who invented the first printing press? A man named Johannes Gutenberg from Mainz, Germany invented it!

Gutenberg's birth date and the date of his death are unknown. Along with that mystery, no known portraits of Gutenberg were ever painted during his lifetime. Hailed as one of the most important inventions in all of history, Gutenberg made it possible to print a block of text using uniform, even letters and a technology which allowed the text to be replicated identically as many times as the operator wanted. What did people do before the printing press? Everything was hand written! Imagine the cost of a manuscript or book written by hand!

In 1454, the book Gutenberg chose to use to showcase his great invention was the Bible. This printed text, known around the world as the Gutenberg Bible, is still considered a masterpiece!

If your student is interested in the process of **typography** (the art of printing texts mechanically), look for more books on the topic at your local library. (Also, be sure to take note of the Fine Arts lesson in this chapter.) *Gutenberg* by Leonard Everett Fisher is an excellent picture book biography, and you can find others at your library or online. Take a little time and discuss what our world would be like today without Gutenberg's invention.

Social Studies: Market Prices Today

Tom knows just what the people buying his paper want to read about. One thing he is careful to include is the "market prices" (page 154). Isn't that interesting? He prints the prices for eggs, butter, chickens and potatoes each week. Does your student know how we learn about market prices today? Use this opportunity to introduce both the commodities market and local advertising.

Market prices for things wholesale (large quantities for resale to consumers) can be studied by using the futures market on the commodity exchange. Weekly, daily, even hourly prices for things like wheat, oats, chickens, cattle, frozen orange juice and pork bellies are posted on the commodities market which is easily found online. Reading commodity prices and understanding how the market works is an extremely complicated lesson. However, you may want to introduce your student to this concept. If your student shows interest in this topic, find some beginner books on the commodity market at your local library, or look online for a simple explanation or video of this advanced topic.

On a more understandable, yet practical level, your student can check market prices for his area each week by looking through the grocery advertisements that come in the mail or are advertised online. Just like Tom, grocery stores today print the going price for food and other goods weekly. Because of competition between stores, these prices may vary but they are always similar.

By examining several stores' advertisements and recording the market prices for a certain item over a period of time, your student can record his findings and create a graph that indicates the rise, or fall, in food costs.

Just like Tom's customers, knowing what things cost is an important bit of news for us today!

Science: Human Anatomy - The Ear

Thomas Edison became partially deaf as the result of his accident on the train (page 158). This is a good opportunity to study the ear and how it works. Get a book that explains the parts of the ear and has excellent pictures. Have your student make a study sheet explaining the way an ear works. Let him label the parts and color it.

Teacher's Note: If you haven't already, you might want to start a teacher's file folder for Anatomy. List what you have covered in this lesson. By keeping a teacher's list you will know what you have studied and in what depth. You can then add to it whenever the subject of Anatomy comes up in your unit study lessons. While studying the subject of hearing impairment, you might also want to research Helen Keller (who will be covered in much greater depth in FIAR Vol. 7) and Ludwig van Beethoven.

Language Arts: Different Styles of Writing

Tom wrote all the articles in his newspaper. What makes writing a news article different from other styles of writing? What should you include? How should you say it? All of these questions can be answered by a lesson in different styles of writing.

Share with your student the classic line, "Just the facts, Ma'am." This statement embodies what a news reporter's goal is when writing an article—to include all the important facts. This means no personal opinions or fancy embellishments. An easy way to remember what to include when you're writing news is to think of the four W's—Who, What, When and Where. If you answer these four questions, you are doing great!

To further explore the different styles of writing, challenge your student to write about a specific incident in three different styles—a personal letter, fiction, and a news article. Here is an example:

Incident: The neighbor's cat was hit by a stranger's car.

Personal Letter

You won't believe what happened yesterday! I was standing in my driveway helping my dad wash the van (you did know my family got a new van, didn't you?) and we heard this horrible screeching sound. I told Eddie later that I didn't even hear the cat meow, just the tires of the car. It was so hot I couldn't run very fast, but I went over to see what had happened. I wish I hadn't. It wasn't a pretty sight. Remember last summer when my dog was hit? I sure miss Fido...

Fiction

The sun was beating down on his baseball cap while Sam scrubbed away on the bumper. Water and suds covered his tennis shoes and his hand swatted at mosquitoes. Sam's dad whistled to himself as Sam emptied the bucket of dirty water and refilled it. Suddenly, they both heard a squeal of tires against pavement and their minds were filled with anxious thoughts. What was going on? Running up the street, Sam and his dad were the first to arrive at the scene. It was awful...

News Report

At approximately four o'clock yesterday, a cat owned by Mrs. Mary Woolsworth, of 1118 Maple, was accidentally hit by a car. The stretch of road on which the incident occurred is at the intersection of 12th and Maple, known to many area residents as a dangerous corner. According to witnesses, the blinding afternoon sun may have played a part in the driver's inability to see properly. Mrs. Woolsworth told police that the cat had been...

The first example (personal letter) is filled with details and comments only a close friend would understand or find interesting. The second example (fictional writing) has many embellishments or extended descriptions, which add great texture to the writing, but aren't really necessary for the reader to understand what happened. The final example (news report) includes just the facts. It answers the questions *Who* (Mrs. Woolsworth's cat), *What* (hit by a car), *When* (about one o'clock) and *Where* (corner of 12th and Maple).

This exercise will truly stretch your student's language art skills! Work together with your student on this activity, and watch as his writing skills increase! You might want to think of a specific incident that has occurred recently in your neighborhood and have your student write about it in the three uniquely different styles discussed. Don't be afraid to repeat this assignment every few weeks with new incidents.

Language Arts: Subscriptions

Tom's *Weekly Herald* is so popular that people want to order by subscription. This may be a new word or concept for your student. A **subscription** means that with a one-time payment, the customer (or subscriber) is promised he will receive something (in Tom's case, a newspaper) for a fixed period of time. In other words, Tom's customers wanted to pay for 52 issues (one full year) of *The Weekly Herald* in one payment. In return for their money, Tom would give them their paper each week for an entire year.

Ask your student what the responsibilities of the publisher or creator of a subscription product are? Tom, just like other publishers, had to make note and list who ordered a subscription. He had to record when each person's subscription began. And most importantly, Tom had to make the money he made on subscriptions last.

Many publishers have gone bankrupt when they spent all their subscription earnings early, and then had to keep producing product through the year. What a lot of responsibility for young Tom Edison!

If possible, show your student an example of a subscription card from a magazine. Generally, the customer can choose between one, two or even three years worth of subscription and can either include payment or be billed by the publisher later.

If there is interest, share with your student all the things people can buy by subscription today—food, flowers, music, science kits, clothing, coffee, hygiene products, pet supplies, puzzles, books—the list is virtually endless. Have your student point out different subscriptions when he encounters them.

Language Arts: Writing and Discussion Questions

1. How do you think Tom knew how to print his own paper?

2. How did Tom know what people wanted to see in a newspaper?

Fine Arts: Making Your Own Newspaper Printing Block

Wouldn't it be fun to have your own printing press? Well, here is a very simple way to make one text block. To do this activity you will need a piece of cardboard, bottled glue, a piece of paper and an inkpad. First, have your student print the word "cat." Take the bottle of glue and have him write this word on the cardboard. Let the letters dry and then write over them again with the glue. Continue this process several times until the "type block" letters are built up.

Then, after pressing the fully dried design into the inkpad, press the block down onto paper and you will have printed a bit of text! But what's wrong? The letters are all backwards! Let your student experiment and do it wrong first with this short word, "cat." Then explain to your student that every letter or character that is to be printed on paper must be put on the press blocks backward. The mirrored image of each letter is then correct and readable on the finished product. Now have your student use his own name or an entire headline. Try it again and see the difference! Have fun with this activity and let your student be as creative as he wishes!

Life Skills: Learning to Communicate with the Deaf*

Thomas Edison was always partially deaf as the result of his accident on the train (page 158). Being deaf makes life more of a challenge, but certainly not impossible! Even for people who are profoundly deaf (can't hear anything), life can be fulfilling and fun! One way deaf people are able to communicate with each other and hearing people is called ASL, or American Sign Language.

Teacher's Note: Be sure to explain the other ways deaf people communicate, as well—lip reading, written communication and sometimes vocal communication.

Perhaps your student knows someone who is hearing impaired and is already familiar with ASL. American Sign Language is made up of hand gestures that express ideas rather than words. Since certain words have no direct translation, there is also a language called the American Manual Alphabet. Using these gestures, ideas or words can be spelled out when a single translation is not available.

Learning sign language is fun because it is both interesting and useful! Even if you just learn the alphabet, you can now communicate with a whole segment

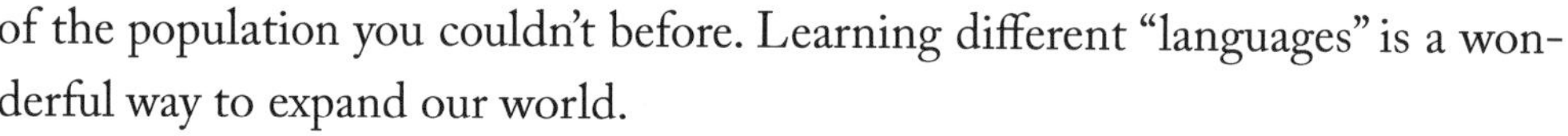

of the population you couldn't before. Learning different "languages" is a wonderful way to expand our world.

Even if your student doesn't have any deaf friends or relatives at the moment, learning the American Manual Alphabet is a great way to communicate with family and friends. There are so many times in life when it is impolite to talk (church, funerals, dinner table with guests, etc.) and by using sign language, your student can communicate quick messages without being disruptive.

If for no other reason than cultural enrichment, encourage your student to explore the realm of deaf communication. It is a creative language form that is both fun to learn and truly useful!

Chapter 15—An Explosion

Teacher Summary

Tom's *Weekly Herald* is gaining in popularity. One day the conductor tells Tom he has a visitor. Tom's unexpected visitor is Mr. George Stephenson from England. Mr. Stephenson tells Tom that *The Weekly Herald* is one of the finest papers he has ever seen. He asks Tom if he can take back one thousand copies to sell in England. Tom is pleased by the praise, and works all night long with James to get the papers ready.

Many months later Mr. Stephenson writes to Tom from London and says the people love Tom's paper and that *The London Times* has printed an article on Tom Edison. Along with the letter, Mr. Stephenson includes a copy of the article about Tom. Tom is very proud.

Tom continues to work in his laboratory on the train, but one day a horrible accident occurs. The train hits rough track and bounces back and forth. Tom's chemicals are knocked to the floor of the car and the phosphorus bursts into flame. Tom and the conductor put out the flames, but the conductor is furious with Tom. He throws Tom off the train along with his printing press and the rest of his laboratory bottles. He tells Tom he never wants to see him again. Tom is heartsick. Eventually, however, he is offered his old job back as long as he doesn't bring his laboratory on board.

Later on in the summer, Tom does a brave deed and saves Mr. Mackenzie's (the telegraph operator) little boy from being hit by a train. To repay him, Mr. Mackenzie offers to teach Tom all he knows about telegraphy. Tom is thrilled and soon he has a job working in the telegraph office.

What we will cover in this chapter:

Social Studies: Career Path - News Editor*
Social Studies: Career Path - Journalist
Language Arts: Writing and Discussion Question
Life Skills: Speaking Words of Praise
Life Skills: Being Brave

Social Studies: Career Path - News Editor*

Tom was the editor of his paper, *The Weekly Herald.* What does an editor of a newspaper or other news source do? Ask your student what he thinks the job involves. Explore this fascinating occupation with your student.

Many people, doing a vast array of different jobs, make up a news staff. The editor is the person in charge of all the writing. Often, if there are many different sections of a newspaper or news source, there will be an editor in charge of each individual section (e.g., food, entertainment, local news, sports, etc.), but there is always a senior editor responsible for the contents of the entire paper. This person's title is usually Editor-in-Chief. This is Tom's job title. Tom has a staff of two. James helps him print and circulate (sell and distribute) the papers, and Tom gathers the news, writes the articles, prints and then sells the papers.

Being the editor-in-chief of a newspaper or news source is an exciting but stressful job. Deadlines for articles, ideas for new articles, gathering facts and verifying quotes, checking the progress of street reporters and giving final approval for the presses to begin the actual printing (or give approval for posting online) are just a few of the daily responsibilities of an editor-in-chief.

If you are able, try to arrange a brief tour of a local newspaper office. Small-town newspaper offices are generally receptive to student tours and even large city papers have a public relations office you can contact.

Social Studies: Career Path - Journalist

If your student is interested in writing, advertising, photography, videography, acting, or just in exploring new ideas, the world of journalism encompasses many career paths. Journalism may be a new word for your student. Journalism is the process of gathering, writing, editing, publishing and circulating news in newspapers, magazines, radio, television, or online. There are so many exciting and different jobs in journalism!

Talk with your student about the following jobs and make a list of more you can think of: news anchor, news writer, news producer, weather person or meteorologist, staff writer, sports writer or commentator, business writer, art director, food critic, movie critic, war correspondent, photojournalist, advertising executive, public relations manager, etc. These jobs can be found in all types of media, whether in print, on radio or television, or online.

For many of these jobs, a person needs a degree in journalism. Most colleges offer a Bachelor of Arts degree in this area and the classes include media-related studies and writing courses. However, many journalists will tell you that on-the-job training is what made them great!

Journalism is a field that often requires a year or two of what is known as an **internship**. Being an intern requires working in the field (at the news station, advertising office, art department, etc.) for little or no money. In this way, you get to "learn the business" and gain valuable experience. Then, after you've proven yourself competent, you may be hired on as an assistant reporter or some other entry-level position.

For more information on journalism and career opportunities in the field, go online or to your local library and do additional research with your student. Being a good journalist requires hard work, dedication, tenacity and a "nose for news." This means knowing what the public wants to hear and where to find that information. Tom Edison had a great nose for news!

Language Arts: Writing and Discussion Question

What do you think Tom was thinking when he saw Jimmie Mackenzie on the train tracks? What would you have done?

Life Skills: Speaking Words of Praise

On page 163 we read about Tom's popularity in London and the article written about his paper in *The London Times*. Mr. Stephenson tells Tom he is doing an excellent job on his paper! Tom is very proud!

Talk with your student about how words of praise make us feel. When someone values us or values what we have accomplished, it makes us feel warm and confident. When someone says, "What an excellent job!" suddenly you feel like you can do even better!

Challenge your student to look for opportunities to speak words of praise to others. It will enrich the person being spoken to and build up your student's character as well! When we hear words of encouragement and praise it helps us through times of frustration. When we're down or sad, we can remember the encouraging word someone said to us! Learning to praise others with our words instead of tearing them down is a major step toward maturity. Who knows? Perhaps if Tom hadn't been encouraged by Mr. Stephenson, he wouldn't have continued to work on his paper to make it the best it could be!

Life Skills: Being Brave

Have your student read pages 167-168 aloud with you. Talk about the frightening incident Tom faces. Imagine seeing a little boy like Jimmie Mackenzie sitting on the railroad tracks and knowing only you could save him! Tom acts heroically.

Ask your student what bravery means to him? Sometimes, being brave means setting aside our own fears in order to help someone in need. But practicing bravery does not mean we must wait for opportunities to "save" a person in distress. Being brave also means facing our own fears.

Learning to swim, playing an instrument in front of an audience at a recital, or telling our parents the truth about something we're nervous about are all examples of acting bravely. Learning to be brave is not a question of age, either. Many adults still have fears in their lives they haven't been able to face yet.

If you have a fear you wish to share with your student, perhaps talking about it will encourage both of you. Discuss with your student things he might need to face with bravery. Being brave is a question of strength and confidence—two things that will improve with practice! Challenge your student to look for opportunities to practice being brave—it will get easier every time.

Chapter 16—Moving Pictures

Teacher Summary

The Wild West Show is in Port Huron! Tom and his friend, James Clancy, are very excited! Before they leave for the show, however, Tom is hard at work on an experiment. By rubbing a glass jar with a piece of silk and then laying cut paper dolls against the glass, Tom can make the dolls "dance" from the static electricity. Tom tells James he wishes he could harness that electricity to their telegraph. Then they wouldn't need batteries!

The boys leave to go the Wild West Show and when they arrive people are already milling about. The panorama show was great! Tom is amazed that some people scream and act frightened just from the drawings on the huge canvas.

After the show, Tom tells James he wants to invent a device that will show people actually moving, instead of just a drawing. James doesn't understand how Tom plans on accomplishing something so amazing, but by now he is used to his inventive friend, Tom Edison!

What we will cover in this chapter:

Social Studies: History - The Wild West Shows
Science: Electricity*
Language Arts: Writing and Discussion Question
Fine Arts: Paper Dolls - As Wild or Winsome as You Wish
Fine Arts: Create Your Own Panorama
Fine Arts: Moving Pictures - A Flip Book
Fine Arts: Tom's Dream - Your Own Movie

Social Studies: History - The Wild West Shows

The panorama picture show Tom and James watch is called a Wild West show. Has your student ever heard of the Wild West? What does it make him think of? Does he know any of the famous names that are synonymous with the Wild West? Look online or find a book at the library and do additional research on topics like the Pony Express, various

Native American tribes, steamships, military forts, famous towns like Tombstone, Arizona; Dodge City, Kansas; Cheyenne, Wyoming, etc.

Also, Buffalo Bill Cody, Annie Oakley and Sitting Bull are particularity associated with the Wild West shows. If you wish, this would be an excellent time to introduce your student to this very unique part of Americana, known as the Wild West. (Your student may already have studied many aspects of the Wild West, especially if you have rowed *Cowboy Charlie* in FIAR Vol. 4. If so, use this lesson for review or to explore new aspects of this colorful time in American history.)

Science: Electricity*

Tom makes his dolls move, almost like magic! (page 174) James is amazed! Ask your student if he has any idea why rubbing glass with a piece of silk would create electricity? Take this opportunity to give your student an introduction into the world of electricity.

Electricity is a form of energy. It is all around us because it is made of tiny particles called electrons. An electron is the smallest unit of electricity—so small, in fact, that not even a microscope can see it! Our bodies, the sky (lightning)—everything is made up in part of electrons. The movement of those electrons is what we call electricity.

There are two types of electricity. **Static electricity** is made up of *non-moving* electrons, usually produced by friction. This is what Tom creates with his paper dolls! If you wish, take a moment and show your student simple examples of static electricity. For instance, when you run a comb through your hair many times your hair will begin to crackle and pop. That is static electricity! If you shuffle your feet across a carpet (in socks) and then touch a metal doorknob or a person, you (and they) may receive a very mild shock. And, just like Tom demonstrates, rubbing glass with a piece of silk will create static electricity, too!

The second type of electricity is called **current electricity**. Current electricity is created by a generator and consists of *moving or flowing* electrons. Almost all of the electricity in the world is generated in one of three ways: 1) generators, 2) batteries, or 3) solar cells.

If your student is interested in this topic, check your local library or online for books, articles, or simple videos on this fascinating topic. Some libraries even have science kits on this and other topics for children. Many resources will include experiments, photographs, and easy-to-understand explanations in a fun and interesting format. Enjoy learning along *with* your student about this fascinating wonder of nature!

Language Arts: Writing and Discussion Question

On page 179 we read that Tom and James "weren't a bit afraid" of the panorama picture show. Do you think this is true?

Fine Arts: Paper Dolls - As Wild or Winsome as You Wish

Tom makes paper dolls (page 172) to prove his experiment in electricity. However, making paper dolls can be a fabulous vehicle for creative design, historical or fanciful recreation, color rendering work and just plain fun!

Your student might wish to begin by cutting the accordion-style dolls just like Tom did. Other options include the more formal version of paper dolls. Begin by creating a cutout cardboard body. Then you can design clothes with little tabs to hold them on. Encourage your student to be as creative as he wishes with these clothed, paper figures. Maybe a doll of Tom Edison would be fun! Perhaps a favorite historic figure or friend. Maybe your student could even create paper replicas of his whole family! Remember, these dolls can be as simple or detailed as your student wishes. Colored pencils, crayons, watercolors, or even tissue paper collage-work can be used to create the doll clothes your student desires. Making paper dolls can be very therapeutic and inspiring—perhaps you may even wish to take part in the fun!

Fine Arts: Create Your Own Panorama

Has your student ever heard of a panorama picture show? Tom and James go to see one, along with people from all over Port Huron and beyond. What is so alluring? Discuss briefly with your student the amazing evolution of entertainment! In the days of kings, people were hired to entertain. Jugglers, mimes, and court jesters were the latest form of entertainment! Later, hand-drawn panoramas like Tom sees became the exciting new form of entertainment.

Imagine, people screaming in fright at an illustration! Today we have movies, videos, virtual reality, video games, high definition television, and much, much more! Our world today is a dizzying array of color and movement—coming at us faster every minute!

For this reason, sometimes it is pleasant to relive and recreate quieter moments of entertainment from days gone by. To help your student create his own panorama, you will need some long white paper.

Unprinted newsprint paper, plain shelf paper, rolled paper from a hobby store, or even the white side of old wrapping paper can be used for this project. Now it's time to draw or paint the pictures and scenes on the paper. Your student's imagination is the best idea-generator there could ever be, but here are few suggestions for the panorama to get you started: scenes from Edison's life; from your student's favorite vacation or dream vacation; scenes from the neighborhood or city where you live; a mini-pictorial of your student's childhood up to this point; or even your student's own version of the Wild West!

When the drawings are complete and the paint is dry, tape each end of the panorama to rods or tubes (wrapping paper or paper towel tubes work great for this!). Then roll all of the paper to one end, leaving the opening scene or title section at the front.

Now, pop some popcorn and watch your student's creation roll by! Perhaps you'd like to invite friends or family for the viewing.

Fine Arts: Moving Pictures - A Flip Book

This lesson illustrates the next stage of entertainment from panorama to the motion picture. Flip books have been around for a long time. Particularly popular in the 1920s and '30s, flip books were highly collectible and often featured famous silent film stars of the day. Has your student ever had the pleasure of seeing a flip book? Take this opportunity to help your student create his own.

To be successful, a flip book must have fairly small pages. Four-inch square pages tend to work well. Explain to your student that the flip book's "movement" is created by drawing a series of pictures, one on each piece of paper. On the first piece of paper, have your student draw the scene—a tree, a flower, a person, a car, a dancer, a family, whatever he wishes. Then, on each successive piece of paper, he needs to draw *almost* the same picture with one bit of the illustration changed. An arm waving, a branch blowing a bit, etc. When the complete scene is finished, staple the pages together at the side and flip away! This is an art project Tom would have loved!

This flip book animation is the basis of cartoons! It is also the way movies and videos work, since each frame is only slightly different from the ones before and after. The tiny amount of movement in each frame creates the illusion of continuous movement when the frames are viewed quickly.

Fine Arts: Tom's Dream - A Movie of Your Own

This activity is the modern culmination of what Tom is wanting—being able to create or record actual moving pictures!

Your student will probably use a cell phone or a digital camera for this activity. Talk to your student about what he needs to think about before he begins filming. There are many types of movies— documentaries, news reports, demonstrative, infomercials and, of course, a filmed screenplay. Let him choose whatever creative form he wishes. Perhaps he would like to try writing his own short script! By involving a friend(s) or family member(s) he can create his own cast and choose his own setting. His "stars" can memorize their lines and he can begin recording!

Another project is filming *"A Day in the Life of..."* his family, his dog, an imaginary friend, whatever! This type of movie can be narrated (telling what is happening, feelings, factual information or the story) by your student while he is recording.

Simple title pages and credits can be drawn on paper and filmed for a short time at the beginning and end of the movie.

Certain children who might lack skill in drawing or sculpture, suddenly discover a whole new world through the eye of a camera! Stephen Spielberg's mother has said in interviews that she couldn't keep a home movie camera out of her son's hands from the time he was a young boy. He loved making movies! Who knows? Perhaps your student is a future film-maker. If not, this is still a fascinating, vibrant art form that is sure to interest and delight your student!

Chapter 17—The Light's Golden Jubilee

Teacher Summary

Thomas Alva Edison, at 22, moved to New York City. Working with a group of friends in an electrical engineering firm, Tom saved enough money to build his first "real" laboratory. He moved to Newark, New Jersey and conducted many experiments. After a time, Tom had so many inventions and so much research underway he was forced to build an even larger laboratory in Menlo Park. It was there, in Menlo Park, along with his friend Francis Jehl, that Tom Edison invented the light bulb—one of the greatest inventions of all time.

The inventions did not stop there. Thomas Edison also invented the phonograph, perfected the telephone mouthpiece, the first motion picture camera and much more. In all, Tom Edison patented over 1,200 inventions during his lifetime!

Years later, as a tribute to the now-great Thomas Alva Edison, his friend Henry Ford "recreated" the Menlo Park Laboratory in Greenfield Village. Down to the most intricate details, Edison's laboratory was perfect and it remains there today. On October 21, 1929, fifty years after the invention of the light bulb, many people gathered at Greenfield Village to watch Mr. Edison "re-enact" the famous discovery. All over the United States people listened to the radio broadcast from Greenfield Village by candlelight. When they heard the radio announcer say Edison had turned on his light bulb, Americans everywhere blew out their candles and turned on their lights!

What we will cover in this chapter:

Social Studies: Geography - Adding to Your Map of Edison's Life
Social Studies: History - President Herbert Hoover
Social Studies: History - The Great Depression and 1929
Science: Edison's Light Bulb - How It Works*

Social Studies: Geography - Adding to Your Map of Edison's Life

Now it's time to complete the map of Tom Edison's life that your student may have begun back in chapter 1. The book tells us that when Tom was 22 years of age he moved to New York City. Then Tom moved to Newark, New Jersey. Both of these cities can be marked on your student's map. If your student wishes to, he can also mark Greenfield Village (located outside of Detroit in Michigan) on his map.

Social Studies: History - President Herbert Hoover

The now-famous Thomas Edison sells a paper to President Hoover on the train ride to Greenfield Village (page 188). Imagine having the president of the United States come to your party and ride a train and ask for your paper! Tom Edison had certainly gained respect and honor worldwide.

President Hoover

Ask your student if he has ever heard of President Hoover? Who was he? What did he do? What do we remember him for? Take this opportunity to introduce your student to our 31st president.

Herbert Hoover was born on August 10, 1874, in West Branch, Iowa. Both his parents died by the time he was nine years old. Sent to live with various relatives after that, Hoover worked many part-time jobs to help pay for his education. Working his way through college by delivering newspapers and doing laundry, Herbert Hoover graduated in 1895 from Leland Stanford University in Palo Alto, California with a degree in mining engineering.

For almost 20 years, Hoover worked on engineering projects in Europe, India, South Africa and Egypt. Considered a genius in mining engineering, Hoover worked as a consultant for other miners all over the world and by the time he was 40 years old he had accumulated enough wealth to retire.

Hoover's success as a businessman was due to the fact he was a master with money and people. Hoover served in a variety of posts as both ambassador and secretary throughout World War I and on through President Coolidge's presidency.

President Coolidge

When Coolidge chose not to run again for the presidency in 1928, Hoover stepped in as the Republican nominee. A hard battle was fought for the victory, but Hoover won on the basis of his promises. Hoover is known for coining the promise "a chicken in every pot." Although America was more prosperous than at any time in history, people are always eager for more. Hoover won in a landslide victory.

Tragic circumstances, however, beyond Hoover's control, were about to develop. On October 24, 1929 (just seven months after Hoover took office), the most devastating stock market crash in history took place. Known forever as Black Thursday, stock prices began to drop rapidly. By the following week, America was facing its greatest challenge since WWI. The Great Depression continued through Hoover's term and into the 1930s.

People often base their opinion of a president on two things: how the economy is doing and whether we are at peace with other countries. For the first time in his life, Hoover was in the wrong place at the wrong time. People immediately began to blame Hoover for causing the economic collapse and any victories he had as president were overshadowed by the Depression.

People were so poor during the Depression that many lived in shanty towns which came to be known as "Hoovervilles." If they were living on the streets, people would use newspapers as blankets and these became known as "Hoover Blankets." The man who had risen to the top was now on his way down, and nothing could stop the fall. In 1932 Franklin Delano Roosevelt defeated the incumbent Hoover in a landslide.

Former President Hoover lived to be 90 years old and wrote several books about his presidency. For more information on President Hoover, look online or find books at your local library. If your student is interested in the Great Depression, go through the following lesson.

Social Studies: History - The Great Depression and 1929

President Hoover buys a paper from the great Tom Edison on October 21, 1929, on his way to a huge party for Edison (page 188). Little did the President know that only three days later, the most tragic economic collapse in history was about to strike the free world. What does your student know about the Great Depression? If you chose to study President Hoover in the previous lesson, you learned that many Americans blamed the president for this nightmare which afflicted the United States for more than a decade.

The Great Depression didn't just happen in one day. Although the huge stock market crash on Black Thursday, October 24, 1929, is considered the beginning of the Depression, many factors occurred leading up to that day, causing the major economic shift. In addition to rapidly falling stock prices, banks became insolvent (unable to pay back depositors) as well. Between January 1930 and March 1933, nearly 9,000 banks went bankrupt and millions of Americans lost all of their savings!

Because of this devastating economic collapse, people began to lose their homes and their possessions and some actually began to starve. People who had a nice home, car and a vacation every year were suddenly on the street. People looked to their president to find an answer.

President Hoover did not move in dramatic government intervention, believing that market forces would quickly solve the struggling economy without direct intervention. It didn't happen. By 1932, Americans chose a new president, Franklin D. Roosevelt, who promised to save America and stop the cycle of the Great Depression. His famous proposal, known as the New Deal, was the exact opposite of what Hoover had suggested.

Roosevelt actively engaged the government in new job and employment mandates, relief for the homeless and starving, and changes in business programs. This is perhaps the most important aspect of the Great Depression—its effects on America in the long term. From that day until this, the United States government has played an ever-increasing role in the lives of both business and individuals.

The Social Security Act was passed in 1935, which provides money for retirement. The attitudes of Americans changed forever after the Great Depression. Many people who had gone through that terrible time in our nation's history were forever preoccupied with obtaining material possessions, food and savings. Today, several generations have passed, and the generations of today don't understand what it was like to live in that type of financial uncertainty and poverty.

If your student is interested in further study on this turning point in American history, find additional books and videos on the topic. If your student has great-grandparents or other relatives who have firsthand or secondhand experience with the Depression, a visit or interview would be most appropriate and educational. Hearing of others' life experiences is always moving and eye opening—particularly for the young. Have your student write a report or "newspaper article" on the basis of his interview.

Science: Edison's Light Bulb - How It Works*

Today, many homes and businesses use light bulbs other than incandescent, such as LED bulbs, halogen bulbs, and compact florescent (CFL) light bulbs. But for well over 100 years, the incandescent light bulb that Thomas Edison invented was the bulb used by virtually everyone. Take this opportunity to explore with your student how an incandescent light bulb works.

Teacher's Note: If possible, obtain a "clear" incandescent light bulb so that you can see the interior without obstruction.

Thomas Edison

Incandescent light bulbs convert electricity into light (and heat too, as a by-product). Electricity is applied to the base of the light bulb and forced through the filament. The filament is the thin, coiled metal wire clearly visible in the bulb. The filament is usually made from tungsten metal. As electricity passes through the filament the wire is heated to nearly 5,000 degrees—this is why incandescent bulbs, unlike more modern light bulbs, feel so hot to the touch after they've been on for some time! As the filament heats up it gives off light. Try looking at a variety of light bulbs including automobile headlights, flashlights, etc.

Encourage your student to check out one or more books on electricity and the light bulb from the library. A three-dimensional model made of clay or cardboard or a drawing explaining the way in which light bulbs convert electricity into light makes a wonderful multi-day science project that is unforgettable.

Also, note that the invention of the light bulb was thrilling, but homes had no electricity! Next, Edison worked on ways to make electric power available to buildings! Imagine trying to find ways to generate power and then developing a system to carry it to homes.

Teacher's Notes

Use this page to jot down relevant info you've found for this *Five in a Row* chapter book, including favorite lessons, go-along resources, field trips, and family memories.

THOMAS A. EDISON: YOUNG INVENTOR

Dates studied:

Student:

Favorite Lesson Topics:

Social Studies:

Science:

Language Arts:

Fine Arts:

Life Skills:

Relevant Library Resources: Books, DVDs, Audio Books

Websites or Video Links:

Related Field Trip Opportunities:

Favorite Quote or Memory During Study:

Great Lakes Regional Map

Name:

Date:

Science: **Scientific Method**

Make copies of this page and use the spaces provided below to record the steps of the scientific method that you see Tom using for each of his inventions. You can also use this page for working through the scientific method with your own discoveries/inventions.

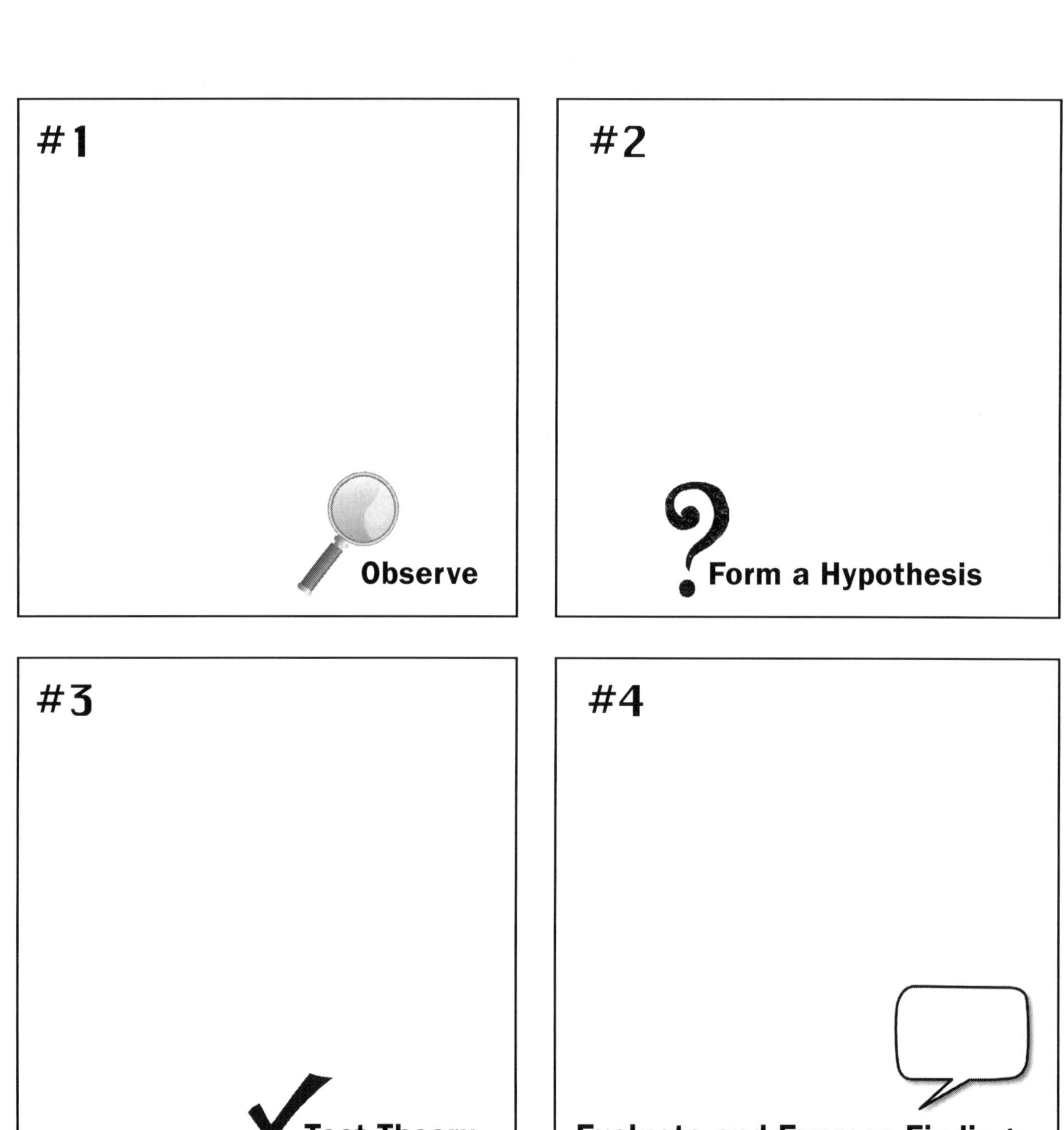

Thomas A. Edison: Young Inventor - Chapter 2

Name:

Date:

Language Arts: **Vocabulary Words**

Use the crossword puzzle below to review the vocabulary words covered in this chapter.

Across

2. a room set aside for entertaining guests

4. the story of your own life, written by you

5. the story of a specific person's life

Down

1. a black, sticky substance made of coal tar and used for waterproofing

3. the distance light travels in one year, 5.88 trillion miles

flip for vocab words: lightyear | autobiography | biography | pitch | parlor

Name:

Date:

History: **Ice Skating Sports**

Research online for each type of skate used in these three ice skating sports. Print and paste a picture of each into the space proided. Note any differences between the skates and the reason for it, (for example, hockey skates are padded to protect the players' feet).

Figure Skating

Speed Skating

Ice Hockey

Thomas A. Edison: Young Inventor - Chapter 4

Name:

Date:

Fine Arts: **Illustrate the Edisons' Home**

Using the description of the Edisons' home from chapter 4 (also listed in the lesson text for **Fine Arts: Drawing Illustrations - The Edison's Home**), draw your illustration onto the book page below.

Name:

Date:

Language Arts: **Famous Sayings - Idioms and Their Meanings**

Some common sayings are **idoms**, like the example in the **Language Arts: Famous Sayings** lesson, "this meal is on the house." An idiom is an expression that has a different meaning from what the literal meaning of the words would be.

Request a book about idioms from the library to use for this activity sheet or search online for common idioms. Write one below along with the acutal meaning. Add an illustration of what the idom sounds like it's saying (for example: an illustration for "this meal is on the house" might look like a plate of food on top of a house).

Idiom: ____

____

Actual Meaning: ____

____

Thomas A. Edison: Young Inventor - Chapter 6

Name:
Date:
History: **Biography - Who Am I?**

After doing the **Social Studies: History - Commodore Perry** lesson, research Matthew Calbraith Perry online.

Print and paste a photograph of Commodore Perry into the frame. Write information gathered through your research into the spaces below.

Name: ______________________________

Lived: ______________________________

Known for: ______________________________

____

____

Connections to story: ______________________________

____

____

Name:

Date:

Language Arts: **Penmanship - Calligraphy**

Calligraphy is the art of writing words with a pen or brush and ink in a decorative way. A calligraphy marker will make it easier to draw the thin/thick lines of the letters shown. Using the alphabet chart below and a piece of tracing paper, try to copy the letters. Or, you could look at them and try to copy them onto a new sheet of paper.

Thomas A. Edison: Young Inventor - Chapter 8

Name:

Date:

Science: **Common Household Compounds and Their Chemical Names**

Search online for "chemical name for ________" (fill in the blank with the common names listed below). Write the chemical name found in the space next to each common compound listed below. Cut out pairs of names and paste onto jars to label if creating your own lab.

* go-along book option - *Why There's Antifreeze in Your Toothpaste: The Chemistry of Household Ingredients* by Simon Quellen Field

white vinegar ____________________

household ammonia ____________________

epsom salts ____________________

baking soda ____________________

washing soda ____________________

table salt ____________________

instant tea ____________________

fruit juice ____________________

borax ____________________

soda water ____________________

Thomas A. Edison: Young Inventor - Chapter 9

Name:

Date:

Language Arts: **Vocabulary Words**

After finishing the ninth chapter, use the crossword puzzle below to review the vocabulary words covered in chapters 3 and 9.

Across

3. (ch. 3) dangerous condition occurring when the body's temperature falls below the normal range of 98.6° F

5. (ch. 3) the term used for ice melting under pressure and refreezing when the pressure is lifted

6. (ch. 3) the lowest temperature at which the air can contain all of its vapors

Down

1. (ch. 9) a person who manages his own business, assuming the risk for the sake of the potential profit

2. (ch. 9) a heavy, bright-red mineral and the principal source of mercury

4. (ch. 3) numbness and possible loss of affected area which occurs when skin is exposed to severe cold

flip for vocab words: hypothermia | regelation | dewpoint | entrepreneur | cinnabar | frostbite

Name:
Date:
History: **Biography - Who Am I?**

After doing the **Social Studies: History - Samuel Morse and the Telegraph** lesson, research Samuel Morse online or read a book from the library about this famous inventor. *Samuel Morse, That's Who!: The Story of the Telegraph and Morse Code* by Tracy Nelson Maurer is an informative biography that celebrates the early technological pioneer.

Print and paste an image of Samuel Morse into the frame. Write information gathered through your research into the spaces below.

Name: ______________________________

Lived: ______________________________

Known for: ______________________________

____

____

Connections to story: ______________________________

____

____

Name:

Date:

Science: **Natural Resources**

Wood, coal, and oil, mentioned in the lesson on steam locomotives, are three important natural resources. Search "natural resources" online and fill in the blanks below with these and other natural resources that you find through your research.

example: wood

____

____

____

____

____

____

____

Bonus Question: Which natural resources are common in your region?

____

____

Name:

Date:

Geography: **Canada**

Use an atlas or look online to find the names and locations of the Canadian provinces and territories. Write them in the correct spaces on the map below.

Name:
Date:
Language Arts: **Biography - Who Am I?**

After doing the **Language Arts: Sherlock Holmes and *The Hound of the Baskervilles*** lesson, research Sir Arthur Conan Doyle online.

Print and paste an image of Sir Aurthur Conan Doyle into the frame. Write information gathered through your research into the spaces below.

Name: ____________________

Lived: ____________________

Known for: ____________________

____

____

Connections to story: ____________________

____

____

Thomas A. Edison: Young Inventor - Chapter 14

Name:

Date:

Life Skills: **Learning to Communicate with the Deaf**

To gain additional understanding of how being deaf could affect someone's daily life, think about the following things that are designed for the hearing and discuss what type of accomadations could make them work for those who are deaf. Search online for answers by searching "how do deaf people use ________." Record your ideas or the answer from your reserach below.

doorbell ______________________________

television ______________________________

telephone ______________________________

smoke detector ______________________________

To the right is the American Manual Alphabet. Using the chart, learn how to sign your name.

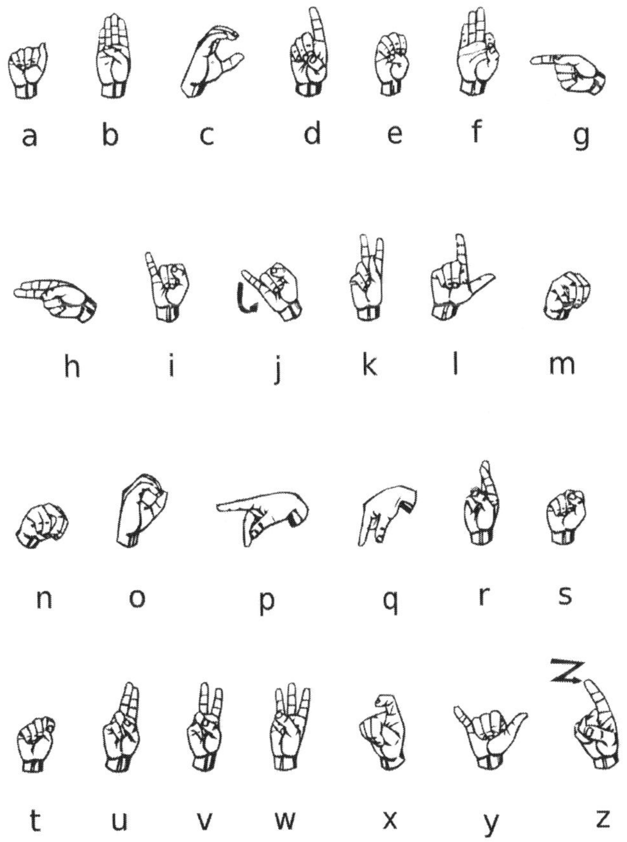

a b c d e f g

h i j k l m

n o p q r s

Z

t u v w x y z

*_Song for a Whale_ by Lynne Kelly is an excellent go-along book for undertanding the daily challenges of living with a hearing imparment.

Name:

Date:

History: **A Newspaper Article**

After doing the **Social Studies: Career Path - News Editor** lesson, try your hand at gathering and writing a short newspaper article like Tom did. Use the article blanks below to guide you.

Newspaper Article

headline

byline (your name)

date

Who, What, When, Where?

quote

photograph

Joke of the Week

Thomas A. Edison: Young Inventor - Chapter 16

Name:

Date:

Science: **Forms of Energy**

In Chapter 16, Tom uses electricity (one form of energy) to make his paper dolls move. Search online for "light (heat, sound, mechanical) energy examples" to find different ways each form of energy appears or opporates. Write in (or illustrate) examples from your research to the right of each icon below.

example: candle

light (radiant)

heat (thermal)

sound (wave motion)

mechanical

Name:

Date:

Science: **Parts of an Incandescent Light Bulb**

After doing the **Science: Edison's Light Bulb - How It Works** lesson, research "parts of an incandescent lightbulb." Use your research and the answers below to fill in the blanks around the light bulb.

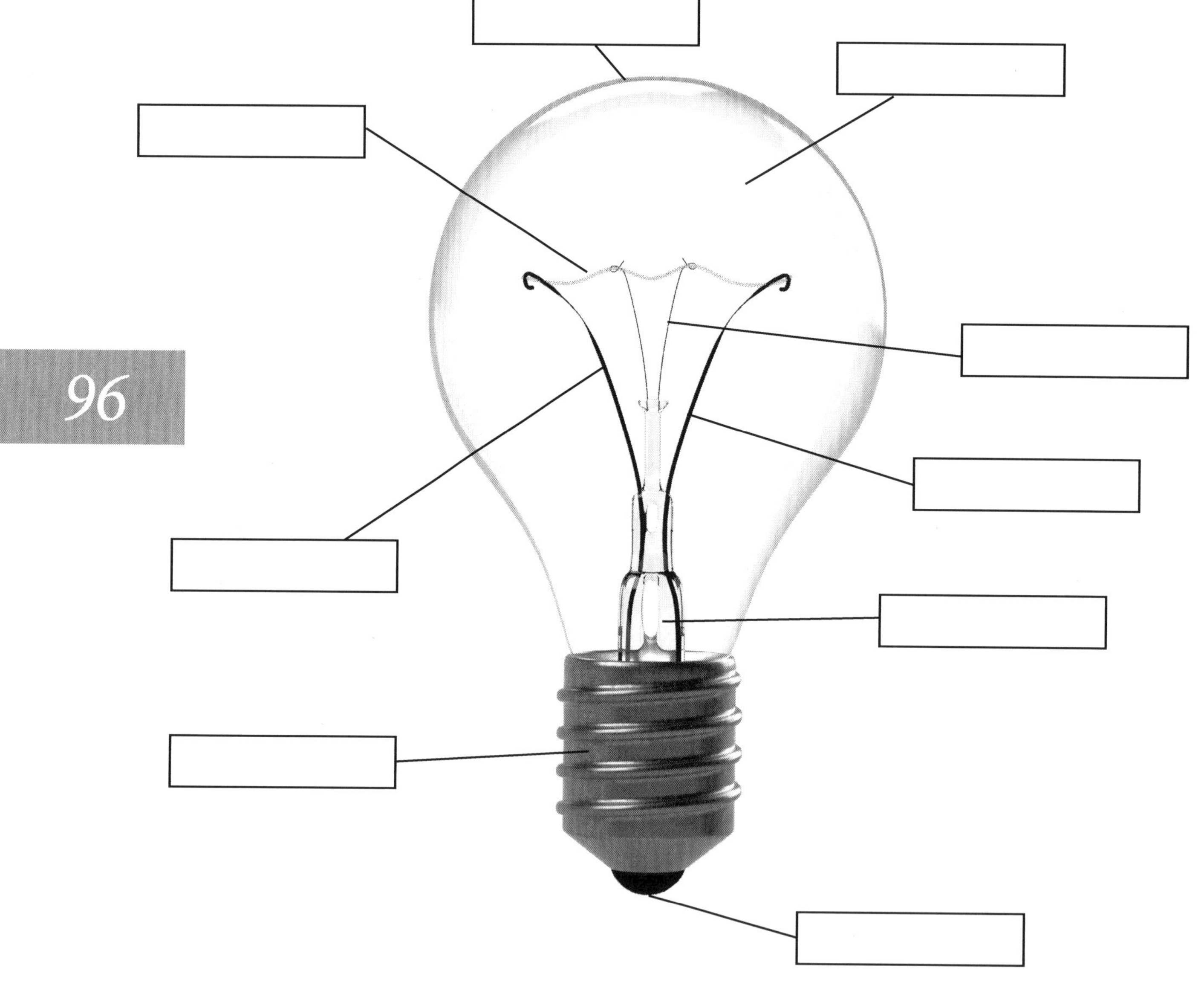

filament contact wire inert gas base contact wire electrical foot contact

support wire glass bulb metal glass

Thomas Alva Edison

Sarah, Plain and Tall

Title: *Sarah, Plain and Tall*
Author: Patricia MacLachlan
Copyright: 1985

Chapter 1

Teacher Summary

Our first chapter begins with an introduction to Caleb and his sister Anna. We find out their mother died when Caleb was born, and now the children live with their father, Jacob Witting, and their two dogs, Nick and Lottie, on the great wide prairie. Caleb, longing to know more about his mother and to remember her, asks Anna about the day he was born. Anna tells him the story as best she can remember. Caleb knows that his mother sang beautiful songs, but he doesn't remember her voice or the times. Anna says she doesn't either. That night, as the family sits down for the evening meal, Papa tells the children some interesting news. He has placed an advertisement for a new wife—a new mother for Anna and Caleb. The children are surprised, and are further surprised that he has received a response. He reads the letter from Sarah Elisabeth Wheaton to the children. Sarah sounds kind in the letter and everyone smiles. Anna, with her arm around Caleb, asks Papa in his next letter to find out if Sarah sings.

What we will cover in this chapter

Social Studies: Geography - Maine and the Eastern United States
Social Studies: Geography - Prairies: Beginning Your Notebook
Science: Babies and Human Development
Science: Rocks - Three Types
Language Arts: MacLachlan's Use of a Continuing Symbol: Singing
Language Arts: Letter Writing - P.S. and R.S.V.P.*
Language Arts: Creative Writing - Writing a Personal Introduction
Language Arts: Avoiding Clichés
Language Arts: Writing and Discussion Question
Fine Arts: Composition in Drawing
Life Skills: Memories
Life Skills: Singing - A Family Activity

Social Studies: Geography - Maine and the Eastern United States

We read in Sarah's letter to Jacob that she lives in Maine. Sarah also notes, "...the sea is as far east as I can go." Draw your student's attention to that phrase. Indeed, Maine is the eastern-most point of the United States. All that is beyond Maine is the Atlantic Ocean. Locate Maine with your student on a United States map. Find Eastport and share with your student that it lies farther to the east than any other city in the United States. At this point, the reader doesn't know what city Sarah is from, but her observation is true. If Sarah is to move to another state, her only options lie further to the west.

Other information regarding Maine can be shared with your student. For example, the capital is Augusta, and Maine's largest city is Portland. The state bird is the chickadee and the state flower is the white pine cone and tassel.

Maine's coast is rocky and sandy, and is dotted by many lighthouses and villages. Because Maine is densely wooded, it is home to a massive wood processing industry. Interesting to note, Maine makes more toothpicks than any other state.

In early New England vernacular, the word "down" was used to refer to "north." To this day, people from Maine are often referred to as "Down Easters'" or "Down Easterners." Sarah might have been called a Down Easter from time to time.

If there is interest, continue studying the eastern coast and Maine. Check your local library for information about this region and state, or look online for pictures of this beautiful area of the country.

Social Studies: Geography - Prairies: Beginning Your Notebook

Teacher's Note: In *Sarah, Plain and Tall*, we will discover and explore many fascinating facts about two specific regions of the United States—the Northeastern seacoast and the prairies. We will learn about the sea, because that is where Sarah is from, and we will explore the prairies because that is where the Wittings live. It would be both educational and entertaining for your student to keep a **Prairie Notebook** and a **Sea Notebook**. Your student can include lists of facts gathered from the story, as well as pictures and notes she makes and collects on her own. The lessons will point out facts as well, so you can be sure to catch all of MacLachlan's descriptions. (We will briefly revisit or recall these notebooks in our study of *Skylark* in FIAR Vol. 7, as well.)

In this chapter, MacLachlan tells us that Papa, Caleb

and Anna live on the prairie. In the Fine Arts section of this chapter's lessons, there is an art lesson devoted to this line: "Outside, the prairie reached out and touched the places where the sky came down." It might be appropriate to have your student copy this sentence down as a first entry in her Prairie Notebook and then, if the art lesson is completed from this chapter as well, to include the artwork in the notebook beneath the quote. In this way, she will be starting what will become a continuing project, as well as "illustrating" her entry with a correlating art lesson.

Encourage your student to decorate the outside of her Prairie Notebook and her Sea Notebook. She can refer to them and add to them as often as she wishes throughout her studies.

As general background information to share with your student, the region known as the "prairie" in the United States extends from central Texas to North Dakota, including the majority of Oklahoma, Kansas, Nebraska, Iowa, Illinois, South Dakota and North Dakota. In general, a prairie is a flat or slightly hilly region covered in tall, wild grasses. When you live on a prairie, the summers can be very hot (100°+ F) and winters are cold (-30° F). Rainfall is moderate, and although the soil is generally rich and fertile, the lack of rain can make growing crops trying during particularly dry seasons.

If your student has read the classic books by Laura Ingalls Wilder, including *Little House on the Prairie*, she may already be familiar with many of the characteristics of this fascinating region. If your student hasn't read that series, now may be a good time to suggest it as supplementary reading.

Science: Babies and Human Development

Caleb wanted Anna to tell him the story of the day he was born. He asks what he looked like. Anna says, "You didn't have any clothes on ... Not enough [hair] to talk about ..." She shows Caleb a ball of pale bread dough and tells him he looked like that.

Babies are fascinating. If your student has an infant sibling currently, or remembers when her siblings were very young, discuss with her how she would describe a baby. Would she compare it to a ball of bread dough, all pale and soft and bald? Have your student write her own idea of an analogy describing a baby. If your student hasn't had the opportunity to be around an infant, perhaps this would be a good time to locate a friend or neighbor with a baby and ask if she could visit.

As a lesson in science, babies can be the appropriate jumping-off point for a discussion regarding human development. Learning about the nine-month human gestation period and the changes that occur at each stage would be a fascinating study. Share as much or as little with your student from the following list of general baby facts as is appropriate and then encourage her to make his own flowchart or poster. She can list each stage of human embryo development and then make her own illustrations to correspond.

A Baby in Development

0. Fertilized Egg: The beginning of a baby, conception, begins with something no larger than a grain of sand. Inside that tiny egg is all the "information" about the baby—hair color, eye color, physical traits (moles, birthmarks, etc.) and much more. (You may wish to explore a simple book on genetics including RNA and DNA from your library as an introduction.)

1. First Two Months: The baby is called an embryo. Cell divisions take place rapidly. By the end of the second month, although the baby is only about one inch long, all her major organs and features are in place. Her brain, heart, legs, arms, fingers, toes and a little bit of a nose are formed.

2. Months Three and Four: The baby is now called a fetus and she is floating freely in the special fluid called amniotic fluid, inside the uterus with the placenta. She is now about 5 inches long and weighs about two ounces.

Teacher's Note: Help make these measurements relative and relevant by showing your student exact lengths and weights.

3. Months Five and Six: The baby can move and kick because she is getting stronger. The mother can feel the baby moving and the baby can hear. She can even recognize her own mother's voice. At this stage, babies even suck their thumb.

4. Month Seven: By now the baby is almost 14 inches in length and will begin to turn herself upside down, getting ready for birth.

5. Months Eight and Nine: The baby continues to gain weight and her lungs develop more fully. When she is ready to be born, she will weigh an average of 7 pounds and be approximately 20 inches in length.

When we look at a baby, we notice several things right away. Many babies do not have much hair at all, cry a lot, sleep a lot and grow very fast! When a baby is born, her body proportions are very different from that of an adult. If you look at most newborn babies, you will notice that their heads make up nearly 1/4 of their entire body's length. In contrast, an adult's head makes up approximately only 1/8 of her total body length. As babies grow and develop, this change in head/body proportion is just one of many physical and mental processes that take place.

Take some time with your student and look at pictures of her when she was a baby. How different she looks! Can she find a picture of herself that looks like she does now? Is there a photograph that has an expression or body movement that she still makes or does?

Also, if there is interest, your student may wish to discuss or study in more depth the topic of human sexual reproduction and how the egg and sperm unite. This is a very specific area of study and, of course, is left entirely to the teacher's discretion.

Science: Rocks - Three Types

Anna turns the bread dough she has been kneading out onto a marble slab on her table. Does your student know what type of rock marble is? What other kinds of rock are there? Take this opportunity to begin a study on rocks—where and how they are formed and the characteristics they possess.

Almost all rocks in the world (98%) are made up of only eight elements: oxygen, silicon, aluminum, iron, calcium, sodium, potassium, and magnesium. (Your student may enjoy finding these elements on the periodic table of elements.) And there are many kinds of rocks! Does your student know there is a kind of rock that floats in water? It is called pumice and it floats when placed in water. The reason a pumice rock floats is that it was once hot volcanic lava, filled with various gases. When the lava cooled, the gas escaped and left rocks with numerous tiny holes that then filled with air. Perhaps you can obtain a piece of pumice rock for your student and let her put it in water and watch it float. (Pumice stones can be used for removing callouses and are often sold at drugstores in the foot care section.)

There are three main types of rock: **igneous**, **metamorphic**, and **sedimentary**. Marble falls into the second category, and is a metamorphic rock. Here are some general notes on each type of rock:

Igneous—Igneous rocks are formed when molten/melted rock materials deep within the earth's core (called magma) are forced to the earth's surface (by means of earthquake, volcanoes, etc.) and then cool and harden. Igneous rocks include pumice (the floating rock), basalt, and granite.

Metamorphic—The word "metamorphic" comes from the Greek word/prefix "meta," meaning to change. Just as the word's origin implies, a metamorphic rock is one whose composition has been altered or changed in some way. For example, slate is a metamorphic rock formed from shale and clay hardening together. Such changes can be caused by heat or pressure. Metamorphic rocks include slate, marble and quartzite.

Sedimentary—Sedimentary rocks are formed from many layers of other substances (various rocks, mineral deposits, plants, animal skeletons, shells) which, as years pass, form rock. Sedimentary rocks include coal, limestone, shale, and flint.

Beginning a rock collection can be a great hands-on way to learn more about rocks. If there is interest, locate a rock/mineral store in your area and visit. If there isn't a specialized store, a visit to a natural history museum is just as valuable. Be sure to collect samples and learn about rocks found in your area!

Language Arts: MacLachlan's Use of a Continuing Symbol: Singing

Caleb wishes Anna would sing. He knows, from Anna and Papa telling him, that his mother sang. He is convinced if they sang the same songs, even now, he could remember her, too. Throughout *Sarah, Plain and Tall*, we will hear the Witting family discuss singing and we will eventually find out if Sarah sings—and what that means to Anna, Caleb and Papa.

Share with your student the idea of a symbol. A symbol is something that represents something else. For example, a graph could be called a symbol. If a child is saving her money for a bicycle and every week she draws a line to the amount she has saved, in relation to the amount she needs, that graph represents her money. It isn't really her dollars and coins, but it shows how much it is growing. The symbol (graph) represents the saved amounts.

Writers often employ a literary device known as symbolism. Coming from the word symbol, symbolism means a phrase, thought, action or set of circumstances which represent to the reader what is happening with the characters and the story. In our story, *Sarah, Plain and Tall*, MacLachlan uses symbolism. As your student will discover, the topic of singing will be a reoccurring theme throughout our story. For Caleb and Anna, singing represents their mother. For us, singing is a "picture" or symbol of how Papa, Anna and Caleb heal from the pain of losing Mrs. Witting and how Sarah helps bring that healing.

For now, just draw your student's attention to the concept of literary symbolism and the many times that singing is mentioned in this first chapter. Then, as the story unfolds over the next several chapters, you can trace the symbolism along with her.

Language Arts: Letter Writing - P.S. and R.S.V.P.*

Sarah Wheaton's letter to the Wittings includes an interesting footnote. Sarah writes, beneath her signature, "P.S. Do you have opinions on cats? I have one." Does your student know what P.S. stands for? Where does it come from? Does she understand R.S.V.P. and what that means? To begin, P.S. stands for postscript—which means "after (post) writing (script)." P.S. is commonly used by people when their letters are complete, and they find they have something more to add. Like Sarah, who probably remembered after the fact that she wished to inquire about cats.

Another common letter abbreviation is R.S.V.P. Used on invitations, it is actually an abbreviation for a phrase in French. It stands for "Respondez s'il vous plait" (re spon DAY see voo play) which translates to "please reply." If you were to send a party invitation and you wished to know how many people were coming to the party, generally you would include this abbreviation at the bottom of the card, and then people would know to inform you of their intentions.

Show your student an example of each of these abbreviations and encourage her to employ them in her own writing.

Language Arts: Creative Writing - Writing a Personal Introduction

Sarah wrote a lovely first letter to the Wittings. It was informative and interesting and she let them get to know her, even though it was a short letter. It must have been difficult for Sarah to decide what to include in her response to the advertisement Papa put out. She has never met Papa or his children.

Ask your student what she would write to a person she has never met. How would she describe herself? How would she describe where she lives? Her family? Her interests? What would she put in a P.S.?

As a creative writing assignment, have your student write a letter, similar to Sarah's. She can make up an imaginary person (someone she has never met) and then write a letter of introduction. It should be the kind of letter someone would want to respond to—full of interesting information about your student.

Language Arts: Avoiding Clichés

As always, when you're working with your student on creative writing, you want to encourage her to avoid clichés (for example, cold as marble, blue as the sky, smooth as silk, etc.). Good writers are creative and come up with interesting, different descriptions that capture their readers' imaginations. MacLachlan uses striking imagery and descriptions in this story. Look at where Anna is remembering the sad day when Mama died. MacLachlan writes, "...remembering the morning that Mama had died, cruel and sunny." Has your student ever thought of the words cruel and sunny together? It is a fascinating description, because it catches the reader off guard, but still accurately describes the scene. Even though the day was bright, Anna saw the light, not as warm or comforting, but as a cruel glare—because of her circumstances.

Then there is another interesting description: "And Maggie had come from Tennessee. Her hair was the color of turnips and she laughed." What is the color of turnips? Perhaps your student doesn't know. When turnips are grown, they have white tops and purple bottoms. We assume our author doesn't mean Maggie's hair was purple; instead, when you peel turnips and mash them, they are a very pale cream color. What an original way to tell us that Maggie's hair is a pale, almost white blonde.

If your student is interested in this description, locate or buy a few turnips and use the following recipe to see what Maggie's hair looked like.

Mashed Turnips

1-2 turnips, peeled and diced (2 cups)
enough water to cover in pot

Simmer for 10-15 minutes, or until fork tender. Drain and mash with some butter and salt. Delicious!

Language Arts: Writing and Discussion Question

In Sarah's letter to Jacob Witting, she says, "I have never been married, but I have been asked." Why would Sarah include this in her letter? What might she be trying to say?

Language Arts: Vocabulary

gestation The process of having young forming in the uterus.

igneous Rock formed by the cooling and solidifying of magma.

metamorphic Rock changed in form by pressure, moisture and heat.

sedimentary Rock formed from sediment.

symbol Something that represents something else.

R.S.V.P. Acronym for French "respondez s'il vous plait." Please respond.

cliché An overused phrase or example.

Fine Arts: Composition in Drawing

With your student, find this beautiful sentence in the chapter: "Outside, the prairie reached out and touched the places where the sky came down." What does your student think that the prairie touching the sky would look like?

If your student is younger, simply using this sentence as a title or description for a picture she can draw or paint could be an excellent art lesson in illustration. If your student is older, more skilled artistically, or interested in learning new ways to draw more effectively, take this opportunity to share with her an introductory lesson in composition, using MacLachlan's beautifully descriptive sentence.

Just as a musician can compose a piece of music, so we, as artists, can compose (design and lay out) our pictures. Although visual arts composition can include many aspects, one major area of decision falls in the category known as the "rule of thirds." Generally, artists compose pictures in thirds. For example, an artist, taking MacLachlan's description, might choose to cover 2/3 of her paper with prairie and 1/3 with sky. Or she could choose the opposite. Most young children, if asked to draw the prairie and the sky, would eye the paper and divide it in half. Seldom does an artist divide a composition directly in half because it makes the work appear less natural. It is more pleasing to the eye and gives a more natural effect to use the rule of thirds. However, often artists "play" with their composition to emphasize various things. For example, if your student read "...where the sky came down" and pictured the sky as massive, she might wish to compose her picture with just a slim strip of prairie at the bottom of the paper and large expanses of sky. Conversely, the picture could be drawn with the prairies reaching nearly the top of the paper and just a sliver of sky at the top.

Share with your student the rule of thirds and let her try it out, using MacLachlan's line as inspiration. Allow her to adjust the horizons and ratios to create pictures with various impacts.

When this lesson is complete, have your student select her favorite drawing and place it in her Prairie Notebook.

Life Skills: Memories

From this first chapter, we can see that Anna and Caleb miss their mother very much. We see Anna's pain that comes from being reminded of things that are now only memories. She can remember the day Caleb was born. She remembers her Mama talking to her. She can remember the singing. Anna has her own set of hurts and longings to overcome, but at least she can remember something.

Caleb, on the other hand, cannot. How sad! To remember something that is gone is painful, but to never know your Mama at all must be worse. That is why he asks Anna to retell the stories, to somehow keep his Mama alive in his heart.

Talk with your student about memories. Perhaps she has had a loved one (grandparent, etc.) pass away and she can remember certain things. What memories stand out? What things have been forgotten? What is your student's earliest memory and how old was she at the time of the event?

Memories that are made with family and friends are wonderful because they allow us to hold on to special times. Make some memories with your student today.

Life Skills: Singing - A Family Activity

Obviously, Anna and Caleb's Mama liked to sing. Singing can be a memorable family time. Singing Christmas carols at Christmas is delightful, but there are other enjoyable songs that can be sung throughout the year. Driving in the car, working in the kitchen, playing in the yard—all sorts of activities can be made more enjoyable and memorable if some songs are shared. Encourage your student to sing more and to learn new songs, as she is able.

Chapter 2

Teacher Summary

Caleb, Anna and Papa all write Sarah letters. Sarah responds, answering questions about herself, Maine, her cat and her brother William. The children, especially Caleb, enjoy the letters immensely. Papa tells the children that Sarah has offered to come for one month to visit and to see how they all get along. The children eagerly give their consent. The days go by and soon Sarah sends her response. It is short and to the point, "Dear Jacob, I will come by train. I will wear a yellow hat. I am plain and tall. Sarah." Caleb notices an extra line at the bottom of the note. Papa smiles and reads it to the children. "Tell them I sing" was all it said.

What we will cover in this chapter:

Social Studies: Geography - North Atlantic Seacoast: Beginning Your Notebook
Science: Fog - What It Is and How It Is Formed
Science: Seals and Whales
Language Arts: Continuing Symbolism - Singing
Language Arts: Reconstructing the Unknown - Learning to Infer
Language Arts: Writing and Discussion Question
Language Arts: Vocabulary*
Fine Arts: Illustrating Envelopes
Fine Arts: The Colors of the Sea

Social Studies: Geography - North Atlantic Seacoast: Beginning Your Notebook

Just as your student should be keeping a Prairie Notebook, she should also keep, as a continuing project for this unit, a notebook about the sea. As our story unfolds, particularly in this chapter, we learn that the sea is an important part of Sarah's life. Throughout the story we gather fascinating facts regarding the colors, animal life, vegetation and culture surrounding the North Atlantic seacoast—all from Sarah's perspective. Encourage your student to compile as many "clues" as she can regarding the sea and record them in whatever way she wishes—as lists, illustrations, pictures found online, etc.

In chapter 2, we learn several key characteristics of the sea and the environment surrounding it. From Sarah's letters we gather the following facts: The colors of the sea are blue, gray and green; the sea can be "fogbound" and a color for which there is no name; her brother is a fisherman and catches flounder, sea bass and bluefish; whales, seals, and sea birds can be seen; the sea is salty and weathers the surrounding buildings.

It is obvious that Sarah's home and life are quite different from that of the Wittings who live on the prairie. Anna and Caleb are both aware that Sarah may miss the sea too much, and not wish to stay with them once she visits. Taking notice of these differences and recording them is an exercise in both observation and cultural enrichment. The author will continue to make occasional notes on the following "clues" we gather about the sea as our story unfolds.

Science: Fog - What It Is and How It Is Formed

In Sarah's letter to Anna, she describes her brother William, the fisherman and the sea. Draw your student's attention to the following sentence: "...he tells me that when he is in the middle of a fogbound sea..." Does your student know what a "fogbound sea" looks like? Fog can greatly reduce visibility; therefore, William's ship was "bound," unable to move safely until the fog lifted. Sailors and fishermen must often deal with weather conditions and adjust their course or plans accordingly. Your student may have studied fog in *Paul Revere's Ride* (FIAR Vol. 3). This lesson expands on that one, or it may be all-new information for your student.

Fog is formed by countless numbers of water droplets that have evaporated from rivers, ponds, lakes or (in William's case) the ocean. As the water evaporates, it expands, cools and becomes water vapor. Air can only contain a specific amount of water at any given temperature. This amount is known as the holding capacity. The warmer air is, the more water vapor it can contain. That is why fog is often seen in the early morning or evening when the air is cooler. As the sun warms the air throughout the day, water vapor is absorbed into the air, and fog is no longer visible.

If there is interest, introduce your student to the four main divisions of fog. They are: advection fog, frontal fog, radiation fog, and upslope fog.

Advection fog is the type of fog that Sarah's brother William described to her when he talked about the "fogbound" sea. Advection fog is created when warm air moves over a large body of water and then hits a cooler area (for example, land or a seacoast). The drop in temperature creates fog.

The second type, **frontal fog**, forms as its name suggests, from a front. When a front (a large air mass of one temperature hitting another air mass with differing air temperature) is formed, raindrops then form, and as they get closer to the ground, they evaporate and form fog.

Radiation fog occurs at night when the ground releases warmth it has absorbed throughout the day (it radiates the heat). When the land cools off, so does the air directly above it. Because cool air can hold less water vapor, fog is formed and hangs close to the ground.

Finally, **upslope fog** is created as warm air travels in a draft and comes to a hill, mountain or slope. As the air is forced up, it cools. Again, the air's ability to hold the water vapor decreases and fog is formed.

If you live in a hilly area (or mountainous region), your student may have seen upslope fog many times, but not known its proper name. Be watching with your student for fog in your area at different times. Try to determine which of the four types you are seeing.

Science: Seals and Whales

Teacher's Note: Seals and sea lions are two different marine mammals that are often confused. Your student may enjoy researching differences and similarities between the two.

Sarah names her cat Seal because "she is gray, like seals that swim offshore in Maine." Seals are beautiful animals, and Sarah is fortunate to live where she can see them in their natural habitat. Has your student ever seen a seal, perhaps at the zoo? Or, if you live on a coast, in the ocean? Has she ever touched one? In Sarah's letter to Anna, she also mentions whales.

Encourage your student to spend some time exploring the fascinating world of these two specific sea animals: seals and whales. Use the following information to begin your discussion. If you are able, visit an area zoo, aquarium or the seashore to see these amazing creatures up close and personal!

Seals are water-dwelling creatures. Most live in salt water (oceans or inland seas), but a few make their home in freshwater. Seals are mammals. They do not have gills (like a fish or shark) so they are unable to breathe underwater. However, seals spend a lot of time in the water and can hold their breath for over 20 minutes! They have hair/fur, are born alive, and nurse their mother's milk when they are born. Seal babies are called pups. Females are cows, males are bulls, and families are called harems, consisting of many females (3-100) and one bull. Baby seals weigh approximately 10 pounds at birth, and generally do not leave the harem (or their mother's care) until they are between three and four months old.

The smallest seal in the world is the ringed seal. It lives in the Arctic and is generally about four feet in length and weighs around 200 pounds. The largest seal is the southern elephant seal. The males can be as large as 21 feet in length and weigh over 8,000 pounds. The only sea mammal larger than the elephant seal is the whale.

Seals keep warm in frigid waters and temperatures by a layer of fat (known as blubber). Blubber also gives them an energy source when food is scarce.

Seals primarily eat other marine life—fish, squid and octopus. Like birds, seals do not chew their food. Instead, they swallow it whole. As they consume their meal, seals also swallow small bits of shell and rock. These pieces remain in the seal's stomach and aid its digestion by grinding the food up after it has been swallowed.

Seals swim very fast, but they generally are quite slow on land. The crabeater is the fastest seal and can move (on land or ice) nearly 15 miles per hour—almost as quickly as humans can run.

Whales are also water-dwelling mammals. They are unable to breathe underwater (they do not have gills) but they do nurse their young.

Teacher's Note: Some children may think of sharks and whales as the same type of animal, but in reality, they are very different. Whales are mammals. They do not have gills and they nurse their young. Sharks, on the other hand, are large, meat-eating fish. They have gills and can breathe underwater. Sharks and whales also swim differently. A shark's tail is vertical, moving from side to side. A whale's tail lies flat and moves up and down.

There are 13 different families of whales. Within the families there are more than 75 species. Dolphins, porpoises and whales are all in the whale family. Some of the most common are orca, sperm, beluga and killer.

A whale is able to hold its breath for nearly 45 minutes when looking for food. Normally, however, whales breathe in air every few minutes. Whales breathe by using a special hole, called a blowhole. A blowhole is a little like one big nostril. When the whale is ready to get air, it comes to the surface of the water and blows out all the water droplets and air in its lungs. This exhale creates a large spray of water and air, known as a "spout." The whale inhales a full intake of fresh air. When the whale is underwater, its blowhole is kept tightly shut with muscles, which prevents it from drowning.

A whale's eyes are located on the sides of its head. Although it can see quite clearly both in water and on land, a whale can only see to the side and a little to the back. A whale cannot see anything directly in front of it. Whales have eyelids, just like humans, and can blink, open and shut their eyes just as we do.

When whales are born, their weight and length vary according to species. The fin whale calf (baby) weighs approximately 3,500 pounds. A blue whale calf can weigh up to 4,400 pounds at birth and can be nearly 25 feet in length. The largest whale in the world is the blue whale. In fact, the blue whale is the largest animal on our planet! Weighing up to 150 tons and longer than 90 feet in length, the blue whale is an impressive sight indeed.

Teacher's Note: To help your student gain a better grasp of these various lengths, go outside and help her measure off 10, 20, 40, and 90 feet outdoors. Then imagine a whale that long! Many whales are nearly 20 times as tall as your student.

Enjoy studying both seals and whales with your student. They are truly beautiful and amazing creatures of the sea!

Language Arts: Continuing Symbolism - Singing

Draw your student's attention to the final sentence in chapter 2. Once again, we see the subject of singing taking a role in our story. Sarah may have understood why the children asked that question. Or perhaps she did not. What we do know is that for Caleb and Anna, learning that Sarah sings is a special thing. Before they have even met her, they already feel a bond with Sarah because her ability to sing reminds them of their mother.

Language Arts: Reconstructing the Unknown - Learning to Infer

From Sarah's letters in this chapter, the reader can infer what Caleb's and Anna's letters must have asked. Invite your student to study Sarah's notes and from them, reconstruct the children's letters. Her letter to Anna includes the following facts:

Sarah can: braid hair, make stew
Sarah likes to: build bookshelves and paint
Favorite colors: blue, gray and green
William, brother: fisherman

Sarah's letter to Caleb includes these notes:

Her cat: Seal, gray like the seals in the sea
She encloses: Seal's paw prints in return
She compliments: the Wittings' house
Sarah's house: tall, shingles made gray from the salt in the sea
Sarah likes: small rooms sometimes
Sarah can: keep a fire going at night
Sarah doesn't know: whether or not she snores

Using these responses, have your student write the letters from the character's point of view (Anna and Caleb) as they might have written them. The following is an example of what Caleb might have written:

Dear Sarah,

My name is Caleb Witting. We have two dogs, Nick and Lottie. Here are their paw prints for Seal to see. Our house is in the prairie, far from anyone and it isn't very large. Do you mind small rooms, Sarah? What is your house like in Maine? It gets cold here in the winter. Do you know how to keep a fire going? One more thing, do you snore?

Yours,
Caleb

As a creative exercise, have your student write her letters on stationery. She can even address envelopes to Caleb and Anna, including a return address from Sarah. If she wishes, she could also draw or stamp the likeness of a paw print from Seal, and two from Lottie and Nick. Have her include the imaginary correspondence in the Prairie Notebook and Sea Notebook, respectively. This will not only be an interesting and creative activity, but will also aid in bringing her study of *Sarah, Plain and Tall* to life.

Language Arts: Writing and Discussion Question

When Caleb writes to Sarah, he wishes to know about things such as snoring and building fires. If you wrote a letter to a relative or stranger who might be coming to live with you, what are the things you would wish to know? If you were Caleb's age, would your questions be different?

Language Arts: Vocabulary*

advection fog Created from warm air moving across water.

frontal fog Formed from two air masses of different temperatures colliding.

upslope fog Formed from warm air traveling up a slope and colliding.

radiation fog Formed from the ground releasing its warmth at night as the land cools off.

holding capacity The specific amount of water vapor the air can contain at any given moment.

blubber The layer of fat on sea animals like seals and whales.

blowhole The hole located on top of a whale's head through which it can breathe in fresh oxygen and exhale moisture.

Fine Arts: Illustrating Envelopes

Sarah drew a picture of a cat on the outside of Caleb's envelope. How delightful! Has your student ever sent someone a letter and drawn or painted a picture on the envelope? Take some time and enjoy a fun art experience with your student by taking Sarah's suggestion. The possibilities are endless: a self-portrait, a picture of a friend or relative, flowers, vines, a ship at sea with waves lapping at the envelope's edges, a colorful border for the front and back, etc. Perhaps your student could write a letter to a grandparent, parent (tucked in the car for them to find in the morning) or to a friend. Allow your student's creativity to blossom. You could even write a letter yourself and illustrate an envelope for a friend and join in the fun!

Fine Arts: The Colors of the Sea

Sarah tells Anna she loves the colors of the sea—blue, gray and green. Create a memorable art project by having your student draw a picture (with colored pencils, paints, pastels or crayons), using only these colors. Talk with your student about the many different values, shades and combinations these three colors can create when mixed. In fact, Sarah probably never saw the sea look one specific color, but always a combination of the three. What does the picture look like when it is completed, using the colors of the sea?

Sarah also tells us the sea sometimes is a color "which has no name." What does that look like? What does your student think that could be? Play with the colors, and create some "nameless" hues with your student.

Chapter 3

Teacher Summary

Sarah comes to the prairie by train. Papa picks her up at the station and brings her home. Anna and Caleb wait for her to come and Caleb spots her yellow bonnet first. Sarah is just as she said—plain and tall. Seal is with her in his own special black case. Sarah gives both children gifts from the sea. For Caleb, a moon snail. For Anna, a sea stone, smooth and white. The children think Sarah already misses the sea, but she gets settled and they both hope she will like them and stay.

What we will cover in this chapter:

Social Studies: Geography - Prairie Notebook Entries
Social Studies: Geography - Sea Notebook Entries
Science: Windbreaks - What They Are and Why They Work
Science: Birds - Hawks
Science: Smooth Stones - Rock Tumblers
Language Arts: Tension - Essential for a Plot*
Language Arts: Creative Writing - A Dog's Life
Language Arts: Writing and Discussion Question
Language Arts: Vocabulary
Life Skills: Wanting to Be Liked

Social Studies: Geography - Prairie Notebook Entries

This chapter offers many more entries for your student's Prairie Notebook. Encourage your student to add these and find pictures of the flowers and animals. She may even wish to draw and illustrate her entries directly in her journal. Depending on your student's ability level and interest, you can ask her to search for "clues" in the chapter or you can go through it together. Here is a list of what you'll find:

Indian paintbrush (red and orange), blue-eyed grass, Russian olive trees, crows, marsh hawks, woodchucks, gophers, windbreaks and dust.

Social Studies: Geography - Sea Notebook Entries

Here are a few more notes for your student's Sea Notebook:

Seagulls, moon snail (shell), and sea stone.

A nice illustration for this entry might be a seascape picture drawing, including all three of these things—the gull, shell and stone.

Science: Windbreaks - What They Are and Why They Work

As we studied in chapter 1, prairie land is very flat, with few trees. Without hills, mountains or even trees, the wind can blow wildly. Nothing stops it. Wind can be a problem for farmers, ruining crops both by blowing seeds away and by bending and breaking the crops as they are growing. From pioneer times through today, people have created their own ways of slowing the wind. Known as windbreaks, people have planted long rows of trees between the fields and around their homes. These trees provide resistance to the wind, and beauty, as well.

In our story, Anna and Caleb's Mama had planted a row of Russian olive trees to form a windbreak near the barn. If you live near the plains or prairie, take your student to see a field and find a windbreak to show her. (If you know where there is a Russian olive tree, show your student that too, or look online.)

Can your student think of a type of jacket that shares the same name as the protective tree line in the field? (windbreaker)

Science: Birds—Hawks

Draw your student's attention to the following sentence, "I saw a marsh hawk wheel down behind the barn." What does "wheel down" mean? Do all hawks do this? What kind of bird is a hawk? Take this opportunity to share a little about this bird of prey with your student.

A marsh hawk is just one of many birds in the hawk family. Hawks are known as birds of prey. (Other birds of prey are vultures, kites, buzzards, eagles, owls, falcons, and harriers.)

Technically, a bird of prey is any bird that lives on other living animals. However, scientists only use this definition with a particular group of birds that have two defining characteristics. First, they must have long, sharp claws, called talons. Talons help a bird in several ways. First, they help kill the prey by striking and piercing it. Second, talons allow a bird to hold onto its killed or captured prey. Finally, they help to hold the meal down while the hawk eats it. The second thing a bird of prey has is a large, hook-shaped beak. This type of beak helps the bird tear the meat/flesh off the dead prey into bite-sized pieces.

When a hawk sees its prey, it often flies faster and faster toward the ground in a downward spiral. This is what Anna saw "wheeling down." All birds of prey spend much time circling slowly in the sky. In this way, the bird can survey a large area of ground and spot animals that represent potential meals.

The hawk Anna saw—the marsh hawk—is only one of many hawks in the world. Like other types of birds, the names of hawks suggest where they're found, or often describe the way they look. Here are some more hawk names: sharp-shinned, Cooper's, red-shouldered, Galapagos, and the sparrow hawk.

Hawks fly fast and see with extraordinary precision. This is what helps them to be such fierce hunters. Some people, called falconers, practice an ancient sport called falconry. Although falcons are commonly used, as the name implies, hawks and even eagles are used as well. Falconers train these birds. In time, they can hunt on command. The birds are each fitted with little custom leather hoods to help keep them calm by making it so they cannot see. When it is "blindfolded," the falcon remains quiet and becomes used to its handler-trainer. The falconer wears thick, special leather gloves, so the claws of the bird won't hurt his or her arms. Falconry takes bravery, care and much patience.

Hawks are beautiful and fascinating creatures. Find some books on this topic and enjoy.

Science: Smooth Stones - Rock Tumblers

Anna's sea stone was indeed very beautiful. How did the sea make it so smooth, so perfect? The constant waves roll the stones back and forth. The stones rub against the sand and other rocks, but the motion of the water against the stone will eventually wear down the edges until they are smooth.

Rocks can be polished smooth without the sea, however. Has your student ever heard of a rock tumbler? Sold in many science stores and hobby shops, rock tumblers can be a source of educational delight for many young, budding scientists. A rock tumbler works on the same principle as the water and sand in the sea (friction). A rock tumbler is a machine with a hollow cylinder, electrically driven to turn over and over. Then, aided by water and coarse grit (just like the sand) it rolls the stones and polishes them smooth. Many rocks can become smooth and beautiful using a rock tumbler. If you are able, secure one of these tumblers and let your student experience the wonder of producing her own polished stones.

Language Arts: Tension - Essential for a Plot*

For a story to be interesting, it must contain a key element—plot. A plot is what happens in the story. Characters tell us whom the plot happened to, while the plot itself is the action happening to the characters. Every plot must contain tension. What's going to happen? What are the characters thinking? What will they do? In our story, *Sarah, Plain and Tall*, tension is created from several directions, but all of it is included in one basic question. *Will Sarah stay?*

Throughout the story, Anna, Caleb, even Jacob wonder this to themselves. As the reader, so do we. Will she miss the sea so much she must return to Maine? Will she learn to love the children and Jacob?

Encourage your student to explore the concept of "tension" in her own stories. Perhaps if you are reading another book together, she can identify the plot and tension in that story. Every good book will include this element. As a project in storywriting, have your student sit down and develop several storyline plots, identifying the tension in each one. These storylines need only be a few sentences long. For example, one storyline could be the story of a boy who finds a stray dog and keeps it in the garage. Story tensions might include: Will the dog recover from its wounds? Will his parents allow him to keep the dog? Will the dog's owners find the dog and claim it? etc. These kinds of story/plot exercises help creative young writers develop an essential skill.

Language Arts: Creative Writing - A Dog's Life

Our story is written in first person, from Anna's perspective. Although we hear the other characters speaking, we only understand what Anna is thinking and feeling. We can read *her* thoughts. But what are the *other* characters thinking? What about Nick and Lottie, the dogs? What do they think of Sarah? What do they think of Seal? Do they like Sarah? Are they excited at the thought of a woman around the house? How will a cat change their lives?

As a creative writing exercise, have your student write chapter 3 over again, this time from the dogs' perspective.Encourage her to give Nick and Lottie as many specific characteristics and feelings as she can. What breed of dogs are they? What do they enjoy

doing? What's their favorite treat? etc.

Teacher's Note: Many classic children's books have been written through the eyes of an animal, such as *Charlotte's Web*, *The Incredible Journey* and *The Tale of Despereaux*. Together with your student, explore some of these much-loved stories.

Language Arts: Writing and Discussion Question

Think about an experience you may have had when you met someone new and you didn't know how the two of you would get along. Were you nervous? What happened? Write down your feelings and describe the experience.

Language Arts: Vocabulary

windbreak Rows of trees or buildings that provide shelter from the wind.

bird of prey A bird with talons and a hook-shaped beak, who feeds on other animals.

talons Sharp claws, especially belonging to a bird of prey.

falconry An ancient sport (still practiced today) where birds of prey are tamed and trained to hunt on command.

Life Skills: Wanting to Be Liked

Caleb and Anna would love to have a new mother. It is obvious. They are both concerned Sarah may not like the prairie, their home, or even them. This tension is a common feeling. Has your student ever met someone new and longed to be her friend? When you make a new friend you hope she will like you. Making new friends can be scary sometimes. What if the other person doesn't like you? Talk with your student about this insecurity and how to overcome it. Sometimes being shy is the way people act when they are nervous or afraid that they won't be liked. The truth is, not everyone will like us. But it doesn't mean we won't have friends or aren't special. Everyone has someone who loves them. Most of us, if we think about it, have many that do.

Perhaps you've dealt with insecurity in friendships. Discuss with your student how it felt when you experienced it. Certainly, everyone has a strong desire to be loved and liked. Sharing these experiences strengthens our relationships. Share with your student today. And truly *listen* to what she has to say about her own life and dealing with new friends.

Chapter 4

Teacher Summary

Sarah begins to make herself at home with the Wittings. She shows the children how to dry flowers. She tells them about the sea and teaches them a new word from Maine—"Ayuh." It means yes. Sarah cuts Caleb's and Papa's hair. She braids Anna's hair and ties it with a beautiful ribbon. And they sing. Sarah sings "Sumer is icumen in..." and soon Caleb, Anna, and even Papa are all joining in. They sing together and they are happy. But the children still wonder if she will leave and go back to Maine.

What we will cover in this chapter:

Social Studies: Geography - Prairie Notebook Entries
Social Studies: Geography - Sea Notebook Entries
Science: Seashells*
Language Arts: Continuing Symbolism - Singing
Language Arts: Writing and Discussion Question
Life Skills: Origin of Personal Traits

Social Studies: Geography - Prairie Notebook Entries

Here are some additional possibilities from chapter 4 for your student to copy, illustrate and include in her Prairie Notebook:

Clover, prairie violets, wild roses, bride's bonnet, sheep and meadowlark.

Social Studies: Geography - Sea Notebook Entries

Here in chapter 4 we see more sea notes in the story. Here are some terms and references your student may wish to include in her notebook. Can she find more?

Kittiwake, scallop, sea clam, oyster, razor clam, conch, seals, seaside goldenrod, wild asters, woolly ragwort and Ayuh!

Science: Seashells*

Caleb is very fortunate. Sarah brings him a beautiful seashell, a moon snail shell from the sea. She shares with the children her collection: scallops, sea clams, oysters, razor clam and conch shells. Does your student have any seashells? Many people keep shell collections, even those who do not live near an ocean or a large lake.

If your student is interested, this would be a good opportunity to explore the world of seashells. Find a few books from your library or look at pictures online and enjoy the fascination with the variety of colors and shapes found in the shells. Below is some beginning information on shells for your discussion.

Seashells come in a variety of colors and shapes. There is a reason for the diversity. It helps the creature that lives in the shell to hide and blend in with his surroundings. Different kinds of shells are found in specific waters of the world. It might interest your student to know that a person who really knows shells can look at a specific type of shell and tell whether it came from the coast of Florida or the coast of Africa!

Seashells are made of calcium carbonate (limestone).

They come in two basic forms: one piece usually coiled into a spiral-like shape (**univalves**) and those made of two pieces which fit together tightly (**bivalves**). Caleb's moon snail shell was a univalve.

When a mollusk (mussels, clams, scallops) grows, so does its shell. The spiral-type shells can even be used to judge how old the animal is by counting the rings in the spiral.

Collecting seashells can be a lot of fun. Even the names of shells are interesting; here are a few: Green Star, Knobby Top, Bleeding Tooth, Banded Tulip, Baby's Ear and Thorny Slipper. Encourage your student to research shells further and even start some collecting, if she wishes!

In the story, Sarah has Caleb hold his shell to his ear and tells him he can "hear the sea." This is an ancient practice and it is fun! If your student has a seashell (the larger the better), "listen" to the sea with her and then discuss what the sound actually is. When we hear that wave-like, swishing sound, what we are really hearing is the air inside the shell vibrating in the small space. This is called **resonance**.

Language Arts: Continuing Symbolism - Singing

Has your student been following the symbolism of singing? In chapter 4, we see the characters finally taking part in a song together. This is a symbol of good things. Draw your student's attention to where Caleb asks Papa, "You don't sing anymore. Why?" And Papa answers, "I've forgotten the old songs. But maybe there's a way to remember them."

Now in chapter 4, Sarah, Caleb and Anna all sing, including Papa. And we read, "...even Papa, who sang as if he had never stopped singing."

The fact that Sarah has brought song back to the Wittings shows us that she is bringing back happiness—the kind of family fun they haven't been able to enjoy since Mama died.

Continue looking for singing references in upcoming chapters. If you haven't made singing a regular part of your family traditions or classroom activities, look for ways to incorporate singing today!

Language Arts: Writing and Disscussion Question

Caleb makes several comments throughout our story (twice in this chapter) that he is sure Sarah will stay. We know Anna wants Sarah to stay, but we don't see her saying it. Why might she be more hesitant to vocalize her feelings?

Language Arts: Vocabulary

univalve A one-piece shell usually coiled into a spiral-like shape.

bivalve A two-piece shell which fits together tightly.

Life Skills: Origin of Personal Traits

Draw your student's attention to where Anna tells us, "Papa was quiet and shy with Sarah, and so was I. But Caleb talked to Sarah from morning until the light left the sky." Anna was like her father, but Caleb was different.

If we ask our parents or relatives, they will often tell us whom we favor. For example, has your student ever heard, "Oh, you're so much like your father—a chip off the old block." Or, "You're just like your mother. The apple doesn't fall far from the tree." Does your student agree? Does she think she is more like her mother, or her father? The truth is, no child is exactly like one parent. We are each a combination of both of our parents. Often, however, we do take after one more than the other.

If Anna was like her Papa, could we imagine that Caleb was more like his Mama? If so, what must their Mama have been like? She might have been more outgoing than Jacob. More carefree and talkative—more like Caleb perhaps.

Learning about our traits and where we get certain mannerisms (as well as physical traits) can be a special way to connect with our family. Since he never knew his mother, do you think Caleb knows he is like her? Remembering our heritage and sharing similarities is all a special part of growing up with family.

Chapter 5

Teacher Summary

Sarah names the Wittings' sheep after her three favorite aunts—Harriet, Mattie and Lou. One evening, Sarah is drawing pictures to send home to her brother William. While she draws, Anna and Caleb discuss with her their very first words. Caleb's was windmill. Anna's was flower. Sarah's was dune. Caleb wants to know what a dune is and so Sarah explains. Papa surprises all of them by showing them a "dune" out of hay near the barn. All four of them happily slide down the "dune" and later Sarah writes to William, "Sliding down our dune of hay is almost as fine as sliding down the sand dunes into the sea." The children are happy to hear her say the words, "our dune."

What we will cover in this chapter:

Social Studies: Geography - Sea and Prairie Notes
Science: Buzzards and Vultures
Science: Sand and Dunes
Language Arts: Alliteration
Language Arts: Unfolding Information in Your Stories
Language Arts: Writing and Discussion Question
Fine Arts: Thomas Hart Benton - Paintings That Roll Like the Sea*

Life Skills: Grieving - A Natural Emotion
Life Skills: Making Others Smile

Social Studies: Geography - Sea and Prairie Notes

Once again we have more entries for your student's Sea and Prairie Notebooks: dunes, wind, mica, rock cliffs, pine and spruce trees, hay, turkey buzzards, windmills.

Science: Buzzards and Vultures

Just as we learned in chapter 4, a turkey buzzard belongs in the family known as birds of prey. With talons and a hooked beak, **buzzards** are fierce hunters. Unlike hawks and eagles, many buzzards are known as "scavengers." Just as the turkey buzzard fed on the dead lamb in our story, buzzards enjoy feasting on prey which has already been killed or has died on its own. When you see a group of buzzards (or one alone) circling in the sky, often you will find a dead animal below.

Today, the term "turkey buzzard," in the U.S., usually refers to a vulture. **Vultures** very rarely kill their prey, but, instead, feed almost exclusively on the dead carcasses of animals they find. In other areas of the world, the words "buzzard" and "vulture" mean other things. Your student may find it interesting to research the differences between buzzards and vultures and see how identification and language differs according to the country and time period.

Look with your student for buzzards or vultures in your area and, if there is interest, take some time to locate pictures of these common and often mentioned birds of prey. You may also want to contact local zoos, nature centers or animal shelters to see if there are vultures or buzzards you can see up close.

Science: Sand and Dunes

Sarah describes her special dune in Maine beautifully, doesn't she? "It was soft and sparkling with bits of mica, and when we were little we would slide down into the water." Has your student ever seen a dune?

Teacher's Note: If you live in an area where there are sand dunes, this would be a perfect opportunity to take an afternoon field trip. Get away and share Sarah's experience with your student.

Dunes require three key elements: sand, wind and something such as trees, houses, or grassy patches to cause the sand to stop being blown. Share with your student some information about the first element—sand.

Sand is actually a scientific term for a specific size of rock—a very small size. If it is a bit larger, it is called gravel and if it is a bit smaller, it is called silt. Sand, geologists have defined, is smaller than 1/12th of an inch and larger than 1/400th of an inch. Sand is comprised of several ingredients, but the main ingredient is silica.

Teacher's Note: If your student is older, you may wish to elaborate more fully on the definition of silica. Silica is part oxygen and part silicon, which are the two elements most common to the earth's crust.

Depending upon where the sand is located, other ingredients will be present, and those most commonly affect the sand's color. For example, in areas where a lot of coral reefs are located (tropical islands), bits of coral will be included in the sand and will make it pinkish-orange. In areas of the world where great amounts of volcanic ash have been left on the beaches (Greece), the sand appears a dark, bluish-black color.

Take some sand and let your student examine it with a magnifying glass or microscope. What does she see? Probably many different colors and bits. The more sand is rolled by the ocean, sea, or lake, the more perfect and rounded the grains become. Geologists call those grains "mature sand." Or, in other words, older sand.

Does your student know how glass is made? Interesting to note, glass is formed by sand heated to extremely hot temperatures. Today, sand is mixed with many different ingredients (soda, lime, etc.) to achieve different types of glass, but the main ingredient is still sand.

The next key elements for a sand dune are wind and some object to stop the sand from blowing any further. The wind direction determines the type of dune.

Teacher's Note: For the older student, here are the specific terms for the four main divisions of dunes: transverse dunes, barchan dunes, seif dunes and star dunes. Your student may enjoy looking up these different types of dunes online.

As a science experiment, why not allow your student to create her own mini sand dune? (**Teacher's Note:** This exercise should probably take place outdoors to prevent any major messes.) Take a five-pound bag of salt, sugar or play sand. Have your student pour it into the lid of a cardboard box or a jellyroll pan (anything with some surface area and small sides will work). That will be your student's "sand." Next, she'll need something to stop the wind. Twigs, tilted saucers, teacups, a toy soldier or anything else your student wishes can be placed here and there in the sand. Two or three objects are plenty. And now, all your student needs is some wind. By placing or holding a fan or hair dryer near the tray of sand and experimenting with the distance, your student can see her own dunes being created! Encourage your student to try various wind directions to create differently shaped dunes.

Another great way to see a dune effect, even if you live far from any beach, is to observe the snow in your area after a large snowfall. The granules of ice, which comprise snow, will drift according to the wind direction and beautiful dune-like forms will appear.

Have fun studying sand and dunes with your student!

Language Arts: Alliteration

The author of our story, Patricia MacLachlan, is a master with language. Not only is our story interesting and heartwarming, but the author includes many poetic and literary devices to keep the narrative flowing and sounding beautiful.

Draw your student's attention to the first line of chapter 5: "The sheep made Sarah smile."

Two of the five words in this sentence begin with the "s" sound. Have your student say the sentence repeatedly. Sentences where more than one word begin with the same letter create a literary form known as **alliteration**.

A famous poet and writer who used alliteration to his great advantage was a man named Lewis Carroll. Lewis Carroll was the pseudonym (or pen name) of Charles Lutwidge Dodgson, born January 27, 1832, in England. He was a withdrawn man who had a speech impediment called stammering. However, he greatly enjoyed the company of children, with whom he felt he could relax and speak more clearly. His stories and poems are still popular today, particularly his most famous work, *Alice's Adventures in Wonderland*. Before he became an author, he was a brilliant mathematician and lecturer at Oxford University. He died of bronchitis in his sister's home on January 14, 1898.

Here is an example of alliteration in the first stanza of his poem entitled "Size and Tears:"

> When on the sandy shore I sit,
> Beside the salt sea-wave,
> And falling into a weeping fit
> Because I dare not shave—
> A little whisper at my ear
> Enquires the reason of my fear.

The words—sandy, sit, salt, sea-wave, whisper, all include the "s" sound and make an interesting and melodic sounding poem.

Encourage your student to try her own hand at alliteration in either a poem or a few sentences. Remind her to look for this literary device when she sees it being used by MacLachlan in this story and in other reading that she does.

Language Arts: Unfolding Information in Your Stories

When an author introduces a character in a story, she rarely tells the reader all there is to know about that character right away. Instead, bits of information are shared throughout the story. Show your student the following example.

In chapter 4, MacLachlan has Sarah introduce us to her three aunts: "There are three aunts who live near us. They wear silk dresses and no shoes. You would love them." Now, in chapter 5, we learn their names. "She named them [the sheep] after her three favorite aunts, Harriet and Mattie and Lou."

Teacher's Note: Later in FIAR Vol. 7, when we study *Skylark* (the sequel to *Sarah, Plain and Tall*), there will be even more information given about Harriet, Mattie and Lou.

Our author, MacLachlan, first introduced the aunts, and then later told us their names. Imagine how boring and tiring it would be if every time a new character was brought into a story, the author wrote pages describing them in detail. Instead, giving us bits of information here and there is interesting and keeps us learning and involved in the author's story all the time.

Encourage your student to write a story in three parts. In each part, have her write a bit more information about the main character (or sub-characters, depending upon the length of the story).

Language Arts: Writing and Discussion Question

Caleb, Anna and Sarah discuss what their first words were. Does your student know what her first word was? Have her try to find out, and then have her include it in an autobiographical sketch. If her parents don't remember, then have her make up a fictitious word (what she thinks her first word *might* have been) and write a sketch about that.

Language Arts: Vocabulary

dune: A mound of sand heaped up by the wind.

mica: A very thin, almost transparent mineral that flakes easily.

silica: The main mineral component of sand.

alliteration: The repetition of the same first sound or first letter in a group.

Fine Arts: Thomas Hart Benton - Paintings That Roll Like the Sea*

In chapter 5, we find Sarah making drawings to send to Maine of the things she sees on the prairie. We read, "...drawing of the fields, rolling like the sea rolled." We see Sarah compares the fields of grass to the sea. Take this time to introduce your student to an artist named Thomas Hart Benton. Benton (1889-1975) was born, lived and died in Missouri. The subjects of his paintings ranged from the common (farmers and fields) to the outrageous (abstract compositions). The thread that ties all of Benton's work together is his rolling, sea-like style. His people, buildings, trees and even locomotives all have a rounded, rolled look to them. Obtain a book or look online at some of Benton's work and show your student an artist's interpretation of his world around him. Sarah might have liked Thomas Hart Benton's ocean-like shapes! Encourage your student to try several drawings using Benton's style, causing various objects in her work to be curved, rolling like the sea! (If your student studied the FIAR Vol. 4 title, *The Pumpkin Runner*, recall or revisit the illustrations by Brad Sneed. Brad Sneed is a children's book illustrator whose work has been compared to Benton's. Your student could then compare and contrast these two artists.)

Life Skills: Grieving - A Natural Emotion

The Wittings find a lamb that has died and Sarah finds the death difficult to handle. She shouts and cries. Finally, Jacob has to help her back to the house. Talk with your student about Sarah's display of emotion. Grieving is a natural response to death. Some reactions included in the process of grieving are crying, sadness, loneliness and anger. Even depression can follow the death of a loved one, a pet or even strangers (in a war, tragic accident, etc.).

Share with your student a time when you may have grieved. Then ask her if she has ever experienced a deep sadness. Learning about different emotions and realizing our feelings are valid is part of growing up. Reassure your student by discussing the grieving process and share about it from your point of view. Such discussions may help your student understand her own deep emotions and may also help your student recognize and be more compassionate of others who are grieving.

Life Skills: Making Others Smile

Jacob knows Sarah is missing Maine—particularly when she discusses the dunes. He gives Sarah great joy by showing her the "dune" behind the barn and allowing her to experience, in some measure, her memories of Maine's sandy beaches. Listening to others and hearing, through their words, their feelings allows us to make note of what they are feeling and needing. Sometimes, if we are lucky, these mental "notes" can translate into actions—concrete things we can give back to the person to make them smile.

Doing kind things for others is a part of the glorious thing that makes us human. Encourage your student to listen actively to the people around her and then to look for ways to make their lives better. It will be a good thing for others, and will build character in your student.

Chapter 6

Teacher Summary

As summer progresses, Sarah learns more about the prairie and the Wittings. She learns how to plow the fields behind the horses, Jack and Old Bess. She asks Anna and Caleb many questions about wintertime on the prairie.

One day, Sarah and the children are hotter than usual. Sarah takes them for a special treat. All three head off for the cow pond and she teaches the children how to swim. It is a glorious afternoon, and the children fall asleep in the warm grass next to Sarah.

What we will cover in this chapter:

Science: Water Sources
Language Arts: The Newbery Medal*
Language Arts: Patricia MacLachlan - Writing About What You Know
Language Arts: Hyperbole - Meaning to Exaggerate
Language Arts: Writing and Discussion Question
Language Arts: Vocabulary
Fine Arts: The Killdeer - A Fine Subject for Drawing

Science: Water Sources

In chapter 6, we read, "The cows moved close to the pond, where the water was cool and there were trees." In our studies of the prairie, we know there are not many trees. Why would there be trees by the pond? (Because the pond is a constant water source.)

Remind your student that although there are large groves of trees (forests), generally in places where water is less plentiful, trees grow by the banks of water (river, creek, pond, etc.).

The next time you see trees by the banks of a water source, remind your student of the cow pond in *Sarah, Plain and Tall.* If you'd like, consider planning a field trip to explore the relationship between trees and water sources. You'll find that trees grow most abundantly along streams and rivers, near ponds and lakes. Use the opportunity to explore tree identification and to enjoy a picnic lunch!

Language Arts: The Newbery Medal*

Take a moment and talk with your student about the Newbery Medal. The two most prestigious and famous American children's book awards given each year are the **Caldecott Medal** (for the finest illustrations) and the **Newbery Medal** (for most distinguished contribution to children's literature).

The Newbery Medal was established in 1922 as a tribute to the first English publisher of books for children—John Newbery (1713-1767). Each year the winner of the Newbery Medal is selected by a board of the Association for Library Service to Children (ALSC).

Remind your student that although each book selected for this high honor is written extremely well, the nomination does not always indicate the story's inherent quality of content. Your student should always exercise her own discernment to judge a book's story and meaning.

Sarah, Plain and Tall is truly an amazing story. It was hailed by many critics as the great American children's novel of the 1980s. It is no wonder the ALSC selected this fine book as the Newbery Medal recipient of 1986.

Language Arts: Patricia MacLachlan - Writing About What You Know

Sarah, Plain and Tall is a beautifully written story. Does your student think the details and characters are realistic? How does she think MacLachlan achieves such realism? When writers begin a project, it is often said that they should write about what they know. In this way, the descriptions and people come from the author's experience and not just from imagination. It has even been said, "Every book is an autobiography." No matter what the subject, an author is always going to put some feelings and emotions in the story from her own life and view.

Patricia MacLachlan (1938-2022) was raised on the western prairie—Cheyenne, Wyoming. For many years, she was known to carry a small bag of prairie dirt with her to remind her of her roots. Her 1986 Newbery Award winning book, *Sarah, Plain and Tall,* came from a real story she heard as she was growing up. According to an article written for *Children's Books and Their Creators* (Anita Silvey, editor), MacLachlan said the idea for Sarah came from her youth. There was an older, unmarried woman who lived by the sea where MacLachlan spent her summers. Then one day she traveled to the prairies, where MacLachlan was born. MacLachlan said, of this event, "This woman left her own roots to help a family preserve theirs ... the facts of it haunted me."

Does your student see where MacLachlan may have had a rich reserve of experiences to write from, both of the prairies and of the sea? Of course, not all writers (nor your student) *always* write about things they know personally. However, many of the great writers often give this as their advice to budding authors. Many feel it is more rewarding to write about the things they knew first.

Encourage your student to begin drawing from her own special past and present for story ideas. MacLachlan did and we are all grateful.

Language Arts: Hyperbole - Meaning to Exaggerate

Draw your student's attention to where Anna discusses what she loves about the winter. "Papa builds a warm fire, and we bake hot biscuits and put on hundreds of sweaters." Ask your student if she thinks the children and Papa really wear hundreds of sweaters in the winter? Of course not. That is an exaggeration.

Does your student know that exaggeration in writing prose and poetry has a special name? When an author exaggerates, it is called **hyperbole** [hie PER buh lee]. Authors use hyperbole to give an effect. For example, if your student reads, "He was as strong as an ox," that would be hyperbole. Of course the man wasn't as strong as an ox, but it paints a picture for the reader of a very tough man.

Encourage your student to think up and write a list of sentences using hyperbole. For example:

> I've traveled over every inch of this world.
>
> The wind nearly blew my face off.
>
> Suddenly, there were millions of ants in the bathroom.

Look for good examples of hyperbole when you're with your student (billboards, television, books, online, etc.) and point them out. Then, watch for examples in your own student's writings and congratulate her on particularly nice phrases.

Language Arts: Writing and Discussion Question

Why do you think many authors write about their own experiences? How does this affect their stories?

Language Arts: Vocabulary

Newbery Medal The prestigious American children's book award given annually for excellence in literature.

hyperbole A phrase or word which exaggerates, used in poetry and writing.

Fine Arts: The Killdeer - A Fine Subject for Drawing

As Anna finally floats in the cow pond, lungs full of air, feeling free, she sees crows fly over her head—and then she hears a killdeer cry. Has your student ever seen a killdeer? The killdeer is a small, slender bird that lives on the prairie. Standing only 10" high, the killdeer makes its nest on the ground and this small bird has an ingenious method of protecting its young. When a predator approaches the nest, the parent distracts the predator by acting as though it's wounded—dragging its wing and crying. The predator, knowing an already-wounded bird is an easier catch, is distracted and goes after the parent. After the "wounded" killdeer has lured the predator a safe distance away, it flies off.

Besides being an interesting bird to study from a naturalist's point of view, the killdeer is also an excellent subject for drawing practice. With black and white markings, a slender beak and clean body lines, your student will find it an interesting wildlife subject to draw. Find a good photograph of a killdeer and allow your student to practice sketching this lovely bird.

Chapter 7

Teacher Summary

Matthew, Maggie, and their girls Rose and Violet come to visit the Wittings and to help Jacob plow the fields. Maggie, like Sarah, is a mail-order bride and she understands Sarah's longings for Maine. To cheer Sarah up, and to make her feel more at home, Maggie brings her three red banty chickens ("for eating," she says) and some flowers for a new garden. Maggie and Sarah become fast friends and Sarah is comforted by the presence and understanding of another woman. And just as Anna assumed, the chickens are not for eating—by the evening Sarah already has them in the house and is discussing names.

What we will cover in this chapter:

Social Studies: Geography - Prairie Notebook Entries
Language Arts: Character Compilation - Maggie*
Language Arts: Writing and Discussion Question
Life Skills: Always Something to Miss

Social Studies: Geography - Prairie Notebook Entries

Here are a few more entries for your student's Prairie Notebook, taken from chapters 6 and 7: killdeer, crow, banty chicken, wild dandelions, summer roses, zinnias, marigolds, wild feverfew, nasturtiums, dahlias and columbine.

Teacher's Note: This is the last lesson in *Sarah, Plain and Tall* where your student will be prompted to add to her Prairie and/or Sea Notebooks. (In the FIAR Vol. 7 unit for *Skylark*, the notebooks will be mentioned again with more possible entries, so you might want to keep them handy for that study.) Please remember these notebook text "clues" are only a few of the things your student might choose to include in her notebook. If she desires, quotes, descriptions, outside research, etc., can all be included to make a more richly diversified study tool and keepsake.

Language Arts: Character Compilation - Maggie*

Although we've heard her mentioned, chapter 7 is our first glimpse of Maggie, Matthew's mail-order bride and the Wittings' neighbor. Authors should give us many clues about their characters. Not just by what they say, but by their actions and how others respond to them. What does your student know about Maggie's character after reading this chapter? Have your student create a "character compilation" by making a list of the clues that she discovers about each character as she reads the story.

Teacher's Note: Encourage your student not to stop at the physical traits or circumstances of Maggie and her situation. Rather help your student to infer and explore Maggie's personality, by way of her actions. Example: She must be a woman of generosity to bring Sarah the chickens and plants.

Maggie: She lives to the south of the Wittings, with her husband Matthew and their two daughters, Rose and Violet. She came to the prairie from Tennessee in response to a letter from Matthew, just like Jacob's letter to Sarah. She has blonde, almost white hair. She is industrious (she gardens, hitches horses to plows and knows how to drive a wagon). She is a hard worker (she wipes her face in the hot sun, leaving dirt on it). She is generous (she gives Sarah chickens and plants, helps with the meal and shares her heart). She is compassionate (she understands and empathizes with Sarah). She is practical and wise (she tells Sarah, "There is always something to miss, no matter where you are"). She is optimistic (she tells Sarah to try growing nasturtiums even though Sarah's not sure they'll do well).

Is your student surprised by how many clues MacLachlan gives the reader in her story, even about a minor character like Maggie? That is the sign of a good writer. If your student wishes, she can draw or paint a picture of Maggie (or of Matthew, Rose or Violet) and include it with her assignment.

Language Arts: Writing and Discussion Question

Why did Anna assume Sarah wouldn't eat the chickens? What do we know about Sarah that might lead us to the same conclusion? What are her feelings about animals?

Life Skills: Always Something to Miss

Maggie gives Sarah some very wise advice—a truth to remember: "There are always things to miss. No matter where you are." Has your student ever moved to a different city or neighborhood? What does she think of Maggie's words? Do they hold true? If you have lived in several places, share with your student specific things you miss. Together, come up with a list of things you'd miss if you moved from the place you live now. Examples: restaurants, parks, neighbors, theaters, events, city holiday traditions, a particular room in your house, etc. To help us avoid disappointment and disillusionment in life, we should remember Maggie's words. No matter where you go, you will miss certain things. Remember, the new place you're going will also hold things you will learn to love.

Chapter 8

Teacher Summary

Sarah convinces Jacob to teach her to drive the wagon. She wishes to go to town alone. Anna and Caleb grow frightened. What if she wants to go to town alone in order to leave them?

Sarah also shocks Caleb by wearing a pair of man's overalls. The rains come and as a storm is inevitable, Jacob decides he should fix the house roof. Sarah, still dressed in her overalls, helps Jacob and impresses him with her ability to do carpentry. Just as they are finishing up, a squall blows in and the winds begin. They sleep in the barn all night long, with rain and hail pelting the roof. In the morning, Papa opens the barn door and they are greeted by land covered in hailstones and windblown grass, but they are safe.

What we will cover in this chapter:

Science: Squalls*
Language Arts: Writing and Discussion Question
Language Arts: Vocabulary
Fine Arts: Recreating Your Own Squall through Sound

Science: Squalls*

Has your student ever heard of a squall? When he sees the squall quickly approaching, Papa immediately warns Sarah and the children to take cover. Take this time to share with your student the meteorological events that comprise the storm known as a squall.

Generally, a squall includes the following weather components: strong, cold winds, a storm front (one warm air mass colliding with a cold air mass), several brief, but fierce, rain showers, and sometimes hail and snow.

Teacher's Note: A squall does not necessarily include a dangerous tornado funnel cloud. However, it is wise to note that the front (or squall line) created by two air masses of different air temperatures can produce a funnel cloud. If a twister forms, the storm is then said to include tornadic activity.

Sarah, Papa and the children are lucky they see the storm coming and are able to get food and the animals and get to the barn in time. Squalls often occur very quickly.

If there is interest, find more books on weather (wind, hail, storms, etc.) for your student to explore.

Language Arts: Writing and Discussion Question

Why do you think Sarah wants to go to town alone? Do you think Anna and Caleb's fears are justified?

Language Arts: Vocabulary

squall A sudden, severe storm, including high winds and often rain.

front Two air masses with different temperatures colliding with each other.

Fine Arts: Recreating Your Own Squall through Sound

Has your student ever listened to an old-time radio program and heard the sound effects? Or has she ever noticed in a movie that has creaks and rattles that they sound remarkably realistic? Creating sound effects is an art form. Children often do this without even knowing it. For example, a child playing with a toy train will often make all the appropriate puffs, whistles and clickety-clack sounds. Sound effects can also be created which are quite sophisticated by using a computer and digitally enhanced sound bites.

What does your student think Sarah, Anna, Papa and Caleb hear outside during the squall? The author tells us there was wild wind, thunder, hail (like stones being tossed) and sheets of rain. How would your student reproduce sounds like that? Encourage her to experiment with different things (i.e., ice chips on a cookie sheet, water through a colander, marbles against a board, a clap against a sheet of metal or tinfoil, a hand fan aimed at the microphone in different directions, etc.)

Once your student has come up with a series of her own sound effects, encourage her to enlist several people to help her in the recording of her "squall." Have her delegate each sound effect to a different person and then run several practice "takes" to see if the storm sounds realistic. Perhaps she wants the wind sound to remain constant throughout the recording and then have the hail, rain, etc., come in at different moments. When she has her sound effects scripted out, and each person knows their part, then the fun can begin.

Have have your student record her "squall" and listen to what she has created. If there are changes to be made, she can re-record her storm as many times as she wishes.

Chapter 9

Teacher Summary

After the storm, Papa keeps his promise to Sarah and teaches her to drive the wagon so she can go to town by herself. Caleb and Anna are frightened. The only reason the children can see for Sarah's trip to town is to leave them. Why else would she want to be by herself? Caleb begins to cry and suggests plans to keep Sarah with them. Maybe they could tie her up. Or make her sick. Anna quiets him, but she is unsure herself.

On the following day, Sarah gets dressed, kisses each of them and leaves for town. The day goes by slowly. Anna and Caleb's only consolation is that Seal is still with them. Evening comes and the children watch for Sarah from the porch. Then, just like the day she first arrived at the Wittings' home, Caleb spies a cloud of dust and her yellow bonnet.

Caleb shares his worries with Sarah—that he thought she would leave them because she missed the sea. Sarah says she would miss Papa and the children more. Then she shows them her purchases from town—colored pencils for their pictures of the sea—blue, gray and green. There are also candles for dinner time, nasturtium seed for her garden and a book of songs to sing.

What we will cover in this chapter:

Language Arts: Conclusions - How to Tie Up Your Story
Language Arts: Writing and Discussion Question
Language Arts: Vocabulary*

Language Arts: Conclusions - How to Tie Up Your Story

Draw your student's attention to the final concluding paragraph of our story. Share with your student how beautifully MacLachlan ties up the ending. She uses bits of information from throughout the entire story.

Take each of the following sentence quotations from the concluding paragraph and assign (or help) your student find in which chapter in the story each item was originally discussed or where it occurred:

Autumn will come, then winter, cold with a wind that blows like the wind off the sea in Maine. (chapter 6)

There will be nests of curls to look for, and dried flowers all winter long. (chapter 4)

When there are storms, Papa will stretch a rope from the door to the barn so we will not be lost when we feed the sheep and the cows and Jack and Old Bess.(chapter 6)

And Sarah's chickens, if they are living in the house. (chapter 7)

There will be Sarah's sea, blue and gray and green, hanging on the wall. (chapter 8)

And songs, old ones and new. (Many chapters, including chapter 9)

And Seal with yellow eyes. And there will be Sarah, plain and tall. (chapter 2, and the title of our book)

Not every author chooses to end her story as MacLachlan does here, with so many bits of information all together. However, it is always a thoughtful literary choice to select some specific subject or saying that is woven through the storyline, to include in the conclusion of a story. It provides closure and allows the reader to immediately reflect back over the entire story.

Encourage your student to try different ways of ending her stories. Perhaps she can mimic MacLachlan's method of story ending in *Sarah, Plain and Tall*, in a story of her own.

Language Arts: Writing and Discussion Question

Why did Papa allow such a young boy as Caleb to take an axe off to chop wood? Do you find this unusual? What was different about the time our story took place and today?

Language Arts: Vocabulary*

conclusion The ending of a story or situation.

Teacher's Note: There is a 1991 Hallmark made-for-TV movie of *Sarah, Plain and Tall* starring Glenn Close and Christopher Walken. Watching the movie together with your student would be a great way to finish up your time with this classic book!

Teacher's Notes

Use this page to jot down relevant info you've found for this *Five in a Row* chapter book, including favorite lessons, go-along resources, field trips, and family memories.

SARAH, PLAIN AND TALL

Dates studied:

Student:

Favorite Lesson Topics:

Social Studies:

Science:

Language Arts:

Fine Arts:

Life Skills:

Relevant Library Resources: Books, DVDs, Audio Books

Websites or Video Links:

Related Field Trip Opportunities:

Favorite Quote or Memory During Study:

Sarah, Plain and Tall - Chapter 1

Name:

Date:

Language Arts: **Anatomy of a Letter**

After finishing the **Language Arts: Letter Writing - P.S. and R.S.V.P** lesson, fill in the blanks below to review parts of a letter and learn a new part of letter writing (the P.S. or postscript). (We are building upon the Anatomy of a Letter lesson that was inlcuded in Five in a Row Volume 5 from *The Boxcar Children*). If you did not use this previous lesson, discuss each section of the Anatomy of a Letter (answers at the bottom of the page).

After you complete this sheet, search online for an example of an invitation that includes an R.S.V.P. by searching "party invitation with rsvp." There are different RSVP methods used which include mailing a reply card to an address, or emailing or texting your response.

September 12th

[ ]

Dear Ben,

[ ]

I think we should ask our parents if we can go play hockey together this weekend. Would Saturday or Sunday be a better day for you to go to the ice rink with me?

[ ]

Maybe we could do a few chores this week and save money to get pizza for dinner afterwards. I need to get new laces for my skates, but I already have money set aside for that and can grab them at the ice rink rental shop.

[ ] Hoping we can go,

[ ] Jack

[ ] Mom said she would make cookies for us to have after dinner.

P.S. Signature Closing Body Greeting Heading

Name:
Date:
Language Arts: **Vocabulary Words**

After finishing the second chapter, use the crossword puzzle below to review the vocabulary words covered in **chapters 1-2**. Clues and vocabulary words are shown on the next page. Black boxes indicate a space between two words.

Sarah, Plain and Tall - Chapter 2 continued

Across

3. (ch. 1) rock formed from sediment

4. (ch. 2) fog created from warm air moving across water

8. (ch. 2) the specific amount of water vapor the air can contain at any given moment

10. (ch. 2) the layer of fat on sea animals like seals and whales

12. (ch. 1) an overused phrase or example

13. (ch. 2) fog formed from warm air traveling up a slope and colliding

14. (ch. 2) the hole located on top of a whale's head through which it can breathe in fresh oxygen and exhale moisture

Down

1. (ch. 2) fog formed from the ground releasing its warmth at night as the land cools

2. (ch. 1) rock changed in form by pressure, moisture and heat

5. (ch. 2) fog formed from two air masses of different temperatures colliding

6. (ch. 1) acronym for French "respondez s'il vous plait." Please respond

7. (ch. 1) something that represents something

9. (ch. 1) rock formed by the cooling and solidifying of magma

11. (ch. 1) the process of having young forming in the uterus

flip for vocab words:

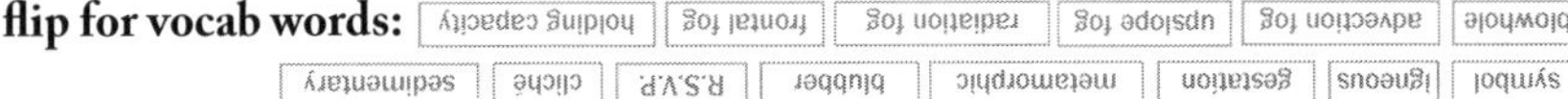

Name:

Date:

Language Arts: **Storyline - Tensions**

As you learned in the **Language Arts: Tension - Essential for a Plot** lesson for a story to be interesting there must be "tension." Use the spaes provided below and prompts to create a storyline and possible story tensions it might contain. A storyline example (as mentioned in the lesson) could be about a boy who finds a stray dog and keeps it in the garage. Story tentions could include: Will his parents allow him to keep the dog? Will the dog's owner find and claim it?

Storyline: ______________________

____

____

____

____

Story Tensions:

1. ______________________

2. ______________________

3. ______________________

Sarah, Plain and Tall - Chapter 4

Name:

Date:

Science: **Seashells**

Search online or use a book from the library to find 4 different seashells. Photocopy or print images, then cut them out and paste them into the spaces provided below. Write the name and any defining features (example: bivalve - a shell with two halves) onto the lines provided below each frame.

Name: ____________________

Features: ____________________

____

Name: ____________________

Features: ____________________

____

Name: ____________________

Features: ____________________

____

Name: ____________________

Features: ____________________

____

Name:

Date:

Fine Arts: **Biography - Who Am I?**

After doing the **Fine Arts: Thomas Hart Benton - Paintings That Roll Like the Sea** lesson, research Thomas Hart Benton online or read a book from the library about this famous painter.

Print and paste an image of a Thomas Hart Benton into the frame on the left and one of his paintings into the frame on the right. Write information gathered through your research into the lines below the frames.

Name: ______________________________

Lived: ______________________________

Known for: ______________________________

____

____

Connections to story: ______________________________

____

____

Sarah, Plain and Tall - Chapter 6

Name:
Date:
Language Arts: **Your Birth Year - Newbery Medal Winner**

After doing the **Language Arts: The Newbery Medal** lesson, search online for the book awarded the Newbery Medal on the year you were born and fill in the information about it below. If this books looks interesting to you, request it from your library and read it.

Year: __________

Title and Author : ____

Story Synopsis (brief summary): ______________________________________

____

____

____

____

If you read it ... rate it with 1 - 5 stars (5 being the best).
Color in the number of stars that you give the story.

Name:

Date:

Language Arts: **Character Compilation**

After doing the **Language Arts: Character Compilation - Maggie** lesson, use this Character Compilation sheet to note character traits for one or more characters in *Sarah, Plain and Tall* or another favorite book or character.

Character's Name: ______________________

Physical Traits: (examples - tall, short, dark haired, rosy cheeked, etc.)

____

____

____

____

____

____

____

____

Personality Traits: (examples - loving, rude, kind to animals, etc.)

____

____

____

____

____

____

____

____

Sarah, Plain and Tall - Chapter 8

Name:

Date:

Science: **Squall Definition**

After doing the **Science: Squalls** lesson, search online to fill in the information blanks below stating what defines a squall. Then search, "photo of weather squall" online and choose an image from the results to print and paste into the frame below.

Squall:

A sudden, strong ___________ that is sustained for at least _____ minutes at a speed of _____ miles per hour. This high wind is often accoumpanied by ___________ and ends quickly.

flip for answers:

wind

1-2 (min.)

18-25 (mph)

rain

Name:
Date:
Language Arts: **Vocabulary Words**

After finishing this chapter, use the crossword puzzle below to review the vocabulary words covered in **chapters 3-9**. Clues and vocabulary words are shown on the next page. Black boxes indicate a space between two words.

Across

1. (ch. 6) a phrase or word which exaggerates, used in poetry and writing

3. (ch. 5) the repetition of the same first sound or first letter in a group of words

4. (ch. 5) the main mineral component of sand

6. (ch. 3) sharp claws, especially belonging to a bird of prey

7. (ch. 8) two air masses with different temperatures colliding with each other

8. (ch. 6) the prestigious American children's book award given annually for excellence in literature

9. (ch. 5) a very thin, almost transparent mineral that flakes easily

10. (ch. 3) rows of trees or buildings that provide shelter from the wind

12. (ch. 4) a two-piece shell which fits together tightly

13. (ch. 4) a one-piece shell usually coiled into a spiral-like shape

Down

2. (ch. 3) a bird with talons and a hook-shaped beak, who feeds on other animals

4. (ch. 8) a sudden, severe storm, including high winds and often rain

5. (ch. 9) the ending of a story or situation

7. (ch. 3) an ancient sport (still practiced today) where birds of prey are tamed and trained to hunt on command

11. (ch. 5) a mound of sand heaped up by the wind

flip for vocab words: 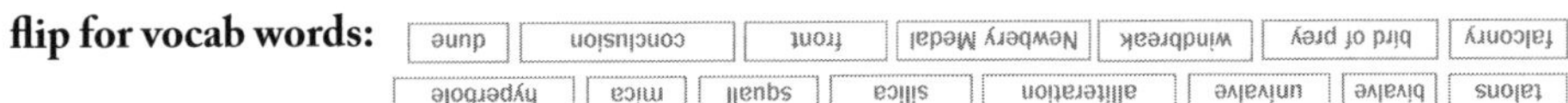

Homer Price

Title: *Homer Price*
Author: Robert McCloskey
Illustrator: Robert McCloskey
Copyright: 1943

Chapter 1—The Case of the Sensational Scent

Teacher Summary

The opening paragraph of Robert McCloskey's book, *Homer Price*, gives the reader a wonderful sense of place through McCloskey's skillful description. We find ourselves in Homer's world. Homer Price lives two miles outside of Centerburg at the junction of Route 56 and Route 56A. His parents own a tourist camp and Homer helps out around the place by pumping gas or helping his mother in the kitchen. In his spare time, Homer enjoys building radios. One night, Homer is busy in his room doing just that. He gets hungry for a snack and heads to the kitchen, being sure to put out a saucer of milk for his cat, Tabby. He feels something brush his skin and reaches down to pet his cat. But it isn't Tabby—it's a skunk! Homer remains very still, knowing skunks can make a terrible stink, and follows the skunk outside. Homer discovers the skunk is living under the house, right beneath his window! Wanting the skunk for a pet, Homer decides to call him Aroma. Homer trains Aroma to listen for a low whistle and climb into Homer's rigged basket pulley system. In this way, Homer can have Aroma in his room each night. Aroma makes his bed in Homer's old suitcase.

One night, Homer finishes a new radio and turns it on. Listening to his radio, Homer hears fabulous news! An area Centerburg resident, Mr. N. W. Blott, has just won $2,000 for writing the best slogan for Dreggs After Shave Lotion. The following week, the radio station is going to broadcast live from Centerburg when they present Mr. Blott with his check and 12 complimentary bottles of after shave lotion. Homer is excited!

The day of the broadcast Homer rides his bicycle to Centerburg to watch the show. Just as Mr. Blott is presented with his prize, four masked men with pistols say, "Put 'em up." Within moments, the four burglars steal all of Mr. Blott's winnings and his after shave lotion! Homer is amazed and that night he tells his parents what happened. The sheriff and his men are unable to apprehend the scoundrels, and Mr. Blott offers half of the money as a reward for finding them.

The next day, Homer and Aroma (in a basket on the bike) go fishing. On their way home, Homer decides to cut through the woods. Suddenly he hears voices and comes upon the four burglars, the money and the after shave lotion! The money and after shave lotion are lying in an open suitcase. While Homer watches the men talk, Aroma spies the suitcase and heads over for a snooze. Curled up in the suitcase, Aroma is immediately seen by one of the burglars. He throws a rock at Aroma, breaking six bottles of after shave lotion and scaring Aroma to death! Emitting a cloud of scent, Aroma permeates everything around him with a foul odor! Homer runs toward his bike and waits for Aroma to catch up.

That evening, Homer is thoughtful. He decides the police will find the burglars and doesn't want to get involved. Later on that night, four men stop and ask Homer for a room. Homer takes them to one of the largest tourist cabins and the men give him a dollar tip. As Homer walks away, he notices the money smells funny—a little like Aroma and a little like the after shave lotion! The burglars!

Homer calls the sheriff in Centerburg, but when no one comes to help, Homer takes matters into his own hands. Coming up with a plan, Homer manages to round up the burglars with one of their own guns, and marches them back into town. Homer saves the day! The story of Homer and the smelly money appears in the newspaper and business picks up for Homer's parents' tourist camp, too. Everybody wants to see the famous skunk, Aroma, who helped identify the burglars!

What we will cover in this chapter:

Social Studies: History - The Famous Homer: A Brief Introduction*
Social Studies: Geography - Highways and Roads of America
Social Studies: History - Tourist Camps: Motels of the Past
Social Studies: History - The Early Roots of Radio and Television
Science: Simple Machines - Pulley
Language Arts: Different Fictional Story Formats
Language Arts: Headlines - Making Them True and Interesting
Language Arts: Advertising Slogans
Language Arts: Writing and Discussion Question
Language Arts: Vocabulary
Fine Arts: What's Wrong with This Picture?
Life Skills: Having Parents Who Understand

Social Studies: History - The Famous Homer: A Brief Introduction*

Draw your student's attention to the first illustration located at the beginning of the book. Here we see a drawing of Homer Price chewing on a hayseed. Homer's head is resting on a broken bust of the famous poet and author, "Homer." But our Homer has written "Price" on the pedestal! Does your student understand what this picture means? Has your student ever heard of the Greek author, Homer? Now is a good time to introduce your student to the *famous* Homer!

Homer, a Greek author of ancient times (approximately 800-700 B.C.) is best known for his work on two poems entitled *The Iliad* and *The Odyssey*. Both of these poems are extremely long **epic poems**. Epic means the poem involves lengthy narrative writing, usually covering a subject of great importance, like a war or a historic figure. Homer's two epic poems center on events occurring during the time of the great Trojan War (approximately mid-1200s B.C.) and mix history with mythology or legend.

No one knows what Homer looked like, when he was born or died, or even where he lived. The legend (an often fictional tale so ancient it is believed to be true) surrounding Homer is that he was blind and illiterate. He is believed to have composed his poems orally, telling them over and over again while other men wrote them down. However, some experts believe Homer never even existed and that someone else wrote these poems!

If your student is interested in learning more about the famous and mysterious Homer, he might enjoy reading portions of the poems themselves. They are filled with excitement and adventure. Many excellent abridged and "student" versions of these two tales are available in bookstores and libraries.

Social Studies: Geography - Highways and Roads of America

In our story, Homer's family lived at the **junction** (where two roads meet) of Route 56 and Route 56A. In the illustration before the chapter begins, the sign by Shady Rest Tourist Camp plainly shows U.S. 56. Can your student find the sign? What does your student know about the roads and highways of America? Show your student a road map of the United States. (A paper map is ideal for this lesson but look at a map online if necessary!) By sharing the basics with your student, he will become more knowledgeable and aware of the streets and roads around him.

There are five main categories of roads in the United States and together (surfaced and unsurfaced) they cover more than 4 million miles. The categories are: city streets, county roads, state highways, U.S. highways, and interstate highways. The different categories dictate who maintains the road. **City streets** are named as well as numbered. Every city sets up its streets in a different way. Some cities have numbered streets running in one direction and named streets running in the other. Some cities, like Lincoln, Nebraska, for example, have their streets lettered in one direction and numbered in the other. A person in Lincoln might have a business located at the intersection of F street and 14th. Cities also often name streets in a common series: Washington, Jefferson, Lincoln, etc., or Oak, Maple, Elm, Walnut, etc., Massachusetts, Alabama, Colorado, etc. What is the name of the street where your student lives? How are your city's streets organized?

The next category of road is the **county road**. Maintained by the county or parish, these roads are generally located on the outskirts of a city, in a more rural area. **State highways**, maintained by the state, are numbered and can be located anywhere.

The two roads intersecting (a junction) at Homer's house are **U.S. highways**. Remind your student that the highway's signs identifying each type of road have specific shapes and colors. Make it a point to watch for the many different types of road and highway signs the next time you're driving.

Finally, there are the big freeways, known as **interstate highways**. Established through federal funding in 1956 during the Eisenhower administration, the interstate highway system is the most advanced and massive road system in the world. While looking at a United States road atlas, draw your student's attention to several interesting facts about the interstate highway system.

An interstate highway is denoted by the letter I and then followed by a number. All the interstate highways running north and south are numbered with odd numbers. They also begin with the lowest digits along the Pacific coast (California has 1-5) and progress toward the east with ever-increasing digits (1-95 runs along the east coast, for instance). The interstate highways running east and west are numbered with even numbers and begin in the south with the lowest number. (I-10 runs across the deep south while 1-90 runs along the northern United States.)

Encourage your student to take notice of the different road signs he sees around him! And maybe the next time your student takes a trip, he'll be able to help the driver navigate!

Social Studies: History - Tourist Camps: Motels of the Past

Draw your student's attention to the picture on the title page of this chapter. In the picture we see the sign for the Prices' business "Shady Rest Tourists Camp—Running Water." The picture also shows us Homer's gas pump, which he uses to fill guest's cars, and the sign over his mother's lunchroom that says "EAT."

Your student may have stayed in a hotel or motel (motel is a combination of the words "motor" and "hotel") at one time or another. If not, he has certainly seen them. Hundreds of motel chains are all over the country. Small tourist camps are largely a thing of the past and the predecessor to today's motels. Share with your student a little bit about this interesting piece of Americana.

Tourist camps were often composed of a series of little cabins or houses called "bungalows." Each cabin had a bed and bathroom and was decorated, cleaned and maintained by the family who owned the camp. Therefore, every tourist camp was different and no two cabins were alike. The "ma and pa"-owned tourist camps often served food cooked by the family (Homer's mother made fried chicken and hamburgers) and often had a gas pump for the motorists' vehicles. Some small towns still have little tourist camps like Shady Rest, but most of these family-owned businesses have given way to the competition of large motel chains.

Does your student think it would be fun to stay in a tourist camp? What would he like better about the tourist camp compared to a large motel or hotel? What would he not like as well? Maybe your student would like to come up with a name for his own imaginary Tourist Camp just like the Prices'. He can draw a map or build a model of the cabins. How many will he have? What kind of food will the lunchroom serve? What road will his tourist camp be located on? Have fun sharing and learning with your student about this unique piece of history.

History and Geography: The Early Roots of Radio and Television

Homer likes to build radios and learn how they work. When the money is stolen from Mr. Blott and a reward is offered, Homer tells Aroma, "If we could just catch those robbers we would have enough money to build lots of radios and even a television receiver."

Have your student look at the copyright date of *Homer Price*. Robert McCloskey wrote our tale in 1943. Were there televisions in 1943? Yes, but they were very, very new! Television was in the experimental stage in the 1930s.

The Radio Corporation of America (RCA) installed television receivers in 150 homes in New York City in 1936. A cartoon of *Felix the Cat* was the first program aired on these experimental televisions. When World War II began in 1941, America largely abandoned television research until 1945. By 1951, television broadcasts were being aired from California to Maine and variety shows, news programs, sporting events and much more became common.

But what did people do for home entertainment before television? That is where radio comes in. No wonder Homer was so interested in radios! In 1943 it was still the primary source of entertainment in most homes. People gathered around the radio in the evening and listened to their favorite programs just the way families often gather around a television set today. Radio programs like *The Lone Ranger*, *Little Orphan Annie*, and *The George Burns and Gracie Allen Show* were popular with old and young alike. Music stars like Duke Ellington, Glenn Miller and Bing Crosby had their own musical programs and people loved it. It was a different kind of entertainment—the pictures you saw were in your imagination!

Perhaps the single most famous event in radio occurred on October 30, 1938. Orson Welles' famous book *The War of the Worlds* was being read dramatically over the radio. The book is about Martians coming to earth in their space ship and invading. The radio announcer began the program by saying it was a dramatic reading and it was all fictional, but thousands of people tuned in during the program and thought it was actually happening! People fled their homes and towns, called the police and some suffered such shock they had to be hospitalized! Imagine that!

If your student shows interest, listen to some old-time radio programs online. One famous and funny skit is Abbott and Costello's "Who's on First?" routine about baseball players. Or listen to the original 1938 broadcast of "The War of the Worlds" and see if your student can understand how people might have been misled by it!

In 1943, Homer probably had never seen a television but had certainly heard of one. And coupled with his curiosity and love for electronics, he would certainly have wanted to try to build one for himself! There are many resources available for students who are serious about electronics, like Homer. Many companies have created discovery kits on inventions, building your own radio, having fun with electronics, etc. The age level and price differ on every kit, but many are inexpensive and include all the equipment.

Science: Simple Machines - Pulley

Homer used a pulley system to get Aroma into his room each night. A pulley is one of the six "simple machines," and is made up of a wheel with a groove around its rim so a rope (or other cord) can lay in the groove. When we want to lift a heavy object, it can be attached to one end of the rope. As we pull on the other end, while the rope runs through the pulley, this simple machine enables the weighted object to be moved up or down more easily than if a person just tried to lift it.

Teacher's Note: The other five simple machines are as follows: lever, wedge, inclined plane, wheel and axle, and screw (which is really a spiral inclined plane).

Challenge your student to utilize a pulley in an invention of his own. A great first pulley invention is an "egg cracking machine." There are an infinite number of possible designs. Here is just one list of possible materials that could be used. By gathering a wooden platform, string, a small metal pulley, some fishing weights (or other heavy metal pieces), small pieces of wood for a frame, and the egg, have your student try to invent his own egg-cracking device.

Encourage him to think through his plan and even draw his designs on paper before he begins to build his invention. If his first few attempts are unsuccessful, challenge him to keep trying until it works!

Once his egg-cracking device is operational, perhaps he would enjoy demonstrating it to family and friends. Encourage him to watch for other ways in which pulleys are used.

Language Arts: Different Fictional Story Formats

The first fictional chapter book we read in FIAR Vol. 5 was *The Boxcar Children.* Remind your student of how it was organized with each chapter leading into the next—often with a cliffhanger! It was clearly necessary to read each chapter completely in order to understand the following chapter. Now look at the contents of *Homer Price* and think about how the author organized this first chapter. Instead of tying each chapter together, McCloskey chose to write each chapter as an individual story. You can read the chapters in any order and the story will still make sense.

If your student enjoys the creative writing process and is working on a short story or has an idea for one, perhaps he would enjoy writing a story in this format—each chapter (it could be as short as a page) containing a complete tale with a beginning, middle and ending.

Language Arts: Headlines - Making Them True and Interesting

Wasn't it amazing that Aroma and Homer made the headlines in the paper? Have your student look at the headline again, "Boy and Pet Skunk Trap Shaving Lotion Robbers By Smell."

What should a good news headline do? What should it include? What should it avoid? These are all questions to ask your student as you begin to study and observe various headlines in newspapers or online. The headline about Homer is great because it tells what happens briefly, it makes the reader want to read the article, and it doesn't exaggerate the facts or make false claims.

A headline is intended to catch the reader's eye and make him want to read the article. It should always briefly explain what the article is about. But a headline should never tell an untruth or be sensationalistic in nature. This means to exaggerate the truth. A news journalist's job is to portray accurate, factual stories, not imaginary tales.

Have your student write two or three headlines for the same story—Homer and Aroma saving the day. As you look at other headlines together, have your student tell you what he thinks about each one. Does it tell the truth? Does it make him want to read the article? Is it sensationalistic? Your student can rewrite any questionable headlines by making them more truthful, more interesting or less sensational.

Language Arts: Advertising Slogans

Mr. N. W. Blott won $2,000 and a dozen bottles of lotion when he came up with a slogan for Dreggs After Shave Lotion. That is a lot of money for thinking up one sentence! Advertising, however, is important business and the Dreggs Company knew they would make back all the prize money and more if they had a great slogan!

The word **slogan** may be a new word for your student. A slogan is a specific, short phrase or sentence used to sell a product. It must be "catchy" or memorable so people will like it or remember it and then buy the item you're trying to sell. Mr. N. W. Blott came up with the slogan, "The after shave lotion with the distinctive invigorating smell that keeps you on your toes."

Because *Homer Price* is a book intended to be humorous, Mr. Blott's slogan may not be the best example of a catchy, short phrase that is memorable. However, share with your student successful slogans that were popular in the past. For example: Just Do It (Nike); Where's the Beef? (Wendy's); Breakfast of Champions (Wheaties); Betcha Can't Eat Just One (Lay's); The Quicker Picker Upper (Bounty); I'm Lovin' It (McDonalds); Got Milk? (California milk producers). Or perhaps you have a few favorite or memorable slogans from your childhood. Share these with your student and if there is interest, discuss why each slogan might have appealed to consumers and encouraged them to buy that particular item.

Companies pay a great deal of money to professional advertising agencies to come up with great slogans or commercials for their products. It takes a lot of creative spark and hard work to come up with a catchy phrase. Many successful advertising slogans exhibit the three S's: short, specific, and saucy. The slogan should be to the point (short), about the product or what it can do for you (specific) and have a memorable tone or catchiness to the phrase (saucy).

Talk with your student about some advertising slogans that are popular right now. Do they make him want to buy the products? Does he remember the wording or the jingle? If your student is interested, have him try his hand at the advertising business. See if he can come up with two or three advertisements for the Dreggs After Shave Lotion (or another product). Can he do better than Mr. Blott?

Language Arts: Writing and Discussion Question

When Homer is trying to decide what to do with the robbers, he decides to call the sheriff. The book tells us, "Homer knew that the sheriff would be down at the barber shop in Centerburg playing checkers and talking politics." How does Homer know what the sheriff is doing?

Language Arts: Vocabulary

Homer Greek epic poet from approximately the 8th century B.C., who wrote *The Iliad* and *The Odyssey*.

junction A place or point of crossing, as two highways.

tourist camp An old-time motel, usually family owned and operated.

bungalow A small house or cottage.

sensationalism The use of exaggerated language intended to shock.

slogan A catchphrase used to sell or advertise a product.

validate To make someone feel worthy or important.

Fine Arts: What's Wrong with This Picture?

The burglars are funny! They all mistrust one another so much that they end up sleeping in the same bed in order to keep an eye on one another. Have your student study that illustration. What does he notice? The author tells us there are *four* burglars. How many men are in the bed? What's wrong with this picture? There are *five* people in the drawing! What happened?

Sometimes illustrations are wrong. In the printing process, things get overlooked. And in this case, perhaps McCloskey drew his illustrations a long time before or after he *wrote* the book. Maybe he was *planning* on having five burglars at first, and then later changed to four. Share with your student how interesting it is that even professional, award-winning authors and illustrators might make mistakes sometimes. And encourage your student to double-check the consistency of his own texts and illustrations when he is working on a story. Who knows? This famous author/illustrator might even have made the picture this way on purpose as a humorous touch for his unusually observant readers!

Life Skills: Having Parents Who Understand

Homer is thinking hard about what to do with the burglars. He finally decides he will need to take matters into his own hands and take responsibility. Homer tells his mother he has some important business to take care of and asks her if she can take care of things for awhile. Homer's mother answers, "Well, I think so Homer, but don't stay away too long."

Homer's mother was very understanding. She recognized Homer's need for some time alone and respected his polite request. It's nice to have parents who understand you when you're young. Sometimes, adults forget that children can have plans and feelings of their own. Talk with your student about the importance of understanding each other, parent-to-child and child-to-parent.

When our parents understand us, it makes us feel validated. To **validate** someone means we make them feel valued, important and worth listening to. Everyone wants to feel like that! Challenge your student and yourself to look for more ways to validate one another.

Chapter 2—The Case of the Cosmic Comic

Teacher Summary

Homer and Freddy like to look at the Super-Duper comic books. They are exciting and the boys think the Super-Duper is powerful and very cool! One day, Freddy calls Homer's house with exciting news. The real Super-Duper is coming to Centerburg! A new Super-Duper film is premiering and the actual, "real, honest-to-goodness" Super-Duper will be there! The boys plan a day-trip to Centerburg for the following Saturday. Freddy's horse, Lucy, pulls the boys by wagon to Centerburg. Homer, Freddy, and Freddy's little brother Louis, are all very excited!

The Super-Duper's car is parked outside the movie theater. Long, shiny and red, the boys think it is the best car ever! They see the real Super-Duper, shake his hand and get his autograph. Freddy asks Mr. Super-Duper if he can please fly for them, but the Super-Duper says "not today."

After the movie, the boys head home. As the wagon rounds a corner, they hear a car honking and suddenly see a red and silver "SWOOSH!" go by them. The Super-Duper! Then they hear a loud crash. Freddy thinks perhaps an electric ray got the Super-Duper. They round the corner and see the car smashed against the fence. The boys are thrilled! Now they're going to get to see the Super-Duper pry the bumper off the fence with his little finger! Or lift the entire car back onto the road with one hand! But, the unexpected happens.

The boys hear, "Ouch!" The Super-Duper is hurt! Freddy and Homer help the Super-Duper pull his car back onto the road with the wagon and Lucy. The boys are disappointed in the Super-Duper. He is only human after all!

What we will cover in this chapter:

Science: Chromium
Science: Horsepower - Does That Really Mean a Horse?
Language Arts: Formula Fiction
Language Arts: Monograms
Language Arts: Writing and Discussion Question
Language Arts: Vocabulary*
Fine Arts: Cartooning - A "Funny" Way to Communicate
Fine Arts: The Art of Melodrama
Life Skills: Dealing with Disillusionment

Science: Chromium

The Super-Duper's car was long and red, with chromium trimmings (page 39). What a cool car! But what is **chromium**? If you have introduced your student to the periodic table of elements, here is another new element!

Chromium is a chemical element. It is a strong, hard, gray metal which gets very shiny when polished. For this reason, it is used to cover or coat other metals to give them a durable, glistening finish. The Super-Duper's car had very sparkling trim! In years past, many cars and trucks had "chrome" bumpers and trim. See if your student can spot chrome on older 20th-century vehicles that he sees while out and about. If there is further interest, he may want to research when and why chromium trim was no longer used on cars and and trucks.

A French chemist, Louis Nicolas Vauquelin, discovered and named chromium in 1797. Take a look at the chemical symbol for chromium (Cr), along with its atomic number and weight. Can your student find this element on the periodic table of elements? Your student is gaining more knowledge of the elements every time you cover a lesson like this!

Science: Horsepower - Does That Really Mean a Horse?

Homer and Freddy have to get an early start for Centerburg. Freddy says, "...it takes old Lucy about an hour to go as far as Centerburg."

Does your student remember how far away Homer's house is from Centerburg? (About two miles) Imagine, traveling at two miles per hour! The typical human walking speed is about 3 miles per hour. Lucy, the horse, does not go very fast, does she?

Ask your student if he has ever heard the word "**horsepower**." Does this unit of power really refer to a horse? Well, a famous Scottish engineer named James Watt (1736- 1819) was the man **to coin** (to make up a new word or phrase) the phrase "horsepower." He used it to *loosely* define the power of the new steam engines by comparing them to horses. In other words, he compared the power it took a horse to lift or pull something to the power it took his steam engines to do the same job. One horsepower is defined as "550 foot-pounds of work per second." For this age level, let's simplify the calculation by eliminating the "per second" part of the equation and simply define **foot-pound** as the work required to raise one pound twelve inches.

Teacher's Note: At this point in the lesson, your younger students may get lost. If this is beyond them, simply introduce them to the term and leave it at that. For your older students, the scientific calculations may be challenging and fun.

If an engine lifts a 550-pound object three feet in the air, it is expending 1,650 foot-pounds of energy (550 pounds x 3 feet = 1,650). How much horsepower was required? (Three; 1,650 divided by 550 = 3.) Try to come up with your own calculations using this equation.

You can also calculate the horsepower of a human at work. How much does the person weigh? How high is he climbing? If a 110-pound student is climbing up Thomas Edison's 100-foot boyhood tower, how much horsepower did he use? (110 pounds x 100 feet = 11,000 foot-pounds. 11,000 divided by 550 = 20 horsepower.)

Therefore, in answer to our initial question, "Does horsepower really mean a horse?", the answer is yes and no. Lucy was pulling the wagon carrying Homer and Freddy at approximately one horsepower. However, this old Scottish phrase now defines a much more specific unit of power.

Language Arts: Formula Fiction

Homer notices the Super-Duper stories all seem alike. Freddy disagrees. "No, they're not! Sometimes the Super-Duper smashes airships and sometimes he smashes ocean liners. Then, other times he just breaks up mountains."

Does your student think Freddy's argument is valid? It sounds like all the Super-Duper stories are alike, just like Homer said. Take this opportunity to introduce your student to a type of writing called **formula fiction**.

Just because the Super-Duper stories are all alike doesn't mean they're not exciting and fun to read! In fact, predictability in stories is sometimes relaxing. You know what's going to happen. No shocking surprises, no scary cliffhanger endings.

The term formula fiction is somewhat self-explanatory. A formula is a predictable way of doing something—ending up with the same result every time. Perhaps the most classic formula fiction series are the *Nancy Drew* and *Hardy Boys* books. Written by Carolyn Keene/Franklin W. Dixon (pen names for a variety of authors who worked for the Stratemeyer Syndicate), these stories have become synonymous with formula plots and predictable endings. But, they are also two of the most well-loved, well-known children's mystery series in the world. Critics may argue that the *Nancy Drew* and *Hardy Boys* books are not of the greatest literary quality, but they have survived despite such criticism.

Formula fiction is a *literary device*—a way of writing. If your student enjoys creative writing, perhaps he would like to develop a set of characters and a formula plot of his own. By writing even a few short installments, he can get a firsthand look at formula fiction.

Language Arts: Monograms

In the description of the Super-Duper's car, we read: "It was long and red, with chromium trimmings, and it had the Super-Duper's monogram on the side." Does your student know what a monogram is? A **monogram** is the combination of the first letters of a person's name into a design. A person's monogram is often designed with the first letter from the first name, middle letter (slightly enlarged) from the last name, and the third letter from the middle name. For example, a woman named Sara Louise Brown would have the monogram SBL. Have your student create his own monogram using markers or colored pencils.

Monograms can be found everywhere: embroidered on towels, handkerchiefs, shirt pockets ... etched on

drinking glasses, silverware, stationery ... displayed on the back windows of cars ... and on anything else someone wants personalized.

If your student thinks this is fun, experiment with adding his monogram to something. A pillowcase can be personalized with a monogram and some fabric paint. If your student likes sewing, a simple pillow or handkerchief can be embellished with a monogram. Have fun and encourage your student to be creative!

Language Arts: Writing and Discussion Question

What do you think was going through Homer's mind when he heard the crash of the Super-Duper's car and then saw the situation?

Language Arts: Vocabulary*

chromium A grayish-white, hard, metallic chemical element.

horsepower A unit for measuring the power of motors or engines, equal to 550 foot-pounds of work per second.

to coin To make up or invent a new word or phrase.

foot-pound A unit of energy equal to lifting one pound a distance of one foot.

monogram The first letters of a name combined into a single design.

melodrama A drama concerned with exaggerated conflicts and emotions and stereotyped characters.

disillusionment A feeling of disappointment because something is not as good as you believed it to be.

Fine Arts: Cartooning - A "Funny" Way to Communicate

Homer, Freddy, and little Louis love the Super-Duper comic books! Comic books and cartoon strips (sometimes called the "funnies") were extremely popular years ago and still enjoy a wide audience today. Cartooning utilizes several specific artistic devices to create its trademark look.

First, the figures are usually only "sketched" out and not in full detail. Often the artist will exaggerate a specific feature to make the figure more humorous. Secondly, the spoken words of the characters are often located in what are known as "balloons." Next, cartoons are separated into "panels."

Cartooning is actually two things— an art form and a communication form. Sometimes the best way to express an idea or feeling is by making it funny, and what better way to do that than through the medium of a cartoon? Well-known cartoon strips enjoyed by children and young teens include *Peanuts*, *Garfield*, *Foxtrot*, and *Calvin & Hobbes*. Cartoons have also been used for many years for political satire (making fun of policies and politicians).

To learn more about cartooning, begin by looking at comic strips online or in your local newspaper. You may also want to look at a few political cartoons (in a newspaper, these are usually located on the opinion/editorial page). What does your student notice about them? What is the same in each? What is different?

An excellent source for learning the art of cartooning is called *The Big Yellow Drawing Book: A Workbook Emphasizing the Basic Principles of Learning, Teaching, and Drawing Through Cartooning* by Dan, Marian and Hugh O'Neill. This book was published in 1974 but is still considered the best learn-to-draw cartooning book available. The format is easy enough for the youngest student to enjoy and is set up like a workbook, with panels of examples and then blank panels to try various techniques yourself. A fabulous book!

Your library may have other cartooning books available, as well as age-appropriate comics for your student to enjoy. Search the library catalog and see what you can find!

Fine Arts: The Art of Melodrama

When Homer and Freddy discuss the plots in the Super-Duper comic books, Homer makes the observation that Super-Duper "always rescues the pretty girl and catches the villain on the last page." "Of course," says Freddy, "That's to show that crime doesn't pay." In a nutshell, Freddy and Homer have just described a classic form of theater—the **melodrama**. Introduce your student to this recognizable dramatic form and familiar term.

Melodrama became a highly popular form of theater in the 1800s, involving a predictable (or formula) plot which always included a hero (a person of high moral character who is brave, strong and handsome), a villain (a person of low moral character who is evil, smart but often physically weak, dressed in black and ugly), and a beautiful woman (the damsel in distress who is in love with the hero but imprisoned by the villain and too weak to escape by herself).

Melodrama was loved by the public! They shrieked in terror at the villain's evil laugh while he twirled his long mustache. They swooned at the handsome young hero, and always sighed during the kiss at the end. Happy endings are a must in melodrama, for just the reason Freddy mentioned. Melodramas always prove that crime doesn't pay, the righteous always win and love is the most powerful thing in the world.

Exaggerated as it is, melodrama is still played in theaters all across the United States and the term "melodramatic" is used to define someone who is being overly dramatic. If your student is interested in acting, perhaps he would like to write or stage his own melodrama. Tinny piano playing is usually the background music for melodramas and in this theater form, you can never over-act!

Life Skills: Dealing with Disillusionment

Homer, Freddy and little Louis think a ray-gun or a villain must have hurt the Super-Duper. They are waiting to see him lift the car up with his little finger. They are sure all they have read about him is true. But what do they hear him say? "Ouch!" The Super-Duper is human! He isn't really a superhero at all. And in fact, they have to help him get untangled. Homer and his friends are disappointed!

Sometimes people fail us. They don't meet our expectations and we can feel disillusioned. **Disillusionment** is the feeling of disappointment you get when you disscover that something isn't as good as you believed it to be. Disillusionment is a very real feeling, and it affects adults and children alike. Discuss with your student times in your life when you've felt disillusioned. Has he ever felt that way?

If you are a human being, there is really no way to escape feeling disillusioned sometimes. But there is a way to reduce the number of times we are disillusioned. We need to develop **discernment**. Discernment is the ability to see clearly and to show good judgment. Discernment can be a learned skill. When we begin to exercise discernment we are much less likely to be disillusioned or disappointed.

For example, when we have a friend who has a habit of not telling the truth and exaggerating stories and he tells us that he's going to take all of his friends to Disneyland for his birthday next summer, should we believe him? If we get our hopes up, convinced that we're going to have a wonderful time on this extravagant birthday trip, there's a very good chance we'll be disappointed. But discernment would suggest that this boy has often failed to tell the truth in the past and this is probably another one of those times. We probably shouldn't count on going to Disneyland if we are discerning about our friend.

Explain to your student that discernment and wisdom go hand-in-hand. Even as adults, we sometimes fail to be discerning, but when we continue to practice this skill, we can avoid many of life's disappointments.

Chapter 3—The Doughnuts

Teacher Summary

Homer's Uncle Ulysses owns an up-and-coming lunchroom, updated with all the newest labor saving devices! One day, Homer's mother goes with his Aunt Agnes to sew and knit for the Red Cross. Homer decides to go along and spend some time with his Uncle Ulysses in the lunchroom while the ladies are gone.

When Homer arrives, Uncle Ulysses is shining and cleaning his favorite labor saving device—his automatic doughnut machine. Uncle Ulysses decides to head over to the barbershop for a little while, and asks Homer if he would mind taking care of the customers and making a batch of doughnuts while he is gone. The first customer in the store after Uncle Ulysses leaves is a nice, traveling advertising man named Mr. Gabby. He decides to stay and wait for the fresh doughnuts Homer is about to make. Then a rich lady in a shiny, black car comes in. Homer tells her the doughnuts aren't made yet, and she insists on helping him mix up the batter. The rich lady tells Homer she has a very special recipe and takes over! Homer is amazed at how much batter the lady makes, but doesn't say anything.

When the first few doughnuts come out of the hot oil, everyone says they are delicious! The lady buys some doughnuts and leaves. Homer decides the automatic machine has made enough doughnuts and tries to turn the stop lever. Nothing happens! The doughnuts keep rolling down the chute into the hot fat! Homer tries the start lever without results. He calls Uncle Ulysses and asks him to come back to the lunchroom. Then he and Mr. Gabby work on stacking the doughnuts everywhere they can find. They put a sale sign out saying, "2 Doughnuts for 5¢," but people aren't buying them fast enough! Uncle Ulysses arrives on the scene and is shocked! What is he going to do with all those doughnuts?

Suddenly, the nice rich lady who had made all the batter comes back in the lunchroom, wringing her hands. "My bracelet!" she wails. "My diamond bracelet is gone and I left it here on the counter." They look for the bracelet without success. Then, Homer has an idea! The bracelet must have been mixed into the batter and baked into one of the doughnuts! He quickly creates a sign for Mr. Gabby, advertising the sale on doughnuts and offering a $100 reward for the return of the bracelet! People start buying doughnuts right and left. Soon almost all the doughnuts are gone and then Rupert Black finds the bracelet in his doughnut! The nice rich lady is thrilled to have her bracelet back. Homer is thrilled the batter has finally run out and the machine is finished, and Uncle Ulysses is thrilled all those doughnuts have been sold!

What we will cover in this chapter:

Social Studies: History - Telephones and Operators
Social Studies: History - The Red Cross
Science: New Technology - Labor Saving Devices Today*
Science: Economics - Supply and Demand
Language Arts: Literary Enrichment - Thematic Stories
Language Arts: Writing and Discussion Question
Language Arts: Vocabulary
Fine Arts: Design Your Own Sandwich Board
Fine Arts: Cooking - Make Your Own Doughnuts
Fine Arts: Illustrating Movement

Social Studies: History - Telephones and Operators

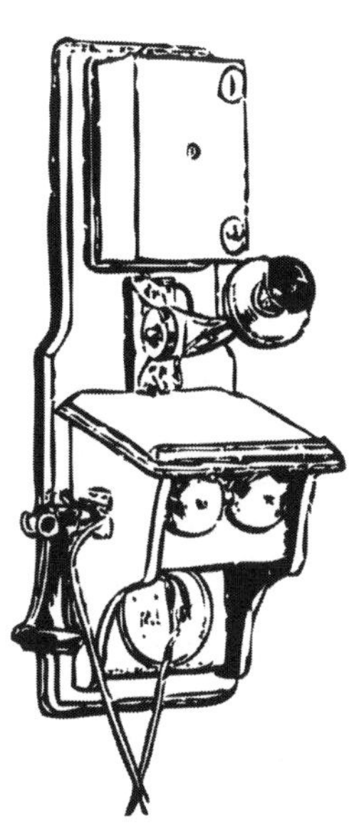

Homer needs Uncle Ulysses' help right away! That automatic doughnut machine won't stop! Homer decides to call his uncle down at the barbershop. The book tells us Homer "gave the number" and then waited for someone to answer. What does it mean to "give the number?" Take this opportunity to share with your student the way in which calls were placed in the first part of the 20th century, especially in rural areas.

In the early days of the telephone, everyone's telephones were all connected on the same line in any given community. When you picked up the telephone handset in your home, if your neighbor down the road was already talking on their phone, you could hear their conversation. All the phones were hooked together on a common line!

The operator (sometimes called "central") would ring each individual family with their own unique ring pattern. For instance, your phone pattern might be "two longs and one short" ring. Everyone in the community could hear the two long and one short phone rings, but you knew that whoever was calling wanted *your* house. If your phone rang with one long and one short ring, you knew that was for your neighbor down the road and so you didn't answer.

Later, as phone systems grew more complex, each phone had a unique phone number, but the operator still placed your call for you. Rather than dialing the barbershop, Homer asked the operator to dial the barbershop for him. Today, of course, each phone has it's own unique phone number and we can dial our own telephone calls directly anywhere in the world. When you see phones in books, on TV and in movies, notice if they have a dialer or if the caller needed an operator to place the call. For instance, in the old Andy Griffith show, Andy had a phone with no dial and always had to ask the operator to get the person he needed.

Take this opportunity to discuss with your student anything he may not know about making phone calls today. Does he know how to use a cell phone to call people whose numbers are stored in the phone already? What about people or businesses he doesn't already know? Does he understand what area codes are and when they're required to make a call or send a text? Also spend some time reviewing the "911" emergency call system, if your community has that option.

Social Studies: History - The Red Cross

Homer's mother and Aunt Agnes help the Red Cross. What does your student know about the Red Cross? Take this opportunity to share with your student the touching story behind this organization of peace and healing. A Swiss philanthropist, Jean Henri Dunant, founded the Red Cross in 1863.

Teacher's Note: You may wish to review the lesson on philanthropy and humanitarianism found in *The Boxcar Children* (FIAR Vol. 5), chapter 10 lessons.

A few years before (in 1859), Dunant was in Italy during the Austro-Sardinian War. To his horror, he saw the field at Solferino the day after nearly 41,000 people had been killed or wounded. He didn't allow himself to be overwhelmed by the vast number of wounded, but instead chose to help in whatever way he was able. Organizing a band of volunteers, Dunant and his group tended to as many of the injured as they could.

This incident changed Dunant's way of thinking. He became driven to find a way to help in other situations like Solferino. In 1862 he published a small booklet entitled *Un Souvenir de Solferino (Recollections of Solferino)*. The last line in the text read "Would it not be possible to fund and organize in all civilized countries permanent societies of volunteers who in time of war would give help to the wounded without regard of their nationality?"

He succeeded in doing just that! His heart-rending plea was looked upon with favor and on October 26, 1863, delegates from 16 countries met to discuss Dunant's plan.

During these meetings, the Red Cross symbol was chosen (the red cross on a white background in honor of Dunant's homeland, Switzerland) and the basic plans for the Red Cross were written out. In the United States, in 1881, Clara Barton founded the American Association of the Red Cross. (Your student might have completed an activity sheet on Clara Barton for *The Boxcar Children,* FIAR Vol. 5, chapter 4). This now famous, dedicated worker was extremely shy as a child and was homeschooled for much of her education.)

Today, the Red Cross's efforts go beyond war relief. Natural disaster relief (floods, volcanoes, tornadoes, fires, etc.), public health services and organizing blood drives are just a few ways the Red Cross maintains an active and helping hand in all aspects of life, worldwide. The Junior Red Cross was founded in 1917 and gives school children a chance to help.

From the late 1800s to around 1950, the citizens of the United States (people like Homer's mother and Aunt Agnes) helped the Red Cross in a *personal* way. Knitting scarves for the soldiers, ripping cloth for bandages, baking tins of cookies, and other things of this nature were ways people could serve their country and the soldiers directly. As late as the 1950s schools and junior organizations had children putting together care packages (washcloth, toothbrush, toothpaste, books, etc.) for the soldiers stationed all over the world.

People can now serve the Red Cross by other means. Whoever is motivated by concern for human life can become active in the Red Cross at the local, national or international level, and serve in many different ways.

Science: New Technology - Labor Saving Devices Today*

Uncle Ulysses is fascinated by labor saving devices! Newer, faster means of doing things are invented every day! Trying to keep up with the latest technology is difficult.

Discuss with your student what types of labor saving devices (sometimes called "time-savers") we have today—things Uncle Ulysses would have loved!

We have snow blowers and leaf blowers, weed eaters, food processors, personal computers, cell phones, smart TVs and watches, the internet, email, rice cookers, dishwashers, microwave ovens, virtual assistants, smart appliances, automatic robotic vacuum cleaners, and much more! Can your student think of any others? Keep a running list. Anyone can add to it and see who can come up with the most unusual or silly labor saving device! You can call the device an "Uncle Ulysses Special." Have fun!

Labor saving devices, however, are more than just fun. They have dramatically changed the face of our culture in the 21st century. Jobs that used to take many hours can now be accomplished in only a few minutes. Imagine handwriting several pages of a book that you wanted to share with a friend, compared to using a copy machine or taking a picture with a smartphone. Imagine cutting a large lawn with a push-type mower compared to using a modern riding mower. As more and more labor saving devices have found their way into American culture, most of us have had more free time for leisure or recreational use. We no longer spend all day mowing on Saturday, but instead we can finish mowing by 10:00 a.m. Uncle Ulysses would have been delighted.

Science: Economics - Supply and Demand

Teacher's Note: The study of economics falls into the category of social sciences, which is the study of individuals and society. It could be categorized as either science or as social studies.

The doughnuts in Uncle Ulysses' lunchroom are out of control! Mr. Gabby, the traveling advertising man, has a great idea! By advertising a sale on doughnuts, they can sell a lot more. Mr. Gabby tells Homer, "You got the doughnuts, ya gotta create a market. ...Understand? ...It's balancing the demand with the supply. ...That sort of thing."

This is an excellent opportunity to share a beginning lesson in economics with your student! The concept of supply and demand is fundamental to all discussions of economics. Even the youngest student can understand the idea of supply and demand.

If you wish, begin with a simple example. In fact, the illustration from our story is perfect! Whether or not you have a product you wish to sell by accident (such as Uncle Ulysses' doughnuts) or you've purposely created a product (such as lemonade for your lemonade stand), you have to make people want it! (Create demand.) Advertising is one common way in which manufacturers increase the demand for their product.

When you have lots of product to sell, you have supply. You have an incentive to keep your price as low as possible to increase demand. In other words, the lower your price, the more people will want to buy of your product. But sometimes there is very little supply. Perhaps you have a very rare Honus Wagner baseball card and there are only a few known to exist. Many people would like to own that baseball card (demand) but there are only a few available (supply). Prices will be very high because of the law of supply and demand. You could sell many Honus Wagner baseball cards for $50 each, fewer of them at $500 each and far fewer still at $5,000 each. As the price goes up, the demand goes down. Fewer people want them.

If you have thousands of the same, identical baseball card to sell, you may have to begin lowering your price in order to convince many, many people to purchase one from you. (This is what Homer had to do—lower the price on his doughnuts in order to convince many, many people to buy them.)

Prices are also controlled by the demand side of the equation. If your baseball card is of someone famous, many, many people will want to own one—big demand. They will compete with one another to purchase a limited supply and force the price to rise. On the other hand, very few people may be interested in buying a baseball card of a rookie who never played in a big league game and is now selling used cars in Arkansas. The low demand for his card means prices will have to be awfully cheap to convince anyone to buy one of his cards.

High prices result from either limited supply or high demand. Low prices result from excess supply or limited demand. This simple economic "law" is the primary force behind most western economies. Whenever you see a "clearance" sale table, you know that either nobody wants that item anymore, or the store has a large supply they need to sell. Likewise, when you see something selling at a higher-than-usual price, you know that either everybody wants one, or there are just very few available for anyone.

For more information on supply and demand, an excellent and popular book is *Whatever Happened to Penny Candy?* by Richard J. Maybury.

Language Arts: Literary Enrichment - Thematic Stories

This chapter in *Homer Price* is an amusing tale of treasure lost and found. Many other stories have a similar theme, and an instructional exercise in literary enrichment is to conduct a thematic study (comparing and contrasting two similar books).

A wonderful book to use for comparative analysis with this third chapter of Homer Price is entitled *Too Many Tamales* by Gary Soto. This is a delightful story of a Mexican-American family's get-together during the Christmas season. Maria, the daughter, helps her mother make a steaming platter of fresh tamales. While her mother steps away for a moment, Maria decides to slip on the diamond ring her mother took off while she was mixing the dough. Later in the evening after the cousins arrive and the presents are piling up under the tree, Maria remembers the ring. She can't remember where she put it and the cousins run downstairs behind her. Staring in dismay at the mound of hot tamales, Maria decides the ring must be in one of them. The cousins begin eating, and soon the floor is littered with paper-thin comhusks and every one of the tamales has been devoured. But no ring! The story ends with a sweet moment between Maria and her mother, Rosa. Rosa tells Maria that she had found the ring and put it back on. All is well and the family makes up another batch of tamales.

The reason this book is such a nice choice for a thematic study is two-fold. First, the story shares the same story line as Uncle Ulysses' doughnut machine disaster. Second, *Too Many Tamales* is an excellent snapshot of another culture and family. A t first, don't tell your student that the story has similarities. Just begin reading the story aloud and see if he comments on the similarities.

For your young student, simply reading the story and discussing the similarities is a great exercise. For your older student, even though *Too Many Tamales* is a picture book, the exercise can be expanded by assigning a written paper. He can develop his paper by comparing and contrasting the two stories, and perhaps discussing differences in the illustrations.

Fine Arts: Design Your Own Sandwich Board

Mr. Gabby wore a sign called a sandwich board. What an interesting way to advertise! Sandwich boards are not seen as often today, but your student might have fun designing and making one. Perhaps, your student could take the advertising slogan he wrote for the last chapter and use that, along with a picture or two, and create his own sandwich board.

By using poster board, cardboard or even a paper grocery bag cut in half, your student can design the back and front. Then add a couple of straps made from fabric or string and you have it!

Fine Arts: Cooking - Make Your Own Doughnuts

Reading this chapter makes you hungry for some fresh doughnuts, doesn't it? Why not take this opportunity to cook something with your student! Beyond the fun bonding time this activity offers, take some time to talk with your student about where a few of the ingredients used in the recipe are grown or gathered. Work on dry and liquid measure. Discuss the fractions involved in the cooking, etc.

Here is a recipe for doughnuts that you can make at home *without* using hot oil; safer and *healthier*!

2 (1/4 oz.) pkgs. dry yeast
1/4 cup warm water
1 1/2 cups warm milk
1/2 cup sugar
1 tsp. salt
1 tsp. nutmeg
1/4 tsp. cinnamon
2 eggs
1/3 cup shortening
4 1/2 cups flour
1/4 cup butter, melted
sugar to decorate

In a large mixing bowl, dissolve the yeast in warm water. Add milk, sugar, salt, nutmeg, cinnamon, eggs, shortening and 2 cups flour (hold the rest of the flour in reserve).

Blend for 30 seconds with a mixer on low speed as you add the remaining flour. Cover the bowl and allow the mixture to rise until doubled in volume (approximately 60 minutes). Turn dough out onto a well-floured surface and roll with a rolling pin until your dough is 1/2" thick. Using a well-floured doughnut cutter (or a large and small drinking glass) cut dough into doughnut shapes. Place your doughnuts on a well-greased baking sheet. Preheat oven to 425° F. Brush the tops with melted butter and allow to rise until the volume of each doughnut has doubled once again (approximately 20 minutes). Bake your doughnuts for 8-10 minutes. Brush once more with melted butter and sprinkle sugar on top. Now enjoy! (Makes 1 1/2 to 2 dozen doughnuts.)

Fine Arts: Illustrating Movement

Robert McCloskey is an award-winning author and illustrator; his illustrations for *Homer Price* are a good example of why. Filled with gentle, sweet faces and pleasing lines, the artwork in this book is exceptional. There are many techniques worth studying (we will be covering more in future lessons), but one of McCloskey's most interesting techniques is the way he illustrates movement.

Show your student the title illustration for this chapter. Homer is mopping the floor. Uncle Ulysses is proudly standing by the automatic doughnut machine, and a Centerburg resident is eating at the counter. Draw your student's attention to the multi-slice toaster behind Uncle Ulysses. How does McCloskey make the toast look like it is actually popping up? (He uses lines drawn in the direction he wants the toast to move.) Isn't that interesting?

Now, look with your student at the illustration of the rich lady mixing up the doughnut batter. Take a moment and look at her jewelry sitting next to the bowl. Notice how the same type of lines can make an object look like it is shiny or glittering. What is different between the "moving lines" McCloskey used to bring the toast to "life" and the "glitter lines" he uses on the jewelry? Talk with your student about the differences and then have him try these simple techniques! Learning drawing methods by studying the work of great illustrators like Robert McCloskey is a great way to improve your own drawings!

Encourage your student to try using McCloskey's techniques to bring *movement* or *sparkle* to a variety of drawings, using either pencil, crayon, colored pencils or markers.

Language Arts: Writing and Discussion Question

What do you think Rupert Black might have done with his $100 reward? What would you have done with such a large reward?

Chapter 4—Mystery Yarn

Teacher Summary

The town of Centerburg is all in a flutter! The annual county fair is coming and instead of trotting races, this year there will be a new kind of contest. Area residents will compete to determine who has the biggest ball of saved string! Homer's Uncle Telemachus (tuh LEH meh kus), the sheriff, and the woman both men have their heart set on, Miss Terwilliger, agree to unroll their collected string balls and set the record straight once and for all. Since both men, Uncle Telemachus and the sheriff, want to marry Miss Terwilliger, they decide the winner will get her hand in marriage. For some time Miss Terwilliger has invited Uncle Telemachus over for fried chicken every Sunday, and the sheriff over for fried chicken every Thursday. She can't seem to make up her mind which one to marry, and the two men figure this contest will put the question to rest once and for all. But as the story turns out, we find Miss Terwilliger with a plan of her own.

The day for the big contest arrives and the rules are explained. Every day of the week-long county fair, from two o'clock till four o'clock, the balls of string will be unrolled around the horserace track. Whoever has the longest piece of string wins the contest and the title of World's Champion String Saver!

The first day of the contest arrives. After the two hours of unrolling, Miss Terwilliger's ball measures 5'9", the sheriff's measures 5'8" and Uncle Telly's measures 5'8" in diameter. Each day, after unrolling the balls of string for the allotted two hours, the contestants measure the string ball remaining. By the end of the week, it seems obvious Miss Terwilliger is going to lose. The town is electric with excitement! What's going to happen?

On the final day of the unrolling, we find out that the sheriff's ball of string has a core of a walnut. Uncle Telemachus' ball is string clear to the center! He's going to win! Suddenly, in a very mysterious way, Miss Terwilliger turns up the winner! Nobody is quite sure how, but Miss Terwilliger wins the title of World's Champion String Saver!

Later, the next week, Miss Terwilliger decides to marry Homer's Uncle Telemachus. It is a beautiful wedding and the best man is the sheriff! A beautiful ending to a wonderful day!

What we will cover in this chapter:

Social Studies: County Fairs
Science: Birds' Eggs*
Language Arts: Writing and Discussion Questions
Fine Arts: Collections
Fine Arts: Trees and Leaves - Art Mediums
Life Skills: Frugality
Life Skills: Special Occasions - Sunday Dinner

Social Studies: County Fairs

The time has come for the county fair in Centerburg. What fun! Has your student ever been to a county fair? There are so many things to see and do! Generally, a county fair includes exhibits and contests for the best livestock (chickens, calves, horses, pigs), vegetables, pies, etc. Often there are rides like Ferris wheels and carousels and lots of yummy things to eat! If your student studied *Daniel's Duck* in FIAR Vol. 3, he may remember elements of an old-fashioned county fair.

One way children can become involved in county and state fairs is through a group called 4-H. 4-H is a national organization supported by county extension offices. It is for both boys and girls, and adults and parents act as volunteer leaders. The children can learn about many subjects including food, art, sports, animals and livestock, sewing, camping, etc. After a child has worked on a specific project, county fairs provide exhibition arenas, divided by age group, for the children to display their work. Awards and ribbons are given out and the whole experience can be a positive, confidence-building vehicle for exposing children to many new things.

4-H is the largest youth development program in the United States. For more information on a chapter in your area, contact your local county extension office.

Whether or not you choose to participate in an organization like 4-H, county fairs are so much fun! If you have the opportunity to attend one, take your student and have a great time!

Science: Birds' Eggs*

Mrs. Terwilliger's special occasion dress was robin's egg blue. Take a moment to look in a field guide, reference book, or online at a robin's egg. What kind of blue is it? Look at other birds' eggs. There is such a variety of color, size and markings! (Does your student remember the cardinals' eggs from *Albert* in FIAR Vol. 4?) Can your student point out a robin's egg and note its difference from a sparrow's egg?

Did you know that some egg designs (especially those in nests on the ground) are colored so as to be camouflaged? Did you know that the unusual and incredible markings on birds' eggs are pigments absorbed by the porous eggshell as it travels through the female bird's oviduct?

There is a great deal to be learned about eggs besides their color. How often does a bird lay eggs? When do birds begin incubating—after the first egg is laid or the entire "clutch?" These questions and many more vary with different birds. Follow this learning trail as far as you would like. There are beautiful and informative books on birds' eggs in your library in both the juvenile and adult sections, as well as plenty of information online. Or plan a visit to a wildlife sanctuary and learn from the guides as much as you can about the birds there.

Language Arts: Writing and Discussion Questions

Miss Terwilliger's ball of yarn had to be removed through the opened side of her house! Imagine a ball of yarn that large! How would you have moved the ball of yarn? Write a description of at least three ways.

Miss Terwilliger won the contest! It seemed impossible! Homer knows how she did it, but the clues are very vague. Do you know how she won? Discuss some of your ideas.

Fine Arts: Collections

Miss Terwilliger, Uncle Telly and the sheriff are serious string collectors! Does your student have any collections? Talk with your student about some of the things people collect: stamps, quilts, old coins, baseball cards, lamps, political pins, ball caps, tea cups, antique cars, dolls, etc. Whatever you can think of, someone probably collects it.

What is the attraction to collecting? You learn a lot about a topic you're interested in and you can become an "expert" in your field. Many people begin an interest in their topic casually, by simply owning a few of something. As the interest grows the real collecting begins. Even children can have entire collections of their own—bird nests, rocks, dolls, pine cones—anything can grow into a collection. Encourage your student to become a collector of something, just like Uncle Telly. It may be the start of a lifelong hobby!

Begin by exploring subjects that interest your student. What does he like? He may choose to collect something that is already popular with collectors, such as baseball cards or model trains. Or, he may prefer to collect something unique such as famous quotes, different types of canning jars, belt buckles or soda pop cans from around the world. The point of collecting is to find an enjoyable avocation and learn about a subject.

Fine Arts: Trees and Leaves - Art Mediums

At the beginning of our chapter, Homer is busy raking the leaves in his yard. Has your student ever helped rake leaves? Do you live in an area where you have deciduous trees (trees which shed their leaves)? If you are doing this lesson in the fall and live in an appropriate region, perhaps you can go with your student to rake some leaves in the yard. Smelling the fresh air and listening to the crunch of leaves underfoot are some of the enjoyable activities of autumn.

To help capture this time of year and for a fun art project, have your student gather several leaves he especially likes. If you live in a region with maples or oaks, colored leaves work especially well for this project. If not, pine needles, green leaves, interesting dry vines, etc., work well, too. The important part is to let your student pick the leaves he finds interesting. Encourage him to look at the shapes, edges, stems, veins, colors, etc., when making his selection. Have him close his eyes and feel the leaves.

After the leaf selections have been made, have your student arrange them in whatever pattern he chooses. He may wish to "frame" a poem he has written or a picture he has drawn with the leaves. When the leaves and whatever else he has chosen to include are laid out in the pattern he has designed, take two pieces of clear contact paper, laying one sticky-side-up. Move the leaves and picture or poem onto the sticky side of the contact paper, pressing down each leaf. When the design is complete, lay the other piece of contact paper on top, being sure to match up the edges and press out any air bubbles. (Use a straight pin to puncture any remaining air bubbles and squeeze the air out.)

Now, your student has either a wall hanging or placemat made from his own gathered leaves! A great gift for a grandparent or neighbor— or you can keep it for yourself! If your student enjoys this project, he may want to work on improving his design and consider making a set as a gift for grandparents or friends.

Life Skills: Frugality

Miss Terwilliger wears the same dress for every special occasion—Sunday church, holidays, and social functions. She wears a simple, knitted, robin's-egg-blue dress. When fashion dictates a shorter skirt, she simply unravels a few inches off the bottom and then saves the yarn for the next time long skirts are in style. Then she knits the yarn back into her skirt and lengthens it once more!

Discuss with your student the concept of **frugality**. Being frugal means you don't spend money unnecessarily or wastefully. When someone is frugal, he is sometimes called "thrifty." Miss Terwilliger may seem too extreme in her frugality, (having only one good dress), but she is, at least, an excellent example of not living an excessive lifestyle.

Encourage your student to find ways to be thrifty. Today, we rarely save things like small pieces of string or yarn, but we can recycle! This is an exceptional way to be thrifty, help the planet and reduce wastefulness. Glass, many plastics, paper and aluminum can all be recycled. Challenge your student to recycle when

possible and to be on the lookout for other ways he can practice a more "frugal" lifestyle. Being wasteful and spending beyond your means shows a lack of wisdom. Miss Terwilliger was a clever woman and had learned to make do with what she had! We can all learn a few things from Miss Terwilliger!

Life Skills: Special Occasions - Sunday Dinner

Miss Terwilliger makes her famous fried chicken every Sunday for Uncle Telemachus and every Thursday for the sheriff. You can create a special occasion with your student and prepare a chicken dinner with all the fixin's including mashed potatoes or potato salad, green beans, rolls, and whatever else you want. You might begin by looking at grocery store ads and noting the price of chicken. You can explain the different ways that chickens are packaged: whole fryers, legs and thighs, breasts only, skinless or boneless, etc., and talk about the differences in price. Then buy the chicken, bring it home and prepare it for frying or baking. If weather permits, taking your chicken dinner on a picnic is a delightful way to enjoy the fresh air—and food always tastes better outside!

You can take this concept a step further by developing your own unique weekly traditions. Just as Miss Terwilliger was known for fixing her famous fried chicken on Sundays and Thursdays, you can think up your own traditions. Perhaps you'd like to always serve waffles on Saturday morning, or always watch a family movie on Friday night. Maybe you'd enjoy always going out for ice cream on Sunday evening or always taking a walk around your neighborhood on a certain day. The tradition you choose isn't important. What matters is developing your own, unique family traditions that build security for children and provide everyone with something special to look forward to each week—just the way Uncle Telly looked forward to dinner with Miss Terwilliger on Sundays!

Chapter 5—Nothing New Under the Sun (Hardly)

Teacher Summary

Not much is happening in Centerburg. The county fair is over and election time hasn't quite arrived. Homer decides to go down to Uncle Ulysses' lunchroom one day and help him serve up blue plate specials. Suddenly an unusual thing is seen in Centerburg. A stranger in a strange truck is coming down the street, rattling and banging with a huge canvas tarp covering whatever is in the back, and pulls up right in front of Uncle Ulysses' lunchroom! Who is the stranger?

What is in his truck? Why are his clothes so tattered? Why is his beard so long? Before long everyone in Centerburg has heard of the strange man. They say he reminds them of Rip Van Winkle, a fictional storybook character. The man seems very shy around adults, but likes children.

Finally, the sheriff and Uncle Ulysses come up with a plan. They send Homer to get to know the fellow and find out what his intentions are in Centerburg—AND to find out what is in his truck!

Homer comes back from his investigation with interesting news. The man's name is Michael Murphy and under his canvas is his invention. It's taken him 30 years to make, but he has finally built a better mousetrap—a real mousetrap! Mr. Murphy's mousetrap plays music and entices the mice into the trap. No harm comes to the mice. As soon as Mr. Murphy is able, he releases them somewhere else.

Centerburg thinks this is a fine plan! The mayor strikes a deal with Mr. Murphy to remove all the mice in Centerburg using his musical mousetrap for only $30. The big day arrives and everyone in Centerburg shows up for the grand mouse evacuation. The children are the most enthralled with the entire spectacle! Soon all the mice in Centerburg are in Mr. Murphy's musical mousetrap and he is starting for the outskirts of town. The children, whistling along with the music, follow the truck. Suddenly, Centerburg's librarian comes running to the mayor and sheriff in a panic!

"We guessed the wrong book...not *Rip Van Winkle*, but another book, *The Pied Piper of Hamelin*!" The librarian is frantic!

Suddenly, everyone is frantic! Uncle Ulysses, the sheriff, the mayor and the librarian all jump into the sheriff's car and zoom off after the procession, screaming out the windows for the children to come back. The sheriff yells, "Let 'em go!" And that is just what Mr. Murphy does. He pulls a lever and all the mice run out of the musical mousetrap, down the ramps and back to their holes in Centerburg. Meanwhile, Homer shows the sheriff and his uncle that he and all the children had cotton in their ears so the music couldn't woo them. All is well and everyone is glad!

What we will cover in this chapter:

Social Studies: History - Political Parties
Social Studies: Career Path - Law Enforcement
Language Arts: Famous Sayings - A New Phrase to Learn*
Language Arts: Washington Irving and "Rip Van Winkle"
Language Arts: Writing and Discussion Question
Life Skills: Making a Good Appearance
Life Skills: Making People Feel Comfortable

Social Studies: History - Political Parties

After the county fair, election time is nearing for Centerburg. Draw your student's attention to the line, "election time, still being a month away, the Democrats and the Republicans are still speaking to one another."

Take this opportunity to discuss with your student the two main political parties in the United States. As background, it is interesting to note that, at the founding of the United States, our forefathers made no mention of any specific parties. In fact, George Washington himself seemed opposed to such definitions, thinking they would bring division to the new country. However, as people are apt to do, different groups began to coalesce based on similar moral beliefs, economic realities and political feelings. These natural polarizations began only three years after the Constitution was written in 1787.

Thomas Jefferson led what first became known as the Democratic-Republican Party (later known as the Democrat Party), supporting a weak central government. Alexander Hamilton was at the forefront of the Federalist Party, supporting strong, influential government. These two parties were the first known political divisions within America. By 1854, the new Republican Party gained momentum over the issue of antislavery, and those who had been affiliated with the Federalists began to align themselves with the Republican Party. By the time Abraham Lincoln was elected in 1860, he was known as the first Republican President.

Draw your student's attention to the illustrations of the party mascots in the margin. Your student may have seen these familiar symbols for the Republican and Democrat Parties already, but he may not have understood their significance. The donkey became associated with the Democratic Party as early as 1820 and had become synonymous with the Democrats by 1880. During the 1828 election campaign people tied Andrew Jackson's name to the donkey symbol and he became known as the "jackass" by his opponents. Many political cartoons and jokes have their origin in this unique symbolism and within a short time the Democrats became recognized by this now-classic symbol.

The Republican Party (also known as the G.O.P., "grand old party"—a self-proclaimed nickname) is recognized by the symbol of an elephant. Interestingly enough, the same political cartoonist who drew a nationally-accepted picture of the Democrat's donkey in 1880, Thomas Nast, also drew the first popular rendering of an elephant in relation to the Republican Party in 1874. Nast's first cartoon to feature this symbol showed a gigantic, obese elephant with the sign "Republican Vote" on its side. All the other animals in the picture had the names of other parties and were uncharacteristically small. It made people laugh and quickly became widely associated with the Republican Party. (For fascinating reading on America's symbols and traditions find *Fireworks, Picnics and Flags* by James Cross Giblin. There is a section on Thomas Nast and many other interesting bits of information, written in an enjoyable style.)

To the extent you choose, discuss with your student the differences between the two major political parties in the United States. Beyond the emotionally charged issues and family-history affiliations, the Democrats and Republicans differ over one specific, fundamental issue—government involvement. The question both parties consistently struggle with is to what extent should the government (and by extension, taxpayer dollars) be in control of individual lives? This question is a fluid, evolving concept that changes with every presidential administration.

Traditionally, the Democratic Party has believed that government should play a significant role in public and private lives, helping protect individual rights and becoming a reliable source to which every American can look for personal well-being. The Republicans, on the other hand, have traditionally held that government is essentially a cumbersome but necessary entity that often unnecessarily complicates the lives of individuals and that in general, "less government is better."

In the U.S., people can vote for a Republican president in one election and a Democratic president in the next. This freedom of political choice also allows what is known as *split-ticket* voting where an individual can even vote for both parties within the same ballot. (Contrast this with *straight-ticket* voting, where a person votes for one party only, all the way down the ballot.)

If your student's family is actively involved in a political party, perhaps contacting the local campaign office and allowing your student to watch what goes into preparing for an election would be great. If your student is older he can help with campaigns, even before he is old enough to vote. Handing out buttons, putting up posters, and helping with mailings are all things your student can do to make a difference and allow him to become an active participant in his country's political life! Becoming involved with politics at an early age can be instrumental in developing a full understanding of America's government and our political system.

Teacher's Note: If you choose, you may continue this discussion by analyzing the concept of third parties in the United States. Parties such as the Libertarian party, Socialist Party, and Green Party are present and vocal but have never come close to winning a presidential election. Perhaps the most significant move by any third party was led by Ross Perot in 1992 against former Presidents George Bush and Bill Clinton. Perot's Independent Party didn't win the election, but caused a tremendous dialogue nationwide and gained more respect than any third party in modern history.

Social Studies: Career Path - Law Enforcement

The sheriff in Centerburg works hard at his job. Does your student think being a sheriff would be an interesting job? Why or why not? Law enforcement is a difficult but rewarding career. Talk with your student about the different job options in this interesting field.

Share with your student the two most common ways a person can become a police officer—civil law enforcement and military law enforcement. If a person goes through the military police (MP) program, his education and training are paid for in exchange for military service. You can also become a police officer by going through a civil police academy program. Ranging in duration from six months to four years, such courses are offered by hundreds of colleges in criminology, psychology, forensics, criminal intelligence and sociology. There are also courses on how to handle a wide variety of weapons.

Within civil law enforcement there are four main divisions. City police departments patrol and maintain order within a city's limits. County sheriffs (just like the sheriff in Centerburg) protect and guard anything within their county lines. State police (called state troopers) have the responsibility for an entire state. Generally, state troopers work on cases involving criminals at large (the criminal might be located anywhere, beyond county jurisdiction) and enforce traffic laws on the major highways (highway patrol). Interestingly, Hawaii is the only state in the United States which does not have a state police department.

Perhaps the most elite police forces in the United States are the federal law enforcement agencies. The two most prestigious federal groups are the Federal Bureau of Investigation (FBI) which enforces federal law, and the Secret Service, which protects the president, the president's family, former presidents and their families, and other government officials.

In order to be a police officer, candidates must be physically fit and have great stamina. The working hours are long and often irregular. A person wanting to be a police officer should have a thorough understanding of the law, be methodical in his or her personal work habits, be courageous and have a strong sense of compassion tempered with justice.

Encourage your student to try to arrange a visit with an area police station. An interview or conversation with an officer who is actually "on the beat" is a great way to get a firsthand look at what the job actually entails. Some agencies will give tours of their facilities. Encourage your student to write a full report on his studies about this interesting career field. If you successfully arrange a tour, as always, try to come up with several specific questions you'd like to have answered.

Language Arts: Famous Sayings - A New Phrase To Learn*

This chapter offers a new phrase to teach your student. Famous sayings or idioms are fun to learn and enable your student to understand more of the world around him.

Homer is busy helping Aunt Aggie and Uncle Ulysses serve up the blue plate specials. A blue plate special is the term for an inexpensive restaurant meal served at a fixed price on a plate (originally it was blue). In most restaurants the blue plate special generally changes daily, but the rest of the menu is set for the week. For example, every Monday the blue plate special might be meatloaf with mashed potatoes and fruit salad. Every Tuesday the blue plate special might consist of baked chicken with green beans and Jell-O®. Every Wednesday the blue plate special might be spaghetti and meatballs with green salad and garlic toast, and so forth. Watch at diners or country restaurants in your area for blue plate specials being offered.

Teacher's Note: If your student worked on the lesson in chapter 1 of *The Boxcar Children* (FIAR Vol. 5) and designed his own imaginary restaurant and menu, encourage him to go back and add a list of blue plate specials. What would he serve? How much would he charge?

Language Arts: Washington Irving and "Rip Van Winkle"

Everyone in Centerburg calls Michael Murphy, "Old Rip." He does seem to be a "Rip-Van-Winklish" sort of character, doesn't he? Does your student know the story of Rip Van Winkle? Does he know who wrote it?

Published in 1819 within a book of short stories entitled *The Sketch Book*, "Rip Van Winkle" is now considered a classic. Written by Washington Irving, the story is an impressionistic journey of one man's unusual experience in a small town. Irving is considered in most literary circles to be the first successful, professional American author. Born in New York City on April 3, 1783, he was the son of a wealthy merchant. Destined for a career in law, Irving soon found he was more proficient at writing.

There are dozens of adaptations and juvenile versions of "Rip Van Winkle." If your student has the patience for more difficult literature, you might suggest that he read the original work, which can be found online or in many American short story collections. The story is written in older English and although the descriptions and narrative are stunning, they can be challenging for even the best readers.

A more practical approach might be to read aloud a small paragraph to your student, so he can get a feel for Irving's style and an appreciation for his use of description. Here is a paragraph example from the original text by Washington Irving:

He now hurried forth and hastened to his old resort, the village inn—but it too was gone. A large, rickety, wooden building in its place, with great gaping windows, some of them broken and mended with old hats and petticoats, and over the door was painted, "the Union Hotel, by Jonathan Doolittle." Instead of the great tree that used to shelter the quiet little Dutch inn of yore, there now was reared a tall, naked pole, with which was singular assemblage of stars and stripes—all this was strange and incomprehensible. He recognized on the sign, however, the ruby face of King George, under which he had smoked so many a peaceful pipe; but even this was singularly metamorphosed. The red coat was changed for one of blue and buff, a sword was held in a hand instead of a scepter, the head was decorated with a cocked hat, and underneath was painted in large characters, GENERAL WASHINGTON.

Have your student pick out what he considers the most descriptive words. Examples might include: rickety, naked, metamorphosed (meaning to change from one thing to another), ruby, etc. Does he like this type of writing?

Interestingly enough, "Rip Van Winkle" goes far beyond being a fairy tale with witty twists and turns. It is Washington Irving's social statement on the Dutch settlers and their early roots in the New York area. Including descriptions of the Catskills, the Hudson River, the Appalachian Mountains and the early Dutch governors, it is a fascinating peek at the background of Irving himself, since this was his early childhood home.

Take some time and study Washington Irving. It will be worthwhile and interesting to both you and your student!

Language Arts: Writing and Discussion Question

We've discussed the fact that it's important to be kind to strangers like Mr. Murphy. But we also need to be cautious around strangers. What are some of the things that you *shouldn't* do with strangers?

Life Skills: Making a Good Appearance

Mr. Michael Murphy is making the town of Centerburg nervous with his appearance. His ripped clothes, patched jacket, uncut hair and beard are all unusual. Even his money is dirty! The citizens begin to make judgments about Mr. Murphy based on his appearance. Talk with your student about the importance of wearing clean, decent clothes and maintaining proper personal hygiene.

It isn't important to keep up with every trend of fashion and look "picture perfect" all the time. But it is important to make a good impression when you meet people, and not be offensive in your appearance. Discuss with your student how different events dictate different clothing choices. What would your family consider appropriate clothing for a day at the park? A wedding or funeral? Going to church? Going to Grandma's? Going to the pool or the beach?

Being aware of your appearance doesn't mean you have to be vain. Encourage your student to dress in a way that makes him, as well as those he is with, feel comfortable. In this way, people won't be offended and your student will have a more pleasant life with those around him. Perhaps your student has heard the saying, "Always make a good first impression." Wearing clean, appropriate clothing and attending to our personal hygiene is one important way to make sure our first impressions are positive.

Life Skills: Making People Feel Comfortable

Mr. Michael Murphy is very shy. He has no friends in Centerburg, and he knows he looks different from everyone else. Uncle Ulysses tries to talk to him, but doesn't want to make him feel uncomfortable. Everyone else in town just stares at Mr. Murphy. What does your student do when he is around someone who is very shy? Or perhaps your student is shy himself.

Learning to make people feel comfortable is an important life skill. When we are around someone who is quiet or shy, being able to ask interesting questions and approach them in a quiet manner can make all the difference in the world. Learning to make jokes on ourselves can sometimes be a simple way to ease tension and bring someone else out of their shell.

Talk with your student about times he has been the shy one and times when he has been the bold one. Coming to the realization that we all feel bashful sometimes can be an encouraging discovery! Everyone has been shy at one time or another and it's just a question of how we handle it in ourselves and with others.

If you wish, do some role-playing games with this issue. Acting out scenarios often helps us realize what we're doing right with people and what we need to work on. Have your student play the shy person and approach him in several different ways—staring, making fun, pointing, ignoring, talking, smiling, introducing yourself, including him in an activity, etc. It will become very apparent what is pleasant and what is not when you're shy or quiet. Now switch roles with your student and have him try it.

Whether we are shy or more outgoing, relating to others and learning kind, appropriate behavior is vital to making and maintaining friendships throughout life!

Challenge your student to work on this issue in his own relationships and get updates on how it's going. Developing interpersonal skills like this takes practice, but the result is very rewarding.

Chapter 6—Wheels of Progress

Teacher Summary

Miss Naomi Enders, the nice, rich lady who helped make all those doughnuts, is helping Centerburg once again. Only this time, she truly is being helpful! Along with Uncle Ulysses' help (a lover of all labor saving devices), Miss Enders has decided to share her wealth with Centerburg by building a new suburb called Enders Heights. The suburb will fcature nice homes at affordable prices. Miss Enders wants everyone in Centerburg to have a home. But this won't just be any suburb. Uncle Ulysses convinces Miss Enders to build all the houses identically. In this way each home, street and the entire neighborhood can be built in a systematic, time-saving fashion. He tells her it is the "modem" way to build homes—mass production! Miss Enders loves the idea and the building soon begins.

Each house in Enders Heights is just alike, complete with the same yard design, fireplace, painting over the fireplace and more. Every Enders Heights home is identical.

With a few mishaps along the way, the neighborhood is soon finished and all of Centerburg turns out for the "One Hundred and Fifty Years of Centerburg Progress Week" celebration!

What we will cover in this chapter:

Social Studies: History - Women's Suffrage
Social Studies: People's Signature Trademarks
Social Studies: Career Path - Landscape Architect
Language Arts: Famous Sayings - Two New Phrases to Learn
Language Arts: New Vocabulary Words - Ideas for Application
Language Arts: Writing and Discussion Question
Language Arts: Vocabulary *
Fine Arts: Design and Make Your Own Checkerboard
Fine Arts: *Whistler's Mother* and James Abbott McNeill Whistler

Social Studies: History - Women's Suffrage

"Uncle Ulysses' pet theories had broken up as many pinochle and checker games as arguing about the World Series and Woman Suffrage put together." Does your student know about women's suffrage? This chapter of *Homer Price* presents an opportunity to introduce this important historical subject.

If you wish, begin with a definition of **suffrage**. Suffrage means the right to vote. A person who works for this goal is called a suffragist. There was a time in America's history when women were not allowed the fundamental right of voting. Two women, Elizabeth Cady Stanton and Susan B. Anthony, were at the forefront of the women's fight for the right to vote. Along with thousands of other women, these two courageous females led the way to the signing of the 19th amendment.

The women handed out flyers, gave lectures and picketed each election in which they were not allowed to vote. The opposition to women's voting was great. Many men believed women didn't have the intelligence or responsibility to handle voting for important government officials. Men also felt that the husband should represent the wife in all legal matters—that a woman couldn't make her own decisions.

Two organizations were formed to fight these myths and beliefs.The National Woman Suffrage Association (led by Susan B. Anthony and Elizabeth Cady Stanton) focused on achieving a national amendment to the constitution. Another organization, the American Woman Suffrage Association, was led by Lucy Stone and her husband Henry Blackwell. This group shared similar beliefs with that of the National Association, but felt the goals would be better reached through a more conservative state-by-state approach. The fight for freedom was not without a price. Women suffragists were beaten, starved, jailed and taken from their families for "illegal" activity. And yet, the bravery of these women was finally realized through the victory of the 19th Amendment. Passed August 1920, the amendment states: *The right of citizens of the United States to vote shall not be denied or abridged by the United States or by any state because of gender.* To this day, the 19th Amendment is sometimes referred to as the Susan B. Anthony Amendment.

Unfortunately several nations still deny women the right to vote, or make it extremely difficult. For the most up-to-date list, research this question online.

All students, whether male or female, should have an understanding of this important topic. Encourage your student to learn more about the history of women's suffrage and find library books or articles on this subject.

Social Studies: People's Signature Trademarks

Does your student remember what Thomas Edison's personal trademark was earlier in this FIAR volume? Right! He pulled at his eyebrow. Can your student tell you from this chapter what Uncle Ulysses' is? Stroking his chin! If you did not do the lesson in chapter 5 of Thomas Edison, go back and read through it. If you did, just mention to your student that this is yet another example of someone's signature trademark.

Social Studies: Career Path - Landscape Architect

Enders Heights is constructed so quickly! "Each front yard had its own climbing rose bush, two dwarf cedars, and maple trees, all planted and sodded round about." Who decides where the trees go? Who designs the yards?

Sometimes the person who owns the house does these types of home improvements, but often a person called a **landscape architect** is called in to do the design work.

Ask your student if he has ever heard of a landscape architect? Landscape architecture holds many career opportunities.

In general, a landscape architect plans and designs outdoor areas. He might design a city park, a walking path, a municipal fountain or a residential neighborhood. The difference between an **architect** and a **landscape architect** is this: the architect designs the actual buildings and a landscape architect designs the outdoor areas surrounding the building and helps determine what effect the building will have on the environment.

Landscape architects go to college where they work toward a BLA (Bachelor of Landscape Architecture) or a BSLA (Bachelor of Science in Landscape Architecture) degree. Master's degrees are also available for those who wish to attend graduate school. Courses you would be required to take include art (drawing, drafting, and sculpting), environmental science, architectural technology, botany, human behavior and media communications. Landscape architecture encompasses a wide variety of academic disciplines.

Have your student draw a simple plan for your home or perhaps an imaginary home. Now have him develop a landscape plan to compliment the building. Encourage him to explore the use of trees, shrubberies, flowers, walkways, ponds, fountains and more. More advanced students can research individual species for their plant material. They might even be interested in building a three-dimensional model of their landscape design.

If your student enjoys being outside, knows and enjoys plants, likes working with people, is concerned about the environment and has a talent for drawing, this career might be worth further exploration!

Language Arts: Famous Sayings - Two New Phrases to Learn

Freddy wants to help in the lunchroom. Homer says, "Uncle Ulysses would like it. He always says the more help the merrier, but Aunt Aggie is a 'Too many cooks spoil the soup' sort of person." Ask your student if he knows what Homer means? Take this opportunity to share two new idioms with your student.

The first, "the more the merrier," is a common saying and it means just what it says. The more people we have involved in the project, the more fun it is! That does sound like Uncle Ulysses, doesn't it?

Homer uses the second phrase to describe Aunt Aggie. "Too many cooks spoil the soup" (or sometimes, "the broth") means the more people who are involved, the more chaotic and messed up things become.

What kind of a person is your student? Is he a "more the merrier" person who enjoys working in groups, or is he a "too many cooks spoil the soup" kind of personality who works best when left alone? What kind of person are you? Talk with your student about issues of flexibility and how both philosophies can be correct in different situations.

Encourage your student to be listening for these common sayings in future conversations. And now that he knows them, he can use them himself!

Language Arts: New Vocabulary Words - Ideas for Application

This chapter of *Homer Price* is unusually rich with new vocabulary words for your student. These words could be used for both spelling exercise and definition comprehension. To give your student more learning retention, be looking for ways to use the words in sentences throughout the day. Encourage your student to try to use them in *his* conversation as well! If you wish, you might have your student write a sentence for each word, using it in context.

Mrs. Enders is financing a new **suburb** for Centerburg. A suburb is an area near the outskirts of a city. A city is known as an **urban** area; and area farther out in the country is known as a **rural** area. Discuss these three terms with your student and perhaps even draw a simple, generic map or a map specific to your own city or town to illustrate them.

Then, find and discuss three more interesting words with your student (definitions are in the Vocabulary lesson that follows):

"Do you think your Uncle Ulysses could use an extra helper today, Homer? Because it isn't **imperative** that I go fishing."

Miss Enders was **receptive** to Uncle Ulysses' up and coming-ness, and, what's more, she had the money to be receptive and up and coming *with.*

"Couldn't you **arbitrate** or something?" suggested Homer.
"Yes," agreed Uncle Ulysses, "I'll write to the President of your Union and ask him..."

Language Arts: Writing and Discussion Question

Everyone in Enders Heights lived in a house just like the next one. What would that be like? Would you like to live in a "cookie-cutter" home like that? Why or why not? Discuss some of the advantages and disadvantages of living in a house identical to your neighbor.

A classic children's picture book that your student may be familiar with would be a great go-along for this lesson. *Mr. Pine's Purple House* by Leonard Kessler has been a favorite for generations of children and explores the topic of living in identical neighborhood houses in an amusing and creative way.

Language Arts: Vocabulary*

suffrage The right to vote.

suburb A residential district on or near the outskirts of a city.

urban Constituting or comprising a city or town.

rural Constituting or comprising the country life.

receptive Able or ready to receive new things and ideas.

imperative Absolutely necessary; urgent; compelling.

arbitrate A decision based on judgment, not rules (an arbitrator).

architect A person who designs and draws plans for buildings.

landscape architect The art and profession of planning or changing the natural scenery of a place for a desired purpose.

Fine Arts: Design and Make Your Own Checkerboard

Uncle Ulysses and the sheriff sure do play checkers a lot, don't they? Why not have your student make his own checkerboard? This game is entertaining and can be as simple or complex as your ability and learning level allows.

The basic board, regardless of how it's made, must involve 64 alternating colored squares.

Each player must have 12 playing pieces. Traditionally red and black discs, these pieces can actually be whatever your student wishes. Oreos and vanilla wafers, pennies and dimes, different colored jelly beans, different colored pieces of paper, stones—whatever he chooses!

To make the actual board, your options for construction are endless! If your student enjoys working with wood, perhaps he would like to make an actual board and wooden checkers. Your student can paint the squares with fabric paint on canvas and make a "roll-away, travel" checkers set. With that type of board, your student could even make cloth playing pieces. By laying sticks or twigs in a grid pattern on a piece of cardboard and forming 64 squares, your student could make an "au naturel" playing board. Stones or seedpods would make great playing pieces for that set.

Let your student's creative juices flow with this activity! And the great part is, after the board is complete the real fun begins—playing checkers! Your student will love the game, and remind him to think of Uncle Ulysses and the barbershop when he plays.

Fine Arts: *Whistler's Mother* and James Abbott McNeill Whistler

Every house in Enders Heights has a print of *Whistler's Mother* over the fireplace. Is your student familiar with *Whistler's Mother*? Does he know who painted it?

Take this opportunity to share with your student about this famous painting. Artist James Abbott McNeill Whistler (1834-1903) was an American artist, but spent most of his life in Europe. Known for his talent in art, quick wit in conversation, and fearless nature, Whistler took on celebrity status quickly.

Find *Whistler's Mother* online and show your student the painting everyone talks about. Commonly called *Whistler's Mother*, the painting's real name is *Arrangement in Gray and Black No. 1: Portrait of the Artist's Mother*. Finished in 1872, the painting features extremely matte, non-dimensional forms and is off-center. His mother is featured sitting in a stiff, wooden chair, with her feet up on a little stool. The etched strokes and dull colors became synonymous with Whistler's style.

Does your student like this painting? Why or why not? As an interesting side note, Whistler, in his day, became as well known for his interior design projects as his paintings. Encourage your student to research more of John Abbott McNeill Whistler's work if he is interested.

Teacher's Note: Did you or your student notice that there are other famous names included in the characters of the story of *Homer Price*? We talked about Homer's name being the name of a famous Greek poet but there are two other names that are significant if you know your Greek writings: Ulysses and Telemachus. Ulysses (in Latin, Odysses in Greek) was a brave hero during the Trojan Wars according to Greek mythology. His son was named Telemachus. So, Robert McCloskey borrowed heavily from these famous Greek myths to find the names for his characters. These examples show why learning about the Greek and Roman myths helps clarify literary allusions and adds fun to reading.

Teacher's Notes

Use this page to jot down relevant info you've found for this *Five in a Row* chapter book, including favorite lessons, go-along resources, field trips, and family memories.

HOMER PRICE

Dates studied:

Student:

Favorite Lesson Topics:

Social Studies:

Science:

Language Arts:

Fine Arts:

Life Skills:

Relevant Library Resources: Books, DVDs, Audio Books

Websites or Video Links:

Related Field Trip Opportunities:

Favorite Quote or Memory During Study:

Homer Price - Chapter 1

Name:

Date:

History: **Biography - Who Am I?**

After doing the **Social Studies: History - The Famous Homer: A Brief Introduction** lesson, research the poet Homer online or read a book from the library about this Greek author.

Print and paste a sketch, illustration, or image of a statue of Homer into the frame. Write information gathered through your research into the spaces below.

Go-along book recommendations include:
Tales From The Odyssey (Parts One and Two) by Mary Pope Osborne
Argos: The Story of Odysseus as Told by His Loyal Dog by Ralph Hardy

Name: ______________________________

Lived: ______________________________

Known for: ______________________________

____

____

Connections to story: ______________________________

____

____

Homer Price - Chapter 2

Name:
Date:
Language Arts: **Vocabulary Words**

After finishing the second chapter, use these clues from **chapters 1-2** to complete the crossword puzzle on the next page.

Across

6. (ch. 2) a unit of energy equal to lifting one pound a distance of one foot (hyphenated word)

10. (ch. 1) a catchphrase used to sell or advertise a product

11. (ch. 2) a feeling of disappointment because something is not as good as you believed it to be

12. (ch. 1) to make someone feel worthy or important

13. (ch. 1) a small house or cottage

14. (ch. 2) a drama concerned with exaggerated conflicts and emotions and stereotyped characters

Down

1. (ch. 2) a grayish-white, hard, metallic chemical element

2. (ch. 1) the use of exaggerated language intended to shock

3. (ch. 1) an old-time motel, usually family-owned and operated; two words (don't use a space)

4. (ch. 2) a unit for measuring the power of motors or engines (equal to 550 foot-pounds of work per second)

5. (ch. 2) to make up or invent a new word or phrase; two words (don't use a space)

7. (ch. 2) the first letters of a name combined into a single design

8. (ch. 1) a place or point of crossing (as two highways)

9. (ch. 1) Greek epic poet from approximately the 8th century B.C., who wrote *The Iliad* and *The Odyssey*

Language Arts: **Vocabulary Words**

After finishing the second chapter, use the crossword puzzle below to review the vocabulary words covered in **chapters 1-2**. Clues are shown on the previous page.

flip for vocab words: Homer | junction | tourist camp | bungalow | sensationalism | slogan | validate | chromium | horsepower | to coin | foot-pound | monogram | melodrama | disillusionment

Name:

Date:

Science: **Labor Saving Device**

After completing the **Science: New Technology - Labor Saving Devices Today** lesson and discussing what types of labor saving devices we have today ... is there a chore or something you must do daily that you wish there was a labor saving device for?

Create your own imaginary labor saving device that would make your life easier. In the space below, write about how your device would work and/or illustrate it.

Homer Price - Chapter 4

Name:
Date:
Fine Arts: **Birds' Eggs**

After doing the **Science: Birds' Eggs** lesson, search online or use the book recommendation below to study different birds' eggs in detail. Look at the color, the texture, the size and shape of the egg. Use the spaces below to illustrate four different birds' eggs. Write in the type of bird on the space below each image. Colored pencils or watercolor paints would be easy mediums to control and would allow you to build color and texture as you illustrate each egg.

Go-along book: *An Egg Is Quiet* by Dianna Hutts Aston

Bird: ________________ Bird: ________________

Bird: ________________ Bird: ________________

Name:
Date:
Fine Arts: **Blue Plate Special**

After completing the **Language Arts: Famous Sayings - A New Phrase to Learn** lesson, spend time brainstorming your favorite meal combinations for a full week's worth of "Blue Plate Specials." Use the spaces below to write out the "menu" or meals on special (in an imaginary restaraunt or diner) for each day of the week. Include prices, if you'd like!

Today's Blue Plate Special

Sunday:

Monday:

Tuesday:

Wednesday:

Thursday:

Friday:

Saturday:

Homer Price - Chapter 6

Name:

Date:

Language Arts: **Vocabulary Words**

After finishing the sixth chapter, use the crossword puzzle below to review the vocabulary words covered in **chapter 6**.

Across

2. (ch. 6) a residential district on or near the outskirts of a city

5. (ch. 6) able or ready to receive new things and ideas

6. (ch. 6) constituting or comprising the country life

7. (ch. 6) a decision based on judgement, not rules

8. (ch. 6) the art and profession of planning or changing the natural scenery of a place for a desired purpose

Down

1. (ch. 6) constituting or comprising a city or town

2. (ch. 6) the right to vote

3. (ch. 6) absolutely necessary; urgent; compelling

4. (ch. 6) a person who designs and draws plans for buildings

flip for vocab words: rural | architect | urban | landscape architect | suburb | arbitrate | imperative | receptive | suffrage

The Saturdays

Title: *The Saturdays*
Author: Elizabeth Enright
Copyright: 1941

Chapter 1—Saturday One

Teacher Summary

Our story begins with an introduction to our four main characters—Mona, Rush, Randy and Oliver Melendy. The four children live in the city (near New York City), with their father and housekeeper, Cuffy. Their mother is not with them anymore (you will find out later she died sometime before).

The Melendy children are bored on this particular Saturday. Nothing seems to hold their interest, so Randy tries to think of something they can do. Suddenly, an idea strikes her. None of them get enough in allowance each week to use for a fun and exciting activity (i.e., museum, circus or theater). But, if they pooled their resources, one of them could do a special thing on the Saturday that is his/her turn to receive the combined allowance.

They decide to form an official club and call it I.S.A.A.C., which stands for Independent Saturday Afternoon Adventure Club. Each child is thrilled and they can't wait to ask their father for permission.

What we will cover in this chapter:

Social Studies: History - Adolf Hitler
Science: Acid and Neutralization
Language Arts: Narration - Hearing Our Author's Voice
Language Arts: Creating a Full Description
Language Arts: New Vocabulary Words*
Language Arts: Writing and Discussion Question
Language Arts: Vocabulary
Fine Arts: Music History - Bach*
Fine Arts: Music History - Tchaikovsky*
Fine Arts: Pen and Ink Drawing
Fine Arts: Clay Art
Life Skills: A Job for Each and Each Job Done Well

Social Studies: History - Adolf Hitler

As Rush and Randy stare at the Office ceiling in boredom, Randy comments on a faded, chipped area in the plaster. She thinks it looks like Adolf Hitler. She says, "See up there? That long fady line is his nose, and those two little chips are his eyes, and that dark place where you threw the plasticine is his mustache."

Has your student heard of Adolf Hitler? Unfortunately, he is not a positive or funny figure in history. For some students, studying Adolf Hitler can be too intense. As the teacher, take into account your student's age and emotional level as you relate this lesson. You may choose to include or delete as much information as you wish. If presented in the appropriate manner, your student can get a glimpse into the life of this political leader and begin to understand his influence.

Adolf Hitler was born on April 20, 1889, in Braunau, Austria. His father was a customs official in Austria, and was over 50 years old when Adolf was born. His mother, Klara Polzi, was only 28. Adolf had three siblings—a sister, Paula, half-brother, Alois, and a half-sister, Angela.

Although Adolf did well in elementary school, his grades began to decline in high school. This discrepancy in performance angered his father, who wanted his son to be a great civil servant. Adolf, however, only wanted to pursue a life in art. He loved painting and drawing. This fundamental disagreement provoked terrible arguments with his father. In his autobiography, *Mein Kampf*, Hitler writes about these arguments.

"How it happened, I myself do not know, but one day it became clear to me that I would become a painter, an artist. There was not doubt as to my talent for drawing...but never in all the world would it have occurred to him [his father] to give me professional training in this direction. On the contrary. When for the first time...I was asked what I myself wanted to be, and I rather abruptly blurted out the decision I had made, my father for the moment was struck speechless. 'Painter? Artist? No, never as long as I live.'"

When his father died, Adolf was only 16, and he quickly began devoting more time to his art. He moved to Vienna, but failed to be accepted into the Academy of Fine Arts, not once, but twice. Soon after, his mother died, but Hitler remained in Vienna.

Like many German-speaking Austrians of the day, Hitler became fiercely nationalistic. Discuss with your student what this means. Nationalism includes a strong sense of loyalty, independence and a desire to have your nation governed within itself.

Hitler began to spend time studying the politics in

his country. He couldn't understand how any form of government could last, if it treated people of different nationalities equally. He felt that to be a successful nation, a country had to be made up of one specific group of people—not racially diverse.

Talk with your student about how this belief is in direct opposition to the United States and our beliefs. We believe that a radically diverse nation is stronger because of its differences. We believe that all people should be treated equally.

Adolf Hitler

Hitler entered the military during World War I in 1914. He was twice wounded and twice decorated for bravery. Hitler quickly rose to the rank of corporal. When news of the armistice surfaced in November of 1918, Hitler was angered. During the Treaty of Versailles, it was said that Germany was responsible for the war. Because of this, Germany was forced to pay huge reparations (payments for war damages). Germany, as a nation, was devastated. Hitler believed that Germany should be a unified, strong nation. And for some reason, he felt a compelling need to save Germany—all by himself, if need be.

Hitler began to attend meetings of a small nationalist group called the German Workers' Party. He quickly became the group's leader and changed the name to the National Socialist German Workers' Party. It was this group which became known as the Nazi Party. Nazis wanted the Treaty of Versailles to be canceled and they also wanted anyone not of German descent (Jews, Slavs, etc.) to be deprived of German citizenship.

Hitler's group, the Nazis, grew in number rapidly. Discuss with your student why it was that so many people wanted to join such a threatening group. After the war, many German people were embarrassed and shamed by the guilt imposed by the Treaty of Versailles. They had lost all their money and their sense of national pride. Hitler and the Nazi Party, however, brought back a sense of the German nationalism from before the war. For this reason, and many others, the German people looked on the Nazi party as a positive thing—something to help rebuild Germany.

Star of David,
a symbol of Jewish identity

It is important to note as well, that Hitler was a compelling orator and a charismatic man. His fiery words and speeches seemed to hypnotize listeners and many Germans looked to him as a friend and protector. They would cheer, "Heil, Hitler!"when they heard him speak. "Heil" is a traditional German greeting meaning "to hail" in English.

Hitler became the dictator (a ruler with total power over a country) of Germany in 1933. Throughout his rule (1933-1945), he wouldn't listen to his advisors, and often overestimated his resources and the Germans' abilities. During World War II, Hitler's plans and military decisions became less and less successful. Finally, as the Allies began to close in on Germany and the end was decided, Hitler killed himself.

Hitler, whose life began relatively peacefully, became a hardened and evil-hearted man as he grew. Hitler spread death and destruction throughout Europe. He told his soldiers and followers, "Have no pity! Act brutally!" Hitler particularly hated Jewish people; he thought they were evil and inferior. By setting up death camps, Hitler persecuted and killed nearly six million Jews and five million additional people who belonged to certain racial, ethnic, religious, or other groups that he felt were threatening. In a negative and horrific way, Hitler left this world much worse off than when he found it.

Teacher's Note: It is strongly encouraged that you present this information to your student *only* if you feel she is emotionally and intellectually old enough to understand and digest it. It is not necessary to go into detail about anything you feel your student isn't ready to hear. Studying Hitler is an important part of world history, but not until your student is ready. Remember that your student will likely study World War II in high school and will learn more about Hitler at that time.

If your student is older and you feel it's appropriate for her at this time, you may wish to find a book or two in the children's section of your library, and take this opportunity to read it with her. Preview the books you find, of course, both for content and pictures.

Science: Acid and Neutralization

Oliver throws a milk of magnesia bottle through the east window of the Office. Has your student ever heard of milk of magnesia? This product was one of the first stomach indigestion medicines to be introduced.

Magnesia is a chemical compound made up of two substances—magnesium and oxygen. Milk of magnesia works to relieve stomach upset because it neutralizes stomach acids.

What is an acid? What do we mean when we say neutralization? Here is a great opportunity to share a simple science lesson with your student.

An acid is a chemical compound which has certain properties. It has a sour taste and will usually produce a stinging or burning sensation when it comes into contact with skin. Has your student ever had a paper cut or scrape, and then accidentally been exposed to lemon juice near the injured area? It hurts! Lemons (and other citrus fruits) are highly acidic. If you have a cold sore or canker sore in your mouth, eating something like pineapple, oranges, or tomatoes can be painful.

Your stomach is filled with acids which aid in the breakdown and digestion of the food you eat. These acids are called hydrochloric acids. Normally, these stomach acids do not hurt you because of the tough stomach lining. Sometimes, however, older or sick people get little sores called ulcers in their stomach linings. When this happens, the stomach acids begin to hurt and burn. Products like milk of magnesia can help the burning go away because they neutralize the acid around the ulcerated area.

The scientific word for something which can neutralize an acid is a base, or alkali. A base is simply a substance which, when combined with an acid, forms a non-harmful, or neutral, compound. Magnesium hydroxide, found in milk of magnesia, is a base or alkali.

Litmus paper tests for acids. Normally, litmus paper is blue, but if it is exposed to acid, it will turn pink or red. If you are able, get some litmus paper strips and let your student touch them to a variety of foods, testing for acid.

Lemons, milk, bread, potatoes, pineapple, oranges and bananas will all have different levels of acidic reaction. Perhaps your student can develop a chart and list each item she tests. Below the name, she can secure the litmus paper strip she used. If she wishes, she can organize her chart to go from least to most acidic.

Now, take a tablespoon of lemon juice and test it with a strip of litmus paper. (It should turn red.) Then add an alkali of some kind—a Tums® or milk of magnesia product—and retest the liquid. If the paper doesn't turn red, the acid has been neutralized!

Language Arts: Narration - Hearing Our Author's Voice

In chapter 1, Elizabeth Enright, our author, writes: "*In addition to various chairs, tables and toy cupboards, there was a big dingy sofa with busted springs, a blackboard, a trapeze and a pair of rings. That was all, but I think you will agree that it was enough.*"

By writing, "*but I think you will agree that it was enough,*" Enright creates a feeling of narration, doesn't she? Suddenly, as the reader, we sense not just a description but a specific voice telling us all about the Melendy's office. Enright isn't a character in the story, but her presence is felt anyway through the use of first person as the storyteller's voice, and the use of "you," referring to the reader.

Encourage your student to look for more examples of Enright's narration throughout our story. And, if she is interested, she may wish to try this form of narration in her own stories.

Language Arts: Creating a Full Description

Our author, Elizabeth Enright, is a masterful writer. She is particularly gifted at writing descriptive phrases, which allow us to see, hear, taste, smell or feel what she is talking about. Your student may have noticed the lengthy and interesting list of objects Enright describes in the Office. Or perhaps, your student enjoyed the description of the upstairs bathroom.

For one example, draw your student's attention to the first line of the book, "*It would have to rain today.*" In the following paragraphs, Enright doesn't just leave that sentence defenseless. Instead, she uses various descriptive words and phrases, allowing the reader to sense exactly what kind of rain was falling.

Words such as sousing, slopping, pouring and wet describe the rain. Enright describes the way the rain comes down the windowpanes ("long curly streams") and the way it sounds ("plinked, splashed and hissed").

In just a few sentences, we have a sense of what that particular Saturday's rain feels like, sounds like, looks like and how it makes the children feel.

Encourage your student to try her own hand at writing a full description—using words to describe as many of the five senses as possible. Reading the works of authors as excellent as Enright helps your student to get a feel for many literary devices, including description.

Language Arts: New Vocabulary Words

Throughout *The Saturdays*, your student will come across many new, exciting and unfamiliar words. Elizabeth Enright uses good, strong words in her writing which may account for more difficult vocabulary. Also, our story was written in 1941. As a result, some words may be older, less fashionable terms. You may wish to use these words for vocabulary building or as spelling lists. It is important, however, to make sure your student has a good understanding of new words and can define their meanings.

Between the Teacher's Notes and the activity sheets at the end of this unit, you'll find a Vocabulary Sorting Exercise that your student can use to keep track of the many vocabulary words in this unit. Or, as an alternate activity, your student may want to create a "*Saturdays* Vocabulary List" in a notebook or perhaps in a card file. Your student should also have fun trying to include these new word acquisitions in her everyday speech. For example, today she should try to use "lugubrious" at least once, correctly. Learning new words is fun!

Language Arts: Writing and Discussion Question

The children have decided on how their new club will work. If you were a part of the Melendy family, what would you do or where would you go with your week's allowance?

Language Arts: Vocabulary

grousing Grumbling, complaining.

truck Clothing, outdoor gear (i.e., hats, gloves, boots, coats, etc.).

rubbers An old-fashioned term for soft rain boots (often going over the regular shoe).

sousing Dripping wet.

lugubrious Overly sad, mournful.

plasticine A plastic-based sculpting product.

rafia Soft, bendable, straw-like ribbon.

Parcheesi A game in which you move pieces according to the roll of a die.

paltry Small, hardly worth counting.

Fine Arts: Music History - Bach*

Rush enjoys playing musical compositions by Bach. Does your student know more about Bach than Rush's sister Randy? Take a few moments and share some information about this famous composer with your student.

Johann Sebastian Bach was a German composer (1685-1750). He is best known for creating and writing music in the baroque period or style, which was very popular during the 1700s. Baroque music is known for its complexity and dramatic movements. Your student may wish to learn two new musical terms, both created by Bach: counterpoint and fugue. Counterpoint occurs in a piece of music when not one, but two melodies are played at the same time. Fugue refers to several instruments playing the same melody, with only slight differences.

Bach was born in 1685 in Eisenach, Germany. His family was a highly musical one, with everyone playing instruments and singing. Bach loved music more than anyone. His father taught him to play the violin and he studied music at church and in school.

Sadly, when he was only 10 years old, Bach's parents both died. Fortunately, he was able to go to live with an older brother. Johann Sebastian's brother, Johann Christoph, was also musical, however, so Johann Sebastian's education was continued.

When he was 15 years old, Bach heard about a school where poor children who were gifted in music could attend for free. He knew that was where he must go. Along with a friend, Johann Sebastian Bach set off for St. Michael's School in the town of Luneburg, Germany. He walked all the way—150 miles!

Johann Sebastian Bach

Bach studied at St. Michael's for two years and then left to play the violin in an orchestra. Over the next several years, Bach continued working as a professional musician at various churches (playing the organ) and orchestras (other instruments). He wrote wonderful organ pieces and cantatas for singers, too. Soon he married Maria Barbara and began a family.

Bach's life, unlike so many other great composers (Mozart, in particular), was different. Instead of being unappreciated and unsuccessful until after his death, Bach enjoyed a popular and successful life. People loved his playing abilities and his compositions.

Unfortunately, after having four children with Bach, Maria Barbara passed away. A short time later, Bach remarried a woman named Anna. It was after this marriage that Bach took a job at the St. Thomas Church as the music director. He wrote many of his famous and beautiful musical pieces, including the B-Minor Mass, during this job appointment.

At the end of his life, Bach had 20 children! Several of them passed away early, but those who lived also enjoyed music very much. Four of his sons (Carl, Wilhelm, Friedrich and Johann Christian) were all famous musicians. But not as famous as their father.

With his children and Anna at his bedside, Bach died in July of 1750. He was 65 years old. Today, we understand not only what a great musician Bach was, but also what a great composer he was, as well. Bach left the world hundreds of compositions, including 300 cantatas for choral singing.

It might be interesting and helpful for your student to compare and take note of other things that were happening in the world during Bach's life. Here are a few examples:

1685 George Frederick Handel was born in Halle, Germany (Two great composers born in the same year! *Messiah* is his most famous work.)

1721 American's first smallpox vaccination in Boston

1732 George Washington was born. Benjamin Franklin published his first "*Poor Richard's Almanac*"

1733 Thomas Jefferson was born in Virginia

Select several pieces of Bach's compositions to listen to. What does your student think? Can she pick out specific moods (i.e., joy, sadness, solemnity, happiness, etc.)? Can she hear a counterpoint (two melodies intertwining) passage? Have fun listening to this great composer's music!

Fine Arts: Music History - Tchaikovsky*

Rush also comments on the music of Tchaikovsky. As with Bach, your student should have at least a brief introduction to this man and his music.

Your student is probably familiar with the famous ballet (usually performed at Christmas), *The Nutcracker*. She may not be aware, however, of who wrote the beautiful story and score.

Peter Ilyich Tchaikovsky was born on May 7, 1840, in Russia. He studied music, taught, and composed for most of his life. He lived a mostly solitary life, composing continuously, but had great trouble performing his compositions. He was a painfully shy and troubled person who found it difficult to even sit in front of people. During one concert, people said he played the piano with one hand while using the other to hold up his chin, because he was shaking so badly.

The style and title of the music Tchaikovsky wrote is called Romantic music. The Romantic movement was a period in music, art and literature. Through music, Romantic composers expressed extremes of feelings in their themes. The Romantic movement lasted from the 1700s to the mid-1800s. Traditionally, in "romantic" stories, there is usually a hero who is fighting against social constraints or evil. Examples of romantic stories include the classic *Grimm's Fairy Tales* and the poetry of William Wordsworth.

Peter Ilyich Tchaikovsky

Tchaikovsky is best known for his beautiful and dramatic ballets including *Swan Lake*, *Romeo and Juliet*, and *The Nutcracker*. He died of cholera in 1893.

It may be interesting to note for your student that Peter Tchaikovsky visited the United States in 1891. The famous philanthropist, Andrew Carnegie, offered Tchaikovsky $25,000 to come and conduct his works in the United States. Tchaikovsky got very sick during his Atlantic voyage, and he felt homesick and nervous when he arrived. He did perform four concerts to mark the opening of the Carnegie Hall in New York. He also went to Washington and Niagara Falls. He returned home, however, glad to be back in familiar surroundings. (You may be able to find at your library a book called *Tchaikovsky Discovers America* by Esther Kalman. There is also an audio performance by the same title produced by Classical Kids.)

It is strongly encouraged, in perhaps a comparison to Bach, that your student listen to several of Tchaikovsky's compositions—particularly from *Swan Lake* and *The Nutcracker*. Does your student notice differences in the musical pieces? How would she describe the differences and similarities between Bach's music and Tchaikovsky's? Your student may also hear folk-song Russian strains in certain sections of Tchaikovsky's music. He loved his country and included it in his music.

Fine Arts: Pen and Ink Drawing

Take some time with your student to study the pen and ink illustrations in *The Saturdays*. Elizabeth Enright is a wonderful illustrator as well as writer, whose work has an open, simple feel.

Look with your student at the illustrations opposite the title page and later in chapter 1. Notice how little detail there is, for example, on the Melendys' clothing. Yet, we certainly can see what each child looks like and how they like to spend their time.

Pen and ink is an interesting and versatile medium for your student to try at home. Many artists and illustrators use pen and ink to achieve many different looks.

Your student may wonder what kind of pen artists use when drawing—many different kinds! Felt-tipped markers (fine to large points), ball-point pens, calligraphy pens (with angled tips), fountain pens and even quill pens dipped in wells of ink are all used to create different effects on paper.

Your student can begin experimenting with pen and ink drawings using any of these tools. Solid, heavy paper is also needed. Any art store or hobby shop will carry pads of paper specifically for pen and ink. Explain to your student that in order to effectively draw with pen and ink (particularly with felt-tip pens or marker) it is important that the paper be "sized." Sizing refers to the surface coating on the paper. If the paper does not have enough sizing, the ink will blot.

If your student uses non-waterproof ink pens, she can try to use her fingertips to create different effects while the ink is still wet. By smudging, blotting and smearing the ink, she can create shadows and smoothness in her drawings. (Fingers, hands and shirts may get smudged as well, so encourage your student to wear a smock!)

Fine Arts: Clay Art

The Melendy's upstairs bathroom is described as a sort of laboratory, with bowls of tropical fish, jars of finger paint and a bathtub full of damp clay! How wonderful for the budding artists!

Your student probably won't have a bathtub filled with wet clay, but that doesn't mean she can't experiment, create and enjoy this art medium just like the Melendys. Art and hobby stores carry a wide variety of clay and molding substances. Some require firing in a kiln, but many others air dry or can be baked in an ordinary kitchen oven.

Regardless of the type of clay product your student chooses to use, remind her of the importance of kneading the clay before she begins shaping or sculpting. By kneading the clay, she is softening the product and reducing the air bubbles so her final pieces will dry without cracking.

After the kneading is complete, let your student's imagination run wild. If she is wanting to sculpt or mold a three-dimensional figure or pot, remind her that it is just that—three dimensional. This means that she needs to add detail or finishing to all sides.

Beautiful and unique pots and vases can be created easily (even by the youngest of students) by methods called "pinching" and "coiling." For a pinch pot, your student can begin by forming a small (or large) ball of clay. Then, by using her fingers or thumbs to create a small impression in the top of the ball, your student can then begin to pinch the sides of the pot. Slowly, but surely, the walls of the pot will begin to thin out and build as the thumb impression deepens and becomes the bottom of the pot.

Coiling can be used to make a variety of pots or vases. First, help your student to form a fairly thick (1/2"-1" thick) base. She can cut this base into whatever shape and size she wishes. This will form the bottom of her vase. Next, she can begin rolling out snake-like ropes of clay. They can be whatever diameter she wishes and in various lengths. As soon as she wants to begin, she can lay a piece of coil on the base, running it around the outside edge. She can smooth it firmly to the base on the inside, using her thumb or finger.

When she has completed the first ring of clay, she can break off extra coil and smooth the ends together. Now she can add a second coil, smoothing this rope to the first. If your student wants the pot to get larger and fatter, she needs to place each new coil a little to the outside of the one before.

Once your student likes the size and shape of the coiled pot, she can begin smoothing all the coils together on the outside, creating a finished look. When the smoothing is complete, she can create texture and decorations by scraping and hatching the clay with various tools (pins, table knife, combs, or sculpting tools). She may even wish to add extra pieces of clay (rolled beads, small ropes and formed shapes) to the outside of the pot.

Sculpting and modeling with clay is a fun, artistic and therapeutic way of creating art! Enjoy it with your student today.

Life Skills: A Job for Each and Each Job Done Well

The Melendy family is a happy one. Everyone has great fun in their own way, and each person also has his or her own job and chores to do. Elizabeth Enright provides us with a nice description of the children's jobs around the house. Even someone as young as Oliver has his own chores to do each day.

Read over that list of chores with your student. Perhaps some of those chores are similar to ones she is required to do each day or week. The Melendys are a good example of a family that works together to get things done, and does so fairly happily.

Learning to do a job well (even if it isn't your favorite thing) is an important part of maturing and getting along well with others. Encourage your student to practice doing her chores happily and well—like the Melendys!

Chapter 2—Saturday Two

Teacher Summary

Randy is so excited she can barely sit still! Today is her day to take the pooled allowances and go out alone. She has decided to see the French painting exhibit at the art gallery. She rushes all morning getting ready, and is soon dressed and out the door.

The pictures are beautiful. Randy tries to take her time and look at each painting slowly and carefully. Sometimes, if she stares long enough, she almost feels as if she's in the picture. Soon, she runs into an old family friend, Mrs. Oliphant. The Melendy children don't really care for Mrs. Oliphant, but Randy is polite.

The older woman turns out to be great fun. She takes Randy to a restaurant and buys her an ice cream sundae. Mrs. Oliphant also tells Randy her exciting story of being kidnapped at a carnival in old Paris. Randy is mesmerized, and loves the thrilling account.

At the end of the afternoon, Randy has made a new friend in Mrs. Oliphant. She promises the old lady that she will visit soon!

What we will cover in this chapter:

Social Studies: History - Benjamin Franklin and Bifocals
Social Studies: Geography - Paris, France*
Social Studies: History - Lucrezia Borgia
Science: Amber
Science: Coatimundis
Science: Camels
Language Arts: Writing and Discussion Question
Language Arts: Vocabulary
Fine Arts: Galleries - What They Hold and How to Enjoy Them
Fine Arts: Cooking - Petits Fours
Life Skills: Enjoying the Companionship of Elderly People

Social Studies: History - Benjamin Franklin and Bifocals

Teacher's Note: If your student completed previous lessons in *Five in a Row*, she has seen several lessons focusing on the inventions and contributions of Benjamin Franklin. A longer overview lesson on Benjamin Franklin is located in FIAR Vol. 5, *Betsy Ross*, chapter 5.

Benjamin Franklin was a prolific writer and inventor. Many of his inventions and discoveries affect our lives every day—one of which was mentioned in our chapter.

Mrs. Oliphant uses bifocal lenses—these lenses were invented by Benjamin Franklin! Share a brief explanation of bifocals with your student. Certain people, as they get older, find it difficult to see things both far away and near. Bifocal eyeglass lenses allow these people to see correctly at both distances. These lenses have one prescription lens in the main part of the frame, and then a second prescription lens toward the bottom of the frame for reading. Often with bifocals, you can see a line where the two different prescription lenses meet. Today, many people have "progressive" lenses, which use the same principle of different prescriptions in one lens, but the lines are not visible.

Can your student think of other scientific discoveries and inventions of Franklin (i.e., lightning rod, Franklin stove, experiments with electricity, etc.)?

Social Studies: Geography - Paris, France*

Mrs. Oliphant's story of her childhood is dramatic, isn't it? She was born and raised in Saint-Germain, near Paris. Take a moment to locate France and Paris on a map with your student. Point out to your student that France is on the western edge of the continent of Europe. France contains several major cities including Paris, Lyon, Merseille, Lille and Nice. The longest river in France is the Loire, which is nearly 628 miles long. Perhaps the most famous river, however, is the Seine, which is 503 miles long and runs through the heart of Paris.

If you have a more detailed map of France available, your student can locate the town where Mrs. Oliphant was raised—Saint-Germain (san zhuhr MAN). Saint-Germain is found on the banks of the Seine River due west of Paris.

Paris is the capital of France and has a long, important and exciting role in the history of Europe and the world. Paris is the main center for the nation's government, business and cultural dealings. It is considered one of the most beautiful cities in the world and includes many elegant boulevards, spacious squares and impressive monuments. At night, spotlights illuminate many of these monuments and structures. The gleaming, beautiful lights have given Paris its nickname—the City of Light.

Several key sights your student may have heard mentioned (or should explore now) include the Eiffel Tower, the Arc de Triomphe, and the Louvre.

The Eiffel Tower (EYE fuhl) is the most famous landmark in Paris. It is a beautiful tower that was built as a symbol for the 1889 World's Fair, called the Universal Exposition. The Eiffel Tower is nearly 1,000 feet tall and was built by a French engineer, Gustave Eiffel. Today, the tower includes shops and restaurants and can be toured throughout the year.

The Arc de Triomphe (ahrk duh tree AWNF) is the largest trimphant arch in the world. The beautiful structure was commissioned by Emperor Napoleon I in 1806 as a tribute to his armies. The arch was completed in 1836, and stands as the world's best example of neoclassical style of the late 1700s to mid-1800s.

Teacher's Note: If your student is interested in art, a study of neoclassical structure may be of great interest and a nice lesson to complement your studies of Paris. As a jumping off point, the neoclassic style is also called the Louis XVI style. It was a return by artists in the 1700s to the roots of Greek and Roman structure design. Instead of numerous curves and swirls, neoclassic designs focused more on straight, strong outlines.

The Louvre (LOO vruh) is one of the largest and most famous art museums in the world. Share with your student that the Louvre covers more than 40 acres and was first built as a royal fort in the 1200s. Then in the 1500s, with expansion, it became a palace residence for the kings of France. Under the reign of Napoleon it received more expansion. It is located on the north banks of the Seine River in Paris, and today houses some of the most spectacular art treasures in the world. Included in the Louvre are nearly eight miles of galleries and over one million pieces of art.

If your student is enjoying learning more about popular sites in Paris, you may wish to continue your discussion by exploring Sacre-Coeur, the Pantheon, Notre Dame and Pompidou Center.

Your student may also enjoy making a simple version of the French treat, petit fours. This activity is located in the Fine Arts section of this chapter.

Social Studies: History - Lucrezia Borgia

Randy loves to draw and paint. She particularly enjoys painting pictures of beautiful princesses, garbed in dramatic headdresses and gowns. Rush teases his sister by saying, "*Don't you ever get tired of drawing Lucrezia Borgia all the time?*" Your student is probably unfamiliar with this reference. As a quick, explanatory lesson, you can share some information on this woman.

Lucrezia Borgia [loo CREE zhuh BAWHR zhuh] was the daughter of Rodrigo Borgia, a Spanish nobleman who later became Pope Alexander VI. Many people hated her father and his use of power. To discredit him, they told terrible lies about Lucrezia. She was used as a pawn in many political decisions of her father's and was not a happy child. She was born in 1480, and in 1501 she married a kind man, the Duke of Ferrara—of Italy. She moved into his home and presided over the court of Ferrara, as the leader of fashion. She worked with artists and seamstresses in the court to create dramatic and beautiful fashion designs that made her legendary. Unlike her father and his advisors, the people of Ferrara liked Lucrezia very much and she was generous and kind to them. She died in 1519 during the birth of her seventh child.

Science: Amber

Randy is dressing in her beautiful brown velveteen dress and getting ready to go. Mona kindly offers to let Randy borrow her "ambers" to wear with the dress. Does your student know what amber is? Or how it is used?

Often used to make beautiful jewelry, amber is not a gemstone, but instead a hardened resin of pine trees. It is golden brown in color and often has "inclusions." These small brown dots and stripes are actually little insects which got trapped in the sticky resin. Some lumps of amber also include little air bubbles.

The greatest deposits of amber are near the Baltic Sea in Europe. Central America, however, has large deposits of amber as well. Amber is most often mined from clay-like soil and is used to make jewelry, instrument mouthpieces and other ornaments.

Science: Coatimundis

Mrs. Oliphant mentions a creature called a "coati-mundi." Even Mrs. Oliphant isn't sure what it is! Your student may enjoy a quick lesson on this interesting and exotic animal.

A coatimundi [koh AH tee MUN dee] is a member of the raccoon family. Using the picture in the margin or a photograph that you find, ask your student what looks similar and what looks different on a coatimundi compared to a raccoon? Coatimundis have longer snouts and very long, strong tails. They are larger than the average raccoon, but have similar coloring and fur texture.

Coatimundis can be found as far north as the wooded areas of Arizona to South America (northern Argentina). Show your student this range of habitat on a map.

Coatimundis eat nearly everything they can catch or find. Things such as insects, snails, spiders, fruit, vegetables, lizards, mice, birds, and more make up their daily diet. Coatimundis' living quarters vary as greatly as their diet. They can make a home on the ground, in caves, in the sand, and in the trees!

The name "coatimundi" comes from an old Indian word meaning "lone coati." The name originally only referred to the males, because male coatimundis always travel alone, leaving the females and young to band together.

Science: Camels

Although Mrs. Oliphant's adventures at the carnival result in frightening and dangerous circumstances, she certainly has a grand time when she first arrives! One particular thing that she seems to enjoy is riding a camel. Having never seen one before, imagine how much courage that must have taken!

Your student may have seen camels at your local zoo. Perhaps she has even ridden on the back of a camel at a zoo or petting area. Camels are interesting, somewhat foreign animals to people in the United States. Explain to your student that in other areas of the world, however, they are as common to children as a pet dog or cat. Take some time and share with your student facts and stories about this fascinating animal.

Camels are large, strong desert animals. Camels generally stand between six and seven feet (at the shoulders) and weigh between 550 and 1,500 pounds when they are fully grown. Camels reach their full size at age 17, and can live over 50 years!

Camels can travel long distances in hot, dry deserts where food or water is scarce. Camels carry food (energy source) in the form of fat on huge humps located on their backs. These humps of fat allow the camel to go without food for days. They can also go without water for days, weeks or even months.

Share with your student that there are two kinds of camels: (1) the Arabian camel, also called dromedary, which has one hump, and (2) the Bactrian camel, which has two humps. (Note that the term dromedary does not refer to all types of camels.)

Using the picture below or a more detailed photograph that you find, go through each of the following physical characteristics of a camel, pause and allow your student to offer a guess as to why a camel might have that particular attribute.

First, draw to your student's attention the unusual facial features. For example, a camel's eyes are located on the sides of its head and are protected by long, curly eyelashes. These lashes help keep out blowing sand and particles as the animal moves through the desert.

Camels also have very thick, bushy eyebrows which help their eyes stay shielded from the hot sun. Camels have very small, round ears located far back on their head. The ears, much like the eyelids, are covered in hair (even on the inside!). The hair keeps dirt and sand out. Camels hear well, but aren't very obedient.

Camels have a unique, split upper lip. This split allows the camel to get his teeth close to the ground so he can eat short grass when it is available. Tough skin on the inside of a camel's mouth helps protect it from rough foods. A camel can eat a thorn-covered twig and not be injured at all. Remind your student that, like cattle, a camel is a ruminant animal.Ruminants have stomachs with three sections, and these animals pull back poorly chewed food called cud to chew it again.

Camels have large feet with two toes like hooves. Each foot has a wide, cushioned pad at the bottom. Their large, round, flat feet allow them to evenly distribute their weight and give them stability when walking in sand.

For millions of people who live in Africa and Asia, camels are an important part of their lives. Camels are used to pull plows, carry grain and other crops, for personal transportation, food, clothing and shelter. Camels need the people too, however, for water that they cannot dig for themselves.

Camels are used for as long as possible as transportation and work animals. They are also used, however, for food and clothing. Camel meat is used as food. The fat in their humps can be melted down and used as oil and butter. Camel's milk can also be drunk and used for cheese. Camel fur can be used for clothing, blankets and cloth. The skin of camels can be used for shoes, water bags and saddles. And finally, camel droppings can be dried and used for fuel.

It might be interesting to note for your student that the U.S. Government imported camels to the United States in the 1850s. They created a work force called the Camel Corps. The army used the camels to transport goods to distant forts in the western states. Soon, however, train tracks were laid and the camels were no longer needed. Many camels were sold to carnivals, circuses and zoos. More were left, however, and were finally turned loose. These poor animals finally died out or were killed. The last "wild" camel to be seen in the United States was in 1941 in California.

If your student is interested in learning more about camels, search online, find books at your local library or go to your local zoo. Camels are among the most interesting and useful animals on Earth.

Language Arts: Writing and Discussion Question

Think for a moment about Mrs. Oliphant's appraisal of Randy. She says, "...you have 'eyes the better to see with, my dear' and 'ears the better to hear with.' Nobody who has them and uses them is likely to find life humdrum very often." What do you think Mrs. Oliphant means by this statement? Do you think you appreciate life like Randy?

Language Arts: Vocabulary

kiting To move about quickly, without plans.

spasm A sudden, involuntary, abnormal contraction of muscles.

enigmatic Baffling, puzzling, mysterious.

camphor A white substance with a strong bitter smell; used to make moth balls to repel moths and other insects.

resilience The power of springing back; the quality of elasticity.

aura An atmosphere; something which surrounds.

dinghy A small rowboat.

launch The largest boat carried by a warship.

albatross A very large sea bird with webbed feet; the albatross is the largest ocean bird and can fly usually long distances.

spinster An older woman who has never married.

cornucopia A horn-shaped container; often represented in art as overflowing with fruit; the horn of plenty.

expostulation An earnest protest or display of opinion.

sarcastic The use of irony in order to mock or show contempt for someone or something.

czarina The wife of a czar; a Russian empress.

Apollo The Greek god of the sun and archery.

Diana The Greek goddess of the hunt.

Fine Arts: Galleries - What They Hold and How to Enjoy Them

Randy decides to use her first Saturday to visit an art museum. Has your student ever been to an art gallery? Galleries hold artwork of all kinds—furniture, sculpture, jewelry, paintings, photography and more. Some galleries concentrate on a specific time period or type of artwork—modern art, neoclassical or sculpture, for example. Art galleries are exciting places to visit. Instead of just studying a painting style or drawing technique, you can stand in front of the actual canvas the artist touched and study their style firsthand.

The author of this FIAR volume remembers fondly visiting her local art gallery with her mother almost weekly as a child. The beautiful paintings and sculptures became more like old friends with each visit, and it created a firm foundation for a lifelong love of art. She still visits that same wonderful gallery and enjoys the art more every year.

If you are at all able, try to set up a field trip to an art gallery with your student sometime during your study of *The Saturdays*. Some younger children find galleries somewhat boring and difficult to endure, but here are some tips to help make the trip enjoyable, memorable and educational for all ages.

1. Take plenty of time to enjoy the gallery. Don't feel like you have to rush. Children tend to go at their own pace, and you don't have to see everything in one visit. If you are visting a large art museum, you will probably want to concentrate on just a few rooms or areas rather than trying to see the whole museum.

2. Take breaks during the day. Eating a snack or lunch can be a welcome lull in the day, or even a quick run around the courtyard or sidewalk can stretch tired legs and wake up tired minds.

3. Wear comfortable clothes and shoes. Dressing up, like Randy, can be fun, but if you plan on being in a museum or gallery for the day, it is better to be comfortable.

4. Read the labels and titles of artwork. Encourage your student to find the title, artist, date and medium of pieces she is particularly drawn to.

5. Record your findings. Your student can take a small notebook or sketchbook with her and record the information she finds on the plaques next to artwork. She may want to study a particular artist later. Or she may, from seeing a work of art, become interested in an event or period of history. Also, your student may see a medium or a technique used by an artist she would like to try. Taking notes helps her remember these kinds of discoveries.

6. Take a sketchbook and drawing utensils. If your student is a budding artist, she may enjoy trying to sketch her own versions of sculptures or pictures she particularly enjoys. Copying the works of masters is a great way to gain greater appreciation and technique.

7. Decide which artwork in a gallery you like best and which you like least. Talk about why. What mood does the artwork make you feel? What do you like about that particular artist's technique?

8. Develop favorite pictures/sculptures/pieces, just like Randy. Encourage your student to make friends with artwork and to study other works by that same artist. No matter what the emphasis is for the day, also visit the old favorite pieces each time.

By exploring and visiting art galleries, your student can broaden her social, historical and cultural awareness. She will begin to appreciate and observe art like never before. Books and the internet are wonderful tools for education, but nothing can compare to standing before the original!

Fine Arts: Cooking - Petits Fours

Mrs. Oliphant generously orders delicious cakes for Randy and herself called "petits fours" (peh TEE for). Our story describes the cakes as "the most wonderful little cakes in frilled paper collars: pink, and pale yellow, and chocolate, with silver peppermint buttons on top."

True petits fours are complex to make, requiring great skill and technique. French bakeries, called "patisseries," excel at making these delectable little cakes. If you have a bakery nearby, you can see if they have petits fours available and purchase some to enjoy during this chapter! Or, your student (with your help) can have fun making her own simpler versions and serving them to family and friends.

By using a cake mix (yellow, white and chocolate are the basic petit four flavors), your student can quickly whip up a nice cake batter. Bake the cake mix, according to the directions, in a square or rectangular pan (not a round pan).

When the cake is cool, wrap it completely in aluminum foil and freeze for at least two hours (or chill in refrigerator overnight). Unwrap the cake and carefully cut it into small squares (approximately 3"x3"). Your student can practice measuring, by using a ruler and scoring the cake before cutting. When the petits fours are cut, you can ice each with pretty icing (the color and flavor can be your student's choice) and decorate with various store-bought cake decorations (silver balls, snow flakes, etc.).

Teacher's Note: If your student is very interested in baking (or is older and ready for more complex cooking techniques), you can ice the petits fours with the traditional style of frosting called fondant. Fondant can be bought at baking supply stores, gourmet food shops and some hobby stores that sell cake decorating kits. Fondant is hardened icing which, when melted, can be poured over each little cake. The fondant hardens slightly into a smooth, beautiful finish—but is still soft enough to eat. Unused fondant can be stored in the refrigerator. Fondant can also be made at home (it is a simple sugar syrup which is cooled and kneaded). Look for fondant recipes online or in baking or French cookbooks.

When your student has her petits fours complete, fix some tea or hot chocolate, arrange some pretty flowers in a vase, and have a delicious snack with your student. Discuss *The Saturdays*, Randy's glorious trip to the gallery, Mrs. Oliphant's wild adventures, or whatever you wish!

Life Skills: Enjoying the Companionship of Elderly People

When Randy first notices Mrs. Oliphant in the gallery, she isn't too excited, is she? Randy, like the other Melendy children, thinks Mrs. Oliphant is nice, but "so far away in her oldness and dignity." Randy hopes Mrs. Oliphant doesn't notice her.

Talk with your student about Randy's first reaction to Mrs. Oliphant and the way she feels about the old woman when the chapter is complete. She enjoys Mrs. Oliphant so much by the end of the story, that she wants to come and visit her soon!

Many times, younger people are frightened or bored by older people. Discuss with your student the rich, wonderful resource older people can be for life lessons, great stories, advice from years of experience, time to spend, and more. Making friends with someone who is older can be such a great thing for children.

If your student doesn't know many elderly people (perhaps she doesn't have a grandparent or one who lives close), why not take an afternoon and go to your local nursing home or retirement center? Call before you go, and confirm what your plans are with the coordinators. Many nursing homes encourage and seek out young people to come and visit with their residents. Games (like bingo, checkers and cards) are often played on a weekly basis. Your student can take part in these events as a volunteer. Your student may just use this project as a community service outreach, but she may form a strong friendship with someone in particular. Learning to appreciate the friendship of older people is something that can bring happiness and wisdom to your student's life!

Chapter 3—Saturday Three

Teacher Summary

Rush decides to go to an opera with his Saturday. He chooses a German opera called *Siegfried* and enjoys it thoroughly. On his way home from the music hall, Rush comes across a wet, lost dog. The poor dog nearly gets hit by a passing car, and doesn't have any tags or a leash. Rush takes the dog home, and after cleaning him up, convinces Mr. Melendy and Cuffy to let him keep the dog. Mr. Melendy insists on posting ads to see if the dog has an owner, but he agrees that the animal can stay if no one claims him. Rush, Randy and the rest of the children are thrilled, and the dog is lovingly dubbed "Isaac."

What we will cover in this chapter:

Social Studies: History - Modernization: Different Jobs for Different People
Science: Snow
Science: Rabies in Animals

Fine Arts: Orchestras*
Fine Arts: *Peter and the Wolf* by Prokofiev*

Social Studies: History - Modernization: Different Jobs for Different People

This chapter offers an excellent opportunity to discuss modernization with your student. Look together at Rush's conversation with the old man, who says, "Nowadays they do it all by machinery. Ain't no work for nobody."

What does your student know about modernization? Through technology, development and science, new inventions and innovations are constantly being offered which make work easier and more efficient. But, does modernization truly put workers out of a job? Sometimes, but not always, as the old man seems to think.

Talk with your student about the subject in our chapter—for example, a machine-operated snowplow versus a horse-pulled snowplow. Certainly, the machines do far more work in a shorter amount of time. Fewer people are hired to operate the machines than were hired to drive the horses. However, who makes the machine snowplows? Who makes all the parts? Who sells them? Who fixes them when they break down?

Often, modernization puts people out of certain jobs, but many other people are hired to fill different, new jobs. Allow your student to follow this train of logic himself by setting up a scenario for him to work through. Let your student select an old-fashioned piece of machinery—spinning wheels, hand set printing presses, or an ax, for example. Encourage your student to think through (and record on paper if he wishes) who was employed with the old machines, and who is employed with the new modern devices (i.e., thread/yarn machines, digital printing, and chainsaws). Which version employs more people?

Also consider changes to the service industry, such as self-serve grocery store checkout lanes, ordering kiosks at fast-food restaurants, and self-serve gas pumps or library checkouts. Talk with your student about how these changes have affected the number of workers needed and if other types of workers would replace them in different ways.

For further study, your student may wish to explore the Industrial Revolution, the work force changes during World War II, or other changes brought on by recent technology.

Science: Snow

Rush is surprised (and delighted!) when he steps out of the music hall and discovers it's been snowing. Snow is beautiful, fun to play in, and interesting to study. Your student may have studied snow with *Snowflake Bentley* in FIAR Vol. 5; use this lesson as a review or as new information.

Snow is a form of precipitation (condensed moisture falling back to Earth in the form of rain, snow, hail or sleet). Snow falls during cold temperatures (32° F. or below) and is made up of tiny ice crystals. These crystals, called snow crystals, are created in the water vapor in very cold clouds. Every snow crystal (or snowflake) has six sides—but no two snowflakes are alike! An innumerable amount of snowflakes fall on any given day of the year somewhere in the world, and not one is the same as another!

Snowflakes vary widely in both shape and size. Your student has probably noticed winter days where the flakes were so big they looked like feathers. Other days, however, the snowflakes are very small. When snowflakes reach sizes of one inch or more, over 100 crystals may be clinging together to form just one snowflake.

Snow is precipitation, just like rain, but it contains much less water than rain. In order to equal one inch of rain water, it takes between six and thirty inches of snow! Despite the lower moisture content, snow is still an important source of water. In regions of the world where snow falls, the melting snow provides water for streams and thereby hydrates plants and animals. Snow is also an excellent and important insulator. It helps protect plants and hibernating animals from winter air.

If your student is doing this lesson during the winter (and there is snow available), take some time and play a little in the snow. At any age, building a snowman or making snow angels is fun and a good workout!Another great snow activity older children enjoy is called "snow painting." For this activity, you will need:

- several spray bottles (available at discount or gardening stores)
- water
- food coloring in various shades
- and of course, snow!

Have your student fill each bottle with water (cold!) and then put in several drops of food coloring. Keep a different bottle for each color and watch out for splashes (old clothes are good for this part of the project). Now your student can take her "palette" of spray bottles out into the yard. Find a smooth snowy patch and begin spraying your picture into the snow. Snow painted pictures can be as simple or elaborate as your student wishes. Take a photograph of the artist and the snow painting to preserve the work!

Science: Rabies in Animals

When Cuffy sees the dog covered in soap suds she begins screaming, "*Mad dog!* MR. MELENDY, THERE'S A MAD DOG!" Does your student understand why Cuffy yells this phrase? She thinks the soap suds are foaming saliva—a sign of rabies in animals. Rabies is a disease that is often feared, but rarely understood. A study of rabies in animals is an excellent science exploration for your student.

Rabies [RAY beez] is an infection caused by a virus. It is a disease which destroys nerve cells in the brain and is often fatal. Mammals, including humans, can be victims of rabies. Animals which are in final stages of rabies often become highly excitable and attack objects or animals which come in their way. This is probably where the name "rabies" came from—it is Latin for "rage" or "fury."

Unfortunately, it isn't always easy to see if an animal has rabies. Mammals can carry the rabies virus in their salivary glands (in the mouth) for long periods of time. If the infected mammal (called a "host") bites another animal or human being (or if any of the saliva enters an open wound or sore), the victim may well develop the disease. Most people contract rabies from unvaccinated dogs and cats and occasionally wild animals. Symptoms of the disease may take from ten days to seven months to develop after the infection is contracted.

Animals suffering from the disease may experience great excitability, difficulty swallowing, over-salivation (causing foaming) and finally, paralysis. (Long ago, rabies used to be called "hydrophobia," which means "fear of water." Animals with rabies appear to exhibit an intense fear of water due to involuntary throat spasms.)

If your student has a pet dog or cat, she may be familiar with rabies vaccinations and the tag her pet wears to signify this inoculation has been given. Vaccinations for house pets is the most effective way we have to control the disease. Because of widespread vaccinations for dogs and cats in the United States, the threat of rabies from pets has been greatly reduced.

Discuss basic animal safety with your student. Never approach or pet a strange animal. If you are in the woods or in an unfamiliar area and a dog or other animal is acting strangely, don't go near but instead, leave the area. Rabies is a dangerous disease, but fortunately it is no longer a widespread problem.

Language Arts: Writing and Discussion Question

Rush isn't sure Cuffy will understand or like his new dog. He tries to clean him up first, so she may be more willing to agree to the new animal. Write about a time when you had an idea or plan and you weren't sure your parents would like it. What did you do to help your case?

Language Arts: Vocabulary

hurdy-gurdy A hand-organ played by turning a handle.

alacrity Brisk and eager action; liveliness.

anvil An iron or steel block on which metals are hammered and shaped.

grotto A cave or cavernous room.

mail A flexible armor made from links of metal loops, forming chains.

aperture An opening.

subterranean Beneath the earth; underground.

minotaur A Greek legend; a monster with a bull's head and man's body.

labyrinth Many connected passageways or tunnels; a maze.

rabies A viral disease which affects mammals and humans; causes paralysis and death.

snow crystal Small frozen water particles which make up a snowflake.

Fine Arts: Orchestras*

Rush is completely delighted by his visit to the music hall. He particularly enjoys watching the orchestra members before the opera begins. Is your student familiar with what makes up an orchestra? What are the instruments and who are the people? How they are organized? Answer all these questions and more by exploring an orchestra with your student.

An orchestra is a group of musicians playing different instruments and playing together. Although there are different definitions of orchestra (string orchestra, jazz orchestra, etc.), the most common definition describes a symphony orchestra. Symphony orchestras, like what Rush heard, can play alone or along with a singer, a ballet, play or opera.

A classic symphony orchestra is made up of four different types of instruments: brass, woodwinds, percussion and strings. Perhaps your student plays one of these:

Brass: tubas, trombones, trumpets, french horns

Woodwinds: flutes, bassoons, clarinets, oboes

Percussion: timpani, triangle, and various drums

Strings: violins, violas, cellos, harp and piano

The musicians and their instruments are placed in specific areas in the orchestra pit or stage. The conductor designs the seating to produce a certain blend of sounds.

To create beautiful music, an orchestra must have gifted musicians and a gifted conductor. The conductor is an integral part of the whole. He or she must direct the musicians and keep time, by using a small pointer (baton) and with facial expressions. A conductor's most important work, however, is completed before the audience ever hears a note. It is the conductor's job to select the musical compositions the orchestra will play. Then it is the conductor's job to decide how the music should be played. This could involve changing the tempo (speed), phrasing (time between notes), or tonal quality (different volumes and instruments). The greatest conductors in the world are able to select compositions, interpret the compositions, inspire their musicians and inspire their audiences.

Enrich this lesson by finding a way for your student to see a conductor and orchestra in action. Attending a live performance is ideal, but watching a video of a symphony orchestra will also work. Remind your student to look for the musicians and the instruments they are holding. Encourage her to draw a representation or picture of where that conductor placed the different instruments. Draw your student's attention to the conductor. Watch closely how much feeling is put into the face, arms and hands. Each musician, no matter where she is sitting, must be able to see the conductor and understand her cue each time.

Learning more about orchestras helps strengthen your student's fine arts appreciation and understanding of the music world!

Fine Arts: *Peter and the Wolf* by Prokofiev*

In the description of the opera's music, we read, "There was a music that was Siegfried's own, and another for his sword, and another for the wanderer, and the Forest Bird..." Many operas (as well as other types of musical productions) have music that is wonderfully intricate. Each different character or mood evokes a specific feeling, and that feeling is reflected in the music.

An excellent example of this principle is the symphonic fairy tale, *Peter and the Wolf*. Written by the Russian composer, Sergei (sehr gay) Prokofiev (proh KOE fee ef), *Peter and the Wolf* is one of the most popular classical works of the 1900s. Locate a recording of *Peter and the Wolf* online or at your library. Both the story and the music are interesting and easily accessible for children.

In *Peter and the Wolf*, Prokofiev gives each character a specific instrument. The narrator tells the story, but the characters never speak. Your student will be able to feel the action of the story through the type of instrument and the compositions. A bassoon, for example, is the instrument for the Grandfather—a deep, solemn-sounding instrument. A flute, on the other hand, represents the Bird. As you listen to the piece with your student, discuss when you hear tension, happiness, confidence, arrogance and more through each of the musical sections.

When Prokofiev wrote about his musical masterpiece, he had this to say, "What was important to me was not to tell a story, but to have the children listen to the music. The story was merely a pretext."

Chapter 4—Saturday Four

Teacher Summary

Mona spends her Saturday in New York City. She enjoys looking at the tall buildings and crowds of people. As she is walking along, she spots a beauty salon advertising three items for one dollar. Immediately, Mona knows what she wants to do with her money. Over the next several hours, Mona gets her hair cut and curled and her nails painted a fire engine red. During the treatments, she spends time talking to her manicurist, Miss Pearl. Miss Pearl tells Mona about her and her brother running away from home to escape a mean stepmother.

When Mona returns home that evening, Willy Sloper doesn't even recognize her. As she suspected, her father and Cuffy aren't happy with her new look. In fact, they are so upset Mona wishes she hadn't gone to the beauty parlor, and Cuffy helps her take the nail polish off.

What we will cover in this chapter:

Social Studies: History - Christopher Columbus
Science: Odors and Your Olfactory Sense
Science: Static Electricity
Language Arts: Creative Writing - Employing New Words*
Language Arts: Writing and Discussion Question
Language Arts: Vocabulary
Life Skills: Avoiding a Vain Attitude
Life Skills: Listening to Your Conscience

Social Studies: History - Christopher Columbus

Miss Pearl and her brother, Perry, left their abusive stepmother and set out into the world on their own. Miss Pearl tells Mona that she and her brother felt like Christopher Columbus. Take this opportunity to discuss exploration and this famous historical figure with your student.

Christopher Columbus lived during the 15th century. He was born in Genoa, Italy in 1451 (we don't know the exact date). His father, Domenico, was a weaver and the young Christopher often helped his father with the business. Because his family was poor and his father needed the help, Columbus didn't get much formal schooling. He was intelligent and motivated, however, and taught himself Latin and Spanish. He also spent many evenings studying scholarly books, maps and charts of the world.

Locate Columbus' birthplace, Genoa, on a map with your student. Genoa is found on the northwestern shores of Italy. As Columbus was growing up, and as it still is today, Genoa was a busy, important port city of industry and trade. (Ask your student if she would like to live in a city that was over 500 years old!) Many, many ships come in and out of Genoa's harbors. Columbus was fascinated by the ships and the men who sailed them. When he was nineteen, as soon as he was able, Columbus joined a war fleet as a sailor and left his family to go and sail the seas.

Christopher Columbus

During his time in service, Columbus learned how to use all the navigating equipment on the ships. Compasses, maps and quadrants helped the sailors track their progress and locate their destinations. Remind your student that during this time in history (the 15th century), most people no longer believed the earth was flat—as they once did! They knew it was a globe, but no one had ventured out far enough into the Atlantic Ocean to see what was on the other side. At that time, Columbus and his contemporaries referred to the Atlantic Ocean as the Sea of Darkness.

Genoa, being a city that survived on trade and industry, did a lot of trading with eastern Asia (at that time, often called "the Orient"). Spices, expensive silks and cloth, jewels and gold were all traded with Asian countries during Columbus' day. Look at a world map again with your student. The only way trading with these countries could be conducted during that time was over land. The businessmen and importers would travel long distances across Europe and back. It worked, but it took many, many days and was very expensive.

Christopher Columbus thought about this problem and came up with an alternate route. Perhaps it would be possible to reach east Asia by sailing due west across the Atlantic Ocean. He was very anxious to try out his idea, but he needed ships, supplies and crew members. All that would take a lot of money! Columbus needed to find a sponsor—someone who was interested enough in his plan that they would pay for it. Christopher Columbus finally decided to approach the King and Queen of Spain—Ferdinand and Isabella. At first, they thought Columbus was crazy. It took Columbus six long years to convince them, but finally they agreed.

Using a globe, if possible, talk with your student about Columbus's plan. Ask your student what Columbus didn't know about his planned trip. What factors was he missing? Columbus wasn't sure how big the circumference of the globe was. He thought it was around 19,000 miles, but in reality it's closer to 25,000! He thought the only land masses were Europe and Asia. He had no idea North or South America existed! He had no idea there was another huge body of water on the other side, what we now call the Pacific Ocean!

The King and Queen of Spain gave Columbus three ships—the *Niña*, the *Pinta*, and the *Santa Maria*. They also helped him stock the ships with food, water, goods for trading and crew members.

Christopher Columbus was also told that he would become governor-general of any lands he discovered and claimed for Spain. He could keep 10% of all the precious gold, silver, spices and other valuables that he might find, too. It was a rich payment, but Columbus was risking a great deal.

On August 3, 1492, the three ships under Columbus's command set out from Spain. Throughout the first few months Columbus dealt with many crew problems. They were convinced they were going to die, and wanted to turn back. Storms were bad, but Columbus insisted they continue to sail west.

Columbus kept detailed diaries and records throughout his journey. Finally, on October 12, the ships reached land—the Bahama Islands, off the southeast coast of North America. Locate these islands on a globe for your student to see. Then point out Indonesia (known as the East Indies), located off the coasts of Japan. Columbus thought he was at *those* islands when he reached the Bahamas. He quickly claimed them for Spain, and called the people who lived there "Indians." Share with your student that to this day, we still refer to the islands off the east coast of America as the West Indies, and until fairly recently, Native Americans were often still referred to as Indians. Both of these names came from Columbus' mistake.

The story of Christopher Columbus is a complicated one. Columbus eventually made three more voyages to the Americas, but never reached Asia or even the North American continent (he did explore many islands, as well as the Central and South American coasts). The question of who "discovered" North America is one that your student may want to investigate now, or possibly wait until later years when she is studying history in more depth. Columbus's methods of exploration and his treatment of native inhabitants are also topics that you may choose to study now, or wait until your student is older.

Although Columbus was an intrepid and experienced sailer and navigator, the King and Queen eventually took away his titles and lost interest in his plans for further voyages. Columbus spent most of the last years of his life trying to convince the King to give him more chances. He died on May 20, 1506, a sad and disillusioned man. He couldn't understand why his plan had failed.

If your student is interested in learning more about Christopher Columbus and his time in history, you might consider finding additional resource books on the following topics: ships, sailing, navigation, the 15th century, the Kings and Queens of Spain, the West Indies, Asia and of course, Columbus himself. Or your student might be interested in finding translations of his diaries and ship's logs.

Science: Odors and Your Olfactory Sense

At the beginning of the chapter, Mona is getting ready for her day out. Even though the lunch dishes are cleaned up, we read that the "odor of baked potatoes and lamb chops lingered comfortably in the house." Does your student know how our noses work? What is an odor and why can we smell it? Ask your student how she thinks all this happens.

Smell is one of the basic five senses of humans and animals. (The other four are sight, hearing, touch and taste.) It is a very important sense, helping animals find food and their home. Explain to your student that just like other topics, scientists have a special name for smelling—olfaction. The way our bodies detect smells is called the olfactory system. To help you student remember this term, encourage her to think of her nose as an "old factory."

People, and land-living animals, smell by breathing in air through their noses. The smells are actually molecules of gas released from different substances. In the Melendy household that day, little molecules of gas from the baked potatoes and lamb chops carried the scent of these foods throughout the house.

Smelling a rose or the delicious aroma of a meal is much more complex than you would think! And yet, it all happens in a split second. Share the amazing job the olfactory system does with your student.

When the molecules of gas reach your nose, they are breathed in and are picked up by the receptor cells of your olfactory nerves. These nerves send informational impulses to your brain and your olfactory bulb (a structure near the front of the brain). From there, the impulses travel toward the brain and you know what the smell is.

Dogs and other animals have very large olfactory bulbs—meaning, they have acute senses of smell. Humans have much smaller olfactory bulbs. Scientists think the size of an animal's olfactory bulb tells us how important the sense of smell is for that creature's survival.

No one really knows how we distinguish between different smells, but scientists do know how the scents get to our brain.

There are many fun, easy and quick-to-prepare activities you can do with your student to complement this lesson. Here are two to choose from. Find one or two (or more!) your student is excited about trying and have fun exploring the sense of smell (olfaction).

Smell, Name and Remember

In this activity, your student will be reminded of the vast array of smells humans recognize and how we often associate certain feelings or memories with those smells. Here is what you'll need:

Things to smell: lemon, orange, bananas, dirt, vanilla, clay, pine needles, chocolate, coffee, onion, crayon, playdough, etc. (anything "smelly" you're able to collect around the house and kitchen).

Blindfold (so your student can't see the item) OR paper-covered jars with holes in the top.

Keep the items separate, and allow your student to sniff each. Have your student (1) identify the smell, (2) rate the smell—strong, pleasant, neutral, etc., and (3) relate any memories or feelings associated with that smell.

Choose and Sniff Game

(This activity is fun for older and younger students. Your student can work on making this game and then can share it with younger siblings.)

This game is a bit like the game Memory. Take index cards and with a small amount of glue or tape, attach a different herb or spice to two of each. For example, you can create two basil, two oregano, two rosemary, two cinnamon, two nutmeg, etc. Let the glue dry completely. When you are ready, arrange the cards on a table in rows, mixing up the smells. Now, your student and her friends can pick a card, close her eyes and sniff. When she has "memorized" the smell, she can replace the card. When her turn comes again, she can pick another card, close her eyes and smell. The object of the game is to find matched pairs of scents.

Science: Static Electricity

Teacher's Note: Your student may have been introduced to static electricity previously in Chapter 16 of *Thomas Edison*, in this volume.

As Mona brushed her hair, it crackled and stood out on end. This movement and sound was created by a kind of electricity called static electricity. Static electricity is a form of electricity made when certain materials are rubbed together.

Share the following interesting fact with your student. Remember that Mona shared her "ambers" necklace with Randy during "Saturday Two." Static electricity was first discovered by the Greeks in around 600 B.C. They used amber to make jewelry and figured out that if you rubbed the lumps of amber on cloth, the cloth attracted small objects. The Greeks called amber, elektron, so what they discovered they called electricity!

Your student has probably seen static electricity and its effects on many occasions. For example, sometimes when we pull clothes out of a hot dryer they crackle and stick together. Show your student static electricity by taking a balloon, inflating it and tying it off. Now hold the balloon against your hair and rub it back and forth. As you pull the balloon away, your hair tries to follow it! Let your student try this simple experiment with her own hair.

Why does this happen? The balloon and your hair produce electricity as they are rubbed together. Static electricity can pull things together (like hair and balloons), and it can also push things apart. Here is another simple experiment. Your student needs a plastic comb and a wool coat, sweater or pants. Rub the comb briskly across the wool. Now quickly hold the comb near a thin stream of water in the bathroom or kitchen sink. Does your student see the stream of water bend toward the comb? The electricity in the comb is pulling the water toward the comb.

These simple experiments show your student static electricity on a very small level. Does she know that lightning is static electricity? When small drops of water and ice inside huge thunderhead clouds rub together, electricity is caused. Lightning bolts are really huge sparks of static electricity. Sometimes these sparks jump from cloud to cloud, and occasionally hit the ground. Lightning can be frightening and destructive, but it can also be beautiful.

For the older student, you may wish to explain further how static electricity happens. To do so, it is important to begin by talking about atoms. Atoms carry neutrons and electrons. When an object gains or loses a large number of electrons, the entire object becomes electrically charged. When objects carry these charges, we call it static electricity.

Static electricity is used every day in important ways. Many copy machines, for example, work using static electricity. They are called electrostatic copiers. The black particles of ink are negatively charged, and they are attracted to positively charged paper. As the particles attach themselves, they create a replica of the original.

Learning more about static electricity helps your student learn more about the world around her!

Language Arts: Creative Writing—Employing New Words*

Our author, Elizabeth Enright, used rich, descriptive words in her writing. She also made her characters in *The Saturdays* smart and well-read children who have excellent vocabularies. Your student has been learning many of these new words throughout our study of this book. Here is an opportunity for her to begin using them in her own writing.

Encourage your student to write a short story, play or descriptive paragraph. However, instead of simply writing whatever she thinks of, have her include five or ten of the new words she has learned in the first four chapters, or in this chapter alone. For example, instruct her to write a one-page story, where the following words must appear at least once: admonition, loathe, bob, fervently and heroine. Depending upon your knowledge of your student's vocabulary skills and level, you may choose the words you think will stretch her the most.

This type of creative writing lesson forces your student to begin using new words correctly and seeing how they fit into her everyday writing. It can be an enjoyable and eye-opening lesson!

Language Arts: Writing and Discussion Question

What do you think Mona would have enjoyed doing with her Saturday if she had not seen the beauty shop? Write about it.

Language Arts: Vocabulary

deftly Quick, skillful.

plaited Braided hair, braided ribbon, etc.

incompatible Not able to live or act together peaceably.

admonition A gentle reproof or warning.

heroine A female hero.

perilous Dangerous.

loathe To dislike strongly, hate, despise.

bob To cut short.

Iago The villain in Shakespeare's *Othello.*

consternation Great dismay, terror.

dexterous Having skill with hands.

tempest A violent windstorm, generally with rain or hail.

fervently Very earnest, with great feeling.

hub The center around which everything revolves.

perdition The loss of one's soul, final ruin.

Life Skills: Avoiding a Vain Attitude

Reread Cuffy's advice to Mona: "Just quit thinking you're the hub of the universe, that's all." "Hub" means the center around which everything revolves. What does Cuffy mean by this statement? Discuss the subject of "vanity"with your student. Mona, like many of us, was worried about herself and her own beauty for much of this chapter. Cuffy understands, as we should, that the world is about more than personal appearance.

If we find that we are feeling sorry for ourselves or acting selfishly, it helps to think of others and what they are going through. Talk with your student about a time when you were caught up in selfish or vain feelings. What did you do? How were you able to shift your focus?

Learning to think of others first, and to put ourselves last, is an important part of growing up and becoming kind, mature adults. No one wants to be around someone who only thinks of how she looks and what she can do for herself. Vanity is really thinking you're better than other people. Instead, remember that we are all human and begin looking for things you can do to help someone else!

Life Skills: Listening to Your Conscience

Mona knows her father and Cuffy won't like what she is about to do! Cutting her hair, fixing it in an older fashion and getting her nails done are all things that will disappoint them. She even thinks about this on several occasions, doesn't she? But Mona decides to ignore "the corner of her mind that never let itself be fooled..."

Ask your student what she thinks that "corner of her mind" really is? It is Mona's conscience. Everyone has a conscience. It is what reminds us of what is right and wrong. Your conscience isn't a physical part of your body. You can't find it in an anatomy guide. But it is real, just the same. Your conscience is a part of being human.

Mona was wrong to ignore her conscience. If she had listened to it, she wouldn't have upset her father and Cuffy, and she would have been so much happier in the end. Talk with your student about how she knows when something is right or wrong. Does she listen to that little "corner of her mind?"

Chapter 5—Saturday Five

Teacher Summary

The Melendy children decide to stay home on Oliver's Saturday. Since he is too young to go out alone, they decide to respect his Saturday and refrain from their own outside activities. Oliver, however, does not feel he is too young to go out. He has carefully saved his last two Saturday allowances, and now has enough to go to the city with a lot left over.

So, on this particular Saturday, Oliver sets out (without telling anyone) to go to the circus! He loves all the animals and acts. He eats way too much junk food, but has a great time. On the way home, however, he gets lost and a mounted policeman rides him home. The Melendys are all tremendously worried about Oliver, and are quite relieved when he gets home safely. Oliver decides he won't go out again alone for a long time.

What we will cover in this chapter:

Social Studies: History – Circuses: Then and Now
Science: Good Nutrition*
Language Arts: Phone Skills
Language Arts: Writing and Discussion Question
Language Arts: Vocabulary
Life Skills: Dealing With Difficult People

Social Studies: History – Circuses: Then and Now

Teacher's Note: If your student has completed previous volumes of Five in a Row, remind her of the circuses she read about in *Another Celebrated Dancing Bear* (Vol. 1), *Mirette on the High Wire* (Vol. 2), and *Andy and the Lion* (Vol. 3). Are there similarities to the circus in this chapter?

Has your student ever been to a circus? Circuses of the type that Oliver attended began in the mid-1700s in Europe. Perhaps the most famous of these kinds of circuses was the Ringling Bros. and Barnum & Bailey traveling circus, which ceased operation in 2017 after 146 years of great popularity. There are still circuses operating in the United States today, but they are quite different in some ways from the kind of circus Oliver snuck out to see.

Go back through chapter 5 of *The Saturdays* with your student and find all of the things that Oliver saw, smelled, heard, touched, and tasted at the circus. Going to the circus in times past was a very exciting experience! From the crunching peanut shells under your feet to the trapeze artists over your head ... from the smell of the elephants and the sticky cotton candy to the shouts of the ringmaster and laughter at the clowns ... from the shiny sequined outfits to the dusty sawdust on the floor, the circus was a feast for the senses.

If you or your student have ever been to a circus, discuss the differences between the circus you saw and the circus that Oliver saw. Circuses today aren't likely to have elephants, seals, camels, lions, or other wild animals (although they might have performers who work with horses, dogs, or even cats—domesticated animals). Today's circuses likely still have a ringmaster and aerial artists on a trapeze, with hoops or rings, or on a tightwire. They still have music, cotton candy, jugglers, and sometimes clowns. Nowadays there may be just one "ring" (for the performers) rather than three, as in years past.

There are many reasons for the decline in circus attendance and loss of popularity, from concern for animal well-being to the many other entertainment options for people to enjoy. If there is interest, have your student find library books or information online about circuses of yesterday and today. And if a circus is in your town, pay a visit and experience the excitement of today's circus!

Science: Good Nutrition*

Oliver doesn't feel so good after he leaves the circus. Review with your student all that Oliver ate while he was there: a whole package of cotton candy, two hot dogs (one with mustard and one with sauerkraut), a bottle of soda pop, and a bag of peanuts. Treats are delicious and wonderful occasionally, but people will feel sick (just like Oliver does) if they eat too many at one time.

This chapter can be a great springboard for your student to think about good nutrition and what she is eating. Many American children and adolescents do not meet the minimum daily nutrition guidelines as put out by the U.S. Food and Nutrition Board. For this reason, it is vital that children talk about, review and remember what good nutrition is all about.

Begin your discussion with your student by talking about what good nutrition is and what makes up a healthy diet. First, a healthy diet consists of a varied diet—one that includes every kind of nutrient. Your student may have heard of the five basic food groups. This is simply a way of organizing food that helps us remember what nutrients each include. The five basic groups are: (1) vegetables, (2) fruits, (3) grains (bread, rice, cereal and pasta, both whole and refined), (4) dairy (milk, yogurt and cheese), and finally, (5) proteins (beef, poultry, fish, eggs and nuts).

Once your student begins to understand the basic food groups, she can look at the actual number of recommended servings.

Dairy .... 2-3 servings
Protein .... 2-3 servings
Vegetables .... 3-5 servings
Fruits ....2-4 servings
Grains .... 6-11 servings

Encourage your student to eat in a more healthful manner by allowing her to help you plan healthy meals. Developing menus (taking into account what nutrients are included) can be a great way for your student to get excited about nutrition. Encourage your student to try new fruits and vegetables. Mangoes, fresh pineapple, kale and different kinds of squash are all great sources of vitamins and delicious, too! If your student enjoys cooking, urge her to look up new ways of preparing these foods in healthy ways.

Another aspect of nutrition your student should explore is food labeling. For the past several decades, all packaged and processed food sold in the U.S. has had consistent nutrition labels. These labels help people compare the nutrients they need each day, with the nutritional value of the foods they eat.

Go to the supermarket with your student and look at similar products and compare their labels. Canned soup, for example: have your student look at the label on a basic cream of mushroom soup, and then the label on a company's "healthy" version of the same soup. What is changed? Less sodium? Less fat? What about the calories?

Your student can even explore the nutritional information of food at fast food and other restaurants. Encourage your student to look for "healthy" alternative meals at these restaurants. What is the best meal she can come up with at each? Eating out can be nutritious and delicious if we choose the right items.

Your student will feel better, smarter and more prepared to eat healthy foods if you discuss nutrition with her. It can be fun and educational.

Language Arts: Phone Skills

Cuffy calls the police when she is worried about Oliver. How much experience has your student had talking on the phone? Has your student ever had to make an emergency call? What has your student learned about other phone skills? Even in an age of texting, emailing, video chats, and other forms of communication, it's still important to develop good verbal phone skills.

Does your student know how to take accurate phone messages for other people? Talk with your student about what she should ask and write down. This information might include the name of the person who called, the time, and/or the reason for the call. If your student needs to leave a message for someone else when she places a call, remind her to leave all the same information. These skills will be important throughout your student's life, whether for social calls, business calls, making appointments, calling various companies, etc. Becoming comfortable with talking on the phone in a clear, pleasant voice is still a valuable skill!

Help your student review any emergency numbers she may need to call. Many cities have one single emergency number—911. Other smaller towns have specific numbers for the police, fire, and poison control. Your student may or may not have a cell phone where these numbers can be stored, but it's important to review basic emergency numbers either way.

Consider posting important numbers somewhere in your home, even if all family members have cell phones. You might want to post all family phone numbers, a close relative and/or neighbor's number, emergency numbers, and even your home address. If there is a fire or someone gets hurt, for example, the emergency responder would want to know your address. Sometimes during times of panic, children can't remember their own address or phone number.

You can help your student practice all of these skills and more by setting up simple scenarios, or "practice sessions."

Language Arts: Writing and Discussion Question

Why do you think Marleen was behaving so badly at the circus? What do you think may have caused her rude, demanding behavior? Write about it.

Language Arts: Vocabulary

apprehension Fear.

portal A door, gate or entrance.

baleful Very evil or harmful.

scrutiny A close examination, a careful inspection.

howdah A seat for persons riding on the back of an elephant or camel, usually equipped with handrails.

Life Skills: Dealing With Difficult People

Poor Oliver! His wonderful trip to the circus is nearly ruined by a mean, selfish little girl named Marleen. Has your student ever dealt with a person like Marleen? Someone who is just not satisfied? Someone who is rude and disruptive? Of course. Everyone has faced people like Marleen. Learning to deal effectively with difficult people is an important and challenging life skill.

Sometimes it helps to try to appease difficult people. For example, if Oliver had known Marleen, he might have shared his cotton candy with the little girl—even though her behavior was rude. Knowing how to compromise and be kind is important when you deal with people who are demanding.

But Oliver decides on a different, equally effective tactic. He simply removes himself from the situation. Instead of being rude back, or yelling, making faces or other immature and mean reactions, Oliver simply found himself a different seat. Knowing when to ignore a person can help you avoid being angry and starting a fight. Talk with your student about other ways she can deal with difficult people.

Chapter 6—Saturday Six

Teacher Summary

The members of the I.S.A.A.C. decide, after Oliver's incident at the circus, that their adventures from now on will be as a group. Their first Saturday adopting the new plan takes them to the Central Park Lake. Mona packs a delicious lunch and the four children rent a rowboat. Unfortunately, Randy falls in the water and the rest of the afternoon is spent trying to get home and conceal the wet evidence from Cuffy.

Later on that night, Rush checks the furnace. He accidentally leaves the door open and the house fills with coal gas. Severe tragedy could have occurred, but Isaac, the dog, smelled the gas and alerted everyone in the house. The Melendys are safe.

What we will cover in this chapter:

Science: Algae
Science: Water Pollution
Science: Safety - Carbon Monoxide
Language Arts: Shakespeare's Plays*
Language Arts: Developing Consistent Characters
Language Arts: Writing and Discussion Question
Language Arts: Vocabulary

Science: Algae

Although our author doesn't describe the Central Park Lake as "green with algae," Enright does use words such as "dark, thick green." That lake almost certainly had algae surrounding the edge of it and floating through its little ripples. Algae is a fascinating life form your student can study and learn about!

Algae [AL jee] are small living organisms that live in all oceans, lakes, rivers, ponds and even mud. Explain to your student that there are all types of algae. Some algae have only one cell, and require a microscope to see them. Others have many cells and are quite large (like seaweed).

Ask your student why she thinks algae look green? It might help to talk about photosynthesis and the leaves on trees and plants. Algae look green for the same reason—chlorophyll. Chlorophyll is the green coloring in plants and is their food source—made up of sugars. All algae contain chlorophyll.

There are several kinds of algae: blue-green algae, brown algae, green algae and even red algae (which is found in subtropical areas where coral is found).

Algae can grow too rapidly in certain ponds and lakes and become thick. As it grows larger and larger, it requires more and more oxygen from the water. If algae grows too much, it can kill fish and other living organisms. If kept in the proper balance, however, algae can provide food for fish and animals. It can also help purify the air and water through photosynthesis.

If you are able, try to locate a little bit of algae and let your student look at it (look at it through a magnifying glass, too). Hold it in your fingers. What can you both see? Try to get algae from a few different locations. What is different about each sample? If you have access to a microscope, put some algae on a slide and look at the amazing forms in the drop of water!

Science: Water Pollution

Randy thinks she sees something in the water—a shell, or maybe an old tin can. Unfortunately, many things can be found in our waterways, lakes and oceans. Water pollution is a serious problem in today's world. Talk with your student about water pollution and ways we can keep from contributing to it.

Water pollution happens when water is contaminated by substances such as human/animal waste, chemicals, metals and oils. Polluted water can be deceiving. Even when it looks clean, it can still contain dangerous, life-threatening materials, germs and chemicals. Governments all over the world, including the United States, have spent billions of dollars working on water pollution research and education.

Remind your student of the four main sources of water pollution: (1) industrial wastes, (2) sewage, (3) agricultural wastes and (4) plastics.

Industrial wastes include chemicals, oil, fuel, etc., that are released from factories and businesses into the water systems. **Sewage** includes the water we flush from our toilets and the water used for laundering and bathing. Globally, about 80% of wastewater flows mostly untreated into oceans and waterways. **Agricultural waste** occurs when melted snow and rain wash the chemicals used in farming away from the fields and into the waterways. And finally, if your student did the pollution lesson in Chapter 5 of *Thomas Edison* earlier in this volume, she'll remember that **discarded plastics** are polluting our oceans and harming marine wildlife.

Water pollution can cause death and disease among people and animals. It also can cause foul odors and floating debris that make the waters ugly and unpleasant. Just like Randy thought she might see a tin can, people find old clothes, soda cans, plastic bags and bottles, and more every day on America's beaches. Littering is a terrible act. Not only does it make our water sources poor looking, but many kinds of litter can choke, entrap and kill fish, dolphins, seals and many other creatures.

If your student is interested (and she can keep her nose pinched shut!), most sewage and water treatment plants offer tours. Your student can learn firsthand what goes into keeping her water clean. You may also wish to locate a few books on the topic, or look online for information about drinking water and how it is made safe.

Science: Safety—Carbon Monoxide

Poor Rush! He thought he was supposed to leave the furnace door open, but unfortunately, he nearly caused a very serious accident by doing so. Throughout the end of this chapter, the Melendys refer to the poisonous gas as "coal gas." Explain to your student, that we now know this is a dangerous gaseous mixture of hydrogen, methane, and carbon monoxide. Carbon monoxide is colorless, tasteless and odorless. It is also potentially fatal.

Teacher's Note: The Melendys smelled the coal gas. Because carbon monoxide is odorless, they probably smelled the bits of burning coal.

Carbon monoxide (chemical formula is CO) is dangerous because it is not easily detected by people. People have often died of CO poisoning during their sleep, without ever realizing they are being poisoned. If people are not asleep, they may feel many of the symptoms Rush and the kids experienced—light-headedness, headaches, hunger and even tunnel vision. This last symptom may account for the odd "dream-like" sequences Rush and Randy thought they saw.

To be safe, it's important (and easy!) to install CO detectors in homes. We now know that just a smoke detector isn't enough. CO detectors are your best bet to fight against this invisible enemy. Look with your student at CO detectors in any discount or hardware store. Find one that is within the right price range and let your student install it. If you already have CO detectors in your home, show them to your student and explain how they work. Learning about the dangers of CO, the symptoms it causes and ways to alert yourself, all help keep you safe and happy!

Language Arts: Shakespeare's Plays*

The Melendy children are intelligent and literate children. They frequently use advanced vocabulary words in their everyday speech. They know about science and the arts, as well as history. Mona, in particular, is well versed in Shakespeare. Your student has undoubtedly noticed many references to the Bard and his writings throughout our story.

William Shakespeare

Here again, in chapter 6, we see Mona quoting lines from *Macbeth*. Your student may have already learned some things about William Shakespeare and his writings. This topic and his plays are far too broad for any one lesson, but it is recommended that you explore at least one of his plays with your student.

Shakespeare wrote some of the most haunting, beautiful and memorable works in literary history. Your student should know that his plays fall into three categories: comedies, tragedies and histories. Try to locate more simple versions of these works, if your student is younger. If she is ready, he may wish to tackle portions of the original. If she finds it difficult, some excellent and helpful books are: *Tales from Shakespeare* by Charles and Mary Lamb (classic retellings); *Tales from Shakespeare* by Marcia Williams (in comic format); and *No Fear Shakespeare* (this series has the original words on one page and the "plain English" version on the opposite page).

Reading and learning Shakespeare can enrich and deepen your student's life, as well as her education.

Language Arts: Developing Consistent Characters

Your student can learn a great deal about writing fiction by reading great authors. Elizabeth Enright, our author for this study, is certainly great. One of her best skills is her ability to create deep, rounded, consistent characters.

Talk with your student about what we mean when we say "round characters." A flat character is a one-dimensional character. We see that person in one scene, perhaps, doing one action. For example, in *The Saturdays* a flat character would be the policeman who helped Oliver find his way home. We hardly know anything about this man except a general description. Every story includes some flat characters, but an author never wants all of her characters to be this thin.

Enright uses excellent descriptions and situations to help create consistent characters. We know all about Mona, don't we? We feel like Rush is a good friend. Ask your student to list the names of the four children on a piece of paper. Now, encourage her to list attributes, likes and dislikes, activities he/she enjoys, etc., about each of the children. Her list might look something like this:

Mona: the oldest (13), thick, blond hair (was long, got it cut), dramatic, loves Shakespeare, wants to be an actress, enjoys getting dressed up and feeling beautiful, reads a lot

Rush: age 12, curly, dark hair, a little bit of a tease, loves music and playing the piano, has a dog named Isaac, wants to be a great pianist and an engineer when he gets older

Miranda: age 10 1/2, curly, brown hair, loves ballet, likes to draw and paint, will try anything—very adventurous, enjoys hearing a good story, fiercely loyal

Oliver: youngest, age 6, mature for his age, calm, quiet, very industrious, enjoys art work, wants to be a train engineer, loves the circus, finds joy in small things, doesn't complain very often

Enright is a master at creating great characters. We aren't surprised when, in chapter 6, Mona breaks into quotations from *Macbeth*. We know that's just Mona. And we aren't surprised at Randy, either, when she gets a little distracted daydreaming and falls into the lake.

Encourage your student to work on creating round characters in her stories through plot and description. Even short stories can have excellent characters if they are given enough to do and we are told enough about them.

Language Arts: Writing and Discussion Question

We never find out what the older man is doing, rowing furiously around in the lake. What do you think he was doing? Write about it.

Language Arts: Vocabulary

campaign A military course of action.

adroitly Ingenious, clever, using one's mind.

laboriously With great effort.

teeming Full of, alive with.

vanquished Removed forever, eliminated.

Chapter 7—Saturday Seven

Teacher Summary

Unfortunately, after the furnace incident, Father decides the Melendy family needs a new oil furnace—one that won't have the same problems and won't cause coal gas poisoning. Father tells everyone how much money the new furnace will cost. They won't be able to afford their country home this year, and will have to stay in the city. The children are disappointed, but they decide to make the best of it.

Later on, Mrs. Oliphant calls up and invites the children for tea at the zoo. While at tea, Randy slips to Mrs. Oliphant that they don't have much money and they can't go to the country all summer. The old woman quickly offers up an idea. She owns a lighthouse at the shore and would love for all the Melendys to come and stay with her. The children are thrilled and quickly go home to ask their father.

What we will cover in this chapter:

Social Studies: Geography - Venice, Italy*
Social Studies: History - 1920s in the United States
Science: How Your Body Keeps Cool
Science: Bird Songs
Science: Heat and Absorption
Language Arts: Henry Wadsworth Longfellow's "The Song of Hiawatha"
Language Arts: Writing and Discussion Question
Language Arts: Vocabulary
Life Skills: Dealing with Embarrassment

Social Studies: Geography - Venice, Italy*

Mona admires Mrs. Oliphant's bracelet, and the old woman tells her it came from Venice. Did your student study *Papa Piccolo* in FIAR Vol. 1? If you have this book available, take a look at it again to remind her about this famous city. Then locate Venice on a map with your student. It is found on the northern shores of the Adriatic Sea, just off the mainland of Italy. Venice is a highly unusual city. Explain to your student that most of Venice (part of the city does lay on the mainland) consists of tiny islands—nearly 120! And instead of streets, Venice has canals of water. People don't drive through town in cars. They float through town in small boats!

Unfortunately, because of this odd water aspect, Venice has been threatened by many floods. Today, there is a great effort being made to help restore the beautiful buildings and artwork which fill Venice and make it the cultural center it is.

Share with your student a few key points of interest they might find in Venice. For example, the city holds an annual regatta. This is a race made up of gondolas—long, narrow boats steered by one man with a pole or an oar.

In the city's center winds the Grand Canal. This is the most famous waterway in Venice. Both sides of the canal are lined with marble and stone palaces built between the 1100s and 1800s!

Although Venice was established as a city of trade and commerce, today its greatest source of economic activity is tourism. Up to 20 million tourists flock to Venice each year.

Your student may wish to study gondolas, gondoliers (the men who steer the great boats), canals, Eastern Italy and more. Venice is certainly an unusual and fascinating city!

Social Studies: History - 1920s in the United States

Randy and Cuffy discuss 1920s fashion, and like many children, Randy expresses disbelief at how different things were long ago. The 1920s was an exciting and pivotal time for Americans. This chapter offers you an excellent opportunity to explore the 1920s more with your student.

First, talk with your student about two common nicknames for the 1920s: the Jazz Age and the Roaring Twenties. What does your student think of when she hears these descriptions? The 1920s in the United States were certainly colorful, dynamic years. World War I had finally ended (1914-1918) and people didn't want to think about death, turmoil or struggle anymore. They wanted to concentrate on having fun, enjoying life and keeping things light. It was a restless time in America. People were anxious to try frivolous, crazy things.

This focus brought about many, many changes. Many people looked on the changes as a breakdown in morality. Americans were wearing more revealing clothing, dancing in new ways, drinking illegal liquor and more. But other things changed which weren't so controversial.

Entertainment, for example, was revolutionized in the 1920s through the birth of radio. Radio programs like *Amos 'n' Andy* and *The Dodge Victory Hour* were wildly successful. These types of programs were also the first that sold advertising spots during their broadcasts. Radio commercials were a new fad, and very effective. Listeners quickly became consumers and the economy boomed. Other new changes in entertainment included motion pictures. Silent movies were big business. Children and adults enjoyed going to the movies and seeing their favorite stars—Charlie Chaplin, Greta Garbo and Will Rogers.

Sports was also big business during the 1920s. Baseball, the great American pastime, was more popular than ever before. Top athletes, such as Babe Ruth, drew thousands of fans to the games.

You can hear some of the early radio programs (such as *Amos 'n' Andy*) online. If you are able, locate a few and let your student listen to the entertainment of the 1920s. You might want to view a silent movie, as well. Seeing the movement and reading the action may be very foreign to your student. It is an unusual type of movie and your student will find it interesting and informative.

If your student enjoys music and literature, the 1920s were alive with new sounds and dramatic writings. Authors such as F. Scott Fitzgerald and Ernest Hemingway began writing during the 1920s and their books reveal much of the abandonment and freedom the decade encouraged. George and Ira Gershwin were perhaps the most famous composers during the 1920s. Their music featured many elements of jazz. A wonderful example of 1920s music is George Gershwin's composition, *Rhapsody in Blue*. Your student will enjoy this piece!

The 1920s were carefree years, but Americans paid for their frivolity. In 1929 the stock market crashed and the Great Depression began. Throughout the years prior, Americans had enjoyed a false sense of prosperity. They began to pay the price for that throughout the 1930s.

If your student is interested in learning more about the 1920s, explore any of the suggestions listed above in music, movies, or even sports footage. Your student may also wish to look further at the administration of President Calvin Coolidge and the effects of World War I (Chapter 17 of *Thomas Edison*, earlier in this volume, contains a lesson on Herbert Hoover that includes Calvin Coolidge).

Science: How Your Body Keeps Cool

Facing a summer spent in the city, Rush and his siblings look at options they have to keep cool and have fun. Rush remembers the hose. They can always hose off to stay cool. Pose this question to your student, "Why does hosing off with water keep your body cool?" The answer is a fascinating part of science and links to the body's own production of moisture—sweat. Explore this topic further with your student.

When you are hot in the summertime, hosing off with water is an excellent way of keeping cool. But why? As the water bathes the skin, the immediate relief is the cool temperature of the water. But, as the water sits on the skin, it slowly evaporates. As it evaporates, each small drop of water draws a small amount of heat from the body. This is what actually cools you down—evaporation.

When you get hot, and you don't have a hose handy, your body doesn't mind. We have a built-in "evaporation cooling system" in our bodies: sweat. Body temperature is controlled by your brain in a region called the hypothalamus. When you get too hot, the hypothalamus tells your body to start cooling off. It tells your sweat glands to start producing extra moisture. As the sweat dries, it draws heat from the body and cools you off!

Explain to your student that there are two kinds of sweat, or perspiration: insensible and sensible perspiration. Our bodies are always producing sweat, even during cool weather. However, the sweat is so small it evaporates nearly immediately. You don't even notice, and that is why we call it insensible. When you are very hot, or exercising, however, your body produces more sweat to keep you cool. You may feel it running down your forehead or back. This is known as sensible perspiration.

Does your student believe that she is always sweating? Why not prove it through a simple experiment. Pick a time when your student is cool and comfortable. Take a clear plastic bag and place it over your student's hand. Now tie off the bag around your student's wrist by using clear tape or a rubber band (not too tight!). Wait 15 minutes. What does your student see? Her body has been giving off moisture constantly and the sweat has begun to bead on the inside of the bag!

Teacher's Note: If you have use of a microscope, you can continue this experiment by taking some of the moisture off the inside of the bag and placing it on a slide. Dye the sweat with a small drop of red food coloring, and look at it under the microscope. Your student will be able to see the sodium chloride (salt) crystals in her own sweat. This is why sweat often tastes salty!

Another easy experiment your student can conduct will show her how evaporation cools the skin. Rubbing alcohol evaporates faster than water, so you will need some alcohol and a cotton ball for this experiment. Have your student put some alcohol on the cotton and then swab the back of her hand. Does the area feel cooler or warmer? Cooler, because the alcohol is drawing warmth as it evaporates.

Evaporation and perspiration are important aspects of our bodies and how they keep us comfortable and healthy! Rush had the right idea!

Science: Bird Songs

Randy loves the call of mourning doves. Mona likes the bobwhite's song. Does your student know and recognize different bird songs? Each and every species has a special way of communicating, and each is unique.

Your student can have great fun bird watching and trying to learn different birds by their calls. Encourage your student to try her hand at describing or copying different birds' calls. There are also excellent resources available for your student to look at which can help her learn what to look for and listen to. Look for birdwatching books that have built-in audio components, such as *The Backyard Birdsong Guide* by Donald Kroodsma. You can also use a free app such as the Merlin Bird ID app from Cornell University to help you identify birds and hear their songs.

Birdwatching is a popular pastime. Armed with a pair of binoculars, a simple bird identification book, and a sketchbook, your student can have a great time trying to find new birds and identifying familiar ones.

Science: Heat and Absorption

The main conflict in chapter 7 is where the children will have to spend the summer. Your student may find this strange. Not many families anymore have summer homes and leave the city for three long months each year. Does your student know that it is actually warmer in the city than it is in the country?

Cities are lined with buildings. They are filled with paved streets. They have busy cars, trains and busses that produce heat and fumes. As the summer sun beats down, the heat is absorbed by each of these things. The buildings, sidewalks and pavements become hot and radiate that heat back into the air. The glass on skyscrapers, buildings and houses reflects the heat back onto the pavements, stone and brick. All of these things trap and increase heat levels around you.

In the country, however, there is little of these things. The heat is absorbed by the ground, but not nearly as much as concrete or asphalt. There aren't as many buildings so the wind can move freely and that helps you keep cool. And trees are able to grow larger so the shade can be more plentiful in the country.

Remind your student that the Melendys did not have central air conditioning. For them, going to the country was a significant way of relaxing, having fun and staying cool in the summer.

If your student wants to see these ideas firsthand, have her step onto a patio or sidewalk on a hot day. Ouch! Her feet get hot quickly, don't they? Now step onto the grass. Much cooler, isn't it? We don't usually think about it, but the Melendys are right. The country is much cooler than the city.

Language Arts: Henry Wadsworth Longfellow's "The Song of Hiawatha"

Oliver enjoys playing make believe, and Rush finds him pretending to be a Native American. Rush calls him "Hiawatha." You can share with your student that years ago, people would have known that Rush was referring to a poem by Henry Wadsworth Longfellow.

The famous American poet named Henry Wadsworth Longellow lived during the 19th century (1807-1882). He wrote many wonderful poems including "The Children's Hour," "The Village Blacksmith" and "Paul Revere's Ride" (which is a book selection in FIAR Vol. 3). He also wrote much longer poems, called epic poems, the most famous of which is "The Song of Hiawatha."

In "The Song of Hiawatha," Longfellow traces the childhood and life of a young Native American boy named Hiawatha. Hiawatha is a hero in the poem, and his life is full of joyful as well as tragic times.

Although this poem is very long, an excellent short section has been illustrated by Susan Jeffers in a picture book called simply, *Hiawatha*. This book is a short excerpt of the poem, covering Hiawatha's childhood. Jeffers' pictures are created by fine-line pen and ink, with dye overlays. Your student may remember Jeffers' work from *Stopping By Woods on a Snowy Evening*, FIAR Vol. 1.

Language Arts: Writing and Discussion Question

Randy got embarrassed during tea with Mrs. Oliphant. She realized after she finished talking, that she hadn't really thought about what she was saying. Write about a time when you were embarrassed. What did you do?

Language Arts: Vocabulary

zeal Eager, earnest, with a lot of enthusiasm.

averted To keep from happening, to stop.

wigwam A hut used by Native Americans for housing; animal skins or bark placed over poles.

monopolizing To get exclusive control all for oneself.

pauper A poor person.

gondola A long, narrow boat used in Venice.

Life Skills: Dealing with Embarrassment

Randy, like many of us, tends to speak before she thinks. When she is talking freely with Mrs. Oliphant, she goes into detail about the Melendy's new furnace and their lack of extra money. Randy is immediately embarrassed when she realizes what she said, and blushes profusely.

Everyone gets embarrassed sometimes. Saying the wrong thing, making a mistake, or being clumsy are all a part of being human. Talk with your student about what she does to deal with embarrassment. Sometimes making light of a situation, telling a joke, etc., helps us to feel better. When we get embarrassed, however, sometimes we get flustered and it takes someone else, like Mona, to help us out of the awkward moment.

Encourage your student to look for ways to help her friends feel better when she sees them embarrassed. Never make fun of someone, particularly when they are already self-conscious. Instead, make them feel better by relating a time when you did something similar. Or just change the subject.

Being embarrassed is a part of life. But we can make it more bearable for ourselves and others by learning that the moment won't last forever.

Chapter 8—Saturday Eight

Teacher Summary

We've reached the end of our story. The Melendys take Mrs. Oliphant's offer and go to stay with her in the lighthouse all summer long. From the moment they arrive, the children know they will have a wonderful time. Even Isaac enjoys swimming in the surf when he finally is brave enough to try it.

The children decide to suspend their I.S.A.A.C. meetings and outings until the following school year. They all agree it was a success, and thank Randy for thinking of it. The children are happy and we leave them, excited to see what their summer brings.

What we will cover in this chapter:

Social Studies: History - WWII Before America Was Involved*
Science: Tide Pools and Sea Life
Language Arts: Listing Descriptions - Enright's Favorite Tool
Language Arts: Writing and Discussion Question
Language Arts: Vocabulary

Social Studies: History - WWII Before America Was Involved*

Your student may have noticed small references to World War II in our story. We read Mr. Melendy's thoughts back in chapter 2 where he says, "It's the people who make the safety on this earth as well as the trouble, unfortunately." We hear Cuffy admonishing Mona to think of the people in Europe, dealing with bombs, air raids and hunger (chapter 4). And here in chapter 8, we see Randy asking Cuffy what it was like when the world was peaceful. Many references, but no direct effects.

Discuss with your student, for a moment, the time before America was involved with World War II. We often think of the Second World War as something that always included American troops and American lives. It didn't, however, for nearly three years!

Draw your student's attention to the copyright date of our story—1941. Enright wrote her story present tense, and we can assume our characters are living and breathing in the summer of that year. Remind your student that the United States didn't enter WWII officially until the attack on Pearl Harbor, on December 7, 1941. Later on in the school year, the Melendy children would feel the real effects of WWII.

If your student enjoyed *The Saturdays*, she should be aware that there are three more books written about the Melendy children and their escapades: *The Four-Story Mistake*, *Then There Were Five*, and

Spiderweb for Two: A Melendy Maze. The Four-Story Mistake and *Then There Were Five* deal directly with World War II. You find out that Mr. Melendy works for the government and his job takes him away from his family a great deal. Rush, Randy and the other children work diligently gathering scrap metal for the soldiers, and buying war bonds.

Science: Tide Pools and Sea Life

Randy enjoys spending time looking at all the small creatures and plants that live in a tidal pool she finds. She sees crabs, small fish, barnacles, seaweed and more. What does your student know about tide pools and marine life?

A tide pool is a pool of water left when the tide is out. It is like the ocean, but in miniature. It is a specific habitat for certain plants and animals. Every creature in a tide pool, just like in other areas of nature, works together to survive. Each plays a special role.

Many kinds of plants live in tide pools, from tiny microscopic algae to large leafy seaweed. These plants live by capturing energy from the sun (photosynthesis) and gathering nutrients from the surrounding waters. In turn, some creatures in the tide pools feast on the plants as well—creatures like limpets and periwinkles (members of the snail family). Other creatures like crabs and prawns eat some of the plants and some of the smaller animals.

Tide pools are just like Randy observed—small jungles of wonderful wildlife. If your student is interested in learning more about tide pools, search online for information or videos, or locate a book on the subject at your local library.

Language Arts: Listing Descriptions - Enright's Favorite Tool

Throughout our study, your student has learned that Elizabeth Enright is a very good writer! Her use of description and details is stunning. Perhaps the single most distinctive tool Enright uses in her writing is her description lists. All through our story, Enright will describe a person or place with phrase after phrase of specific details. Look at this passage with your student, for example.

"All over the house suitcases gaped open hungrily and two ancient trunks were slowly being fed, bit by bit: delicious morsels such as Oliver's overalls, Mona's party dress, assorted bathing suits, six pairs of sneakers, Beethoven's Sonatas, the Milk of Magnesia, the iodine, three rolls of adhesive tape, litters of socks and scores of other things."

There are many similar lists all through *The Saturdays*. Enright lets us know a lot about the Melendys, simply by telling us what they pack, where they like to go, and what their house is filled with. Look back at some other passages with your student. Here are just a few examples:

Chapter 5: Oliver's description of the circus

Chapter 6: The description of Rush's bedroom

Chapter 7: The description of all the things found at the house in the valley

Encourage your student to employ this technique in a short story or essay. Giving your readers specific lists of details helps them picture exactly what you are trying to convey. Enright is a master at this technique!

Language Arts: Writing and Discussion Question

What would you like best about living in Mrs. Oliphant's lighthouse? Write about it.

Language Arts: Vocabulary

surreptitiously Acting with stealth, in secret.

declension A grammar device, giving different endings to nouns and other words appropriate to number, gender, etc.

pongee A kind of soft silk, generally left in its natural color state (a soft yellow), made from thread obtained from silkworm cocoons found in China.

lapis lazuli A deep-blue, opaque, semi-precious stone used for ornament and jewelry.

melancholy A deep sadness.

Teacher's Notes

Use this page to jot down relevant info you've found for this *Five in a Row* chapter book, including favorite lessons, go-along resources, field trips, and family memories.

THE SATURDAYS

Dates studied:

Student:

Favorite Lesson Topics:

Social Studies:

Science:

Language Arts:

Fine Arts:

Life Skills:

Relevant Library Resources: Books, DVDs, Audio Books

Websites or Video Links:

Related Field Trip Opportunities:

Favorite Quote or Memory During Study:

The Saturdays - Directions for Vocabulary Words

Language Arts: **Vocabulary Sorting Exercise**

In some previous FIAR chapter book units, vocabulary words have been made into crossword puzzles for you to complete. *The Saturdays* contains so many wonderful vocabulary words that a crossword puzzle, or even several, is not the best method of learning these words.

For this unit, you will create a flashcard or small piece of paper for each vocabulary word. Write the word on the front of the piece of paper or flashcard and its definition on the back.

Once your vocabulary words for a chapter are written you will then begin a sorting exercise with them. You may choose to sort only the new words for each chapter or add new words to words from the previous chapter(s).

You'll need four pieces of 8.5" x 11" paper. On each you will write a category name on the top or bottom of the paper. There are four basic categories given, but you can also change the categories and resort your words into new categories of your own choosing. You can even resort the words with the same four categories (in this case you will move each word into a different category). Start with the four categories (words written at the top of the paper): **good**, **bad**, **soft**, and **hard**. You could change the categories to anything ... another set of four categories that would work for most words is: **easy**, **difficult**, **stationary**, and **moving**.

The categories are random words that require some thought and reasoning of each vocabulary word and its definition to decide a best fit. The "reasoning" required helps you think through the meaning of the word, which will help you remember the word. There are no right or wrong answers.

For example, sousing: dripping wet (a vocabulary word from chapter 1), could be categorized into the category—**bad** because you wouldn't want to be dripping wet, or, you could sort it into the category—**soft** because wet clothing gets droopy and soft. See example below.

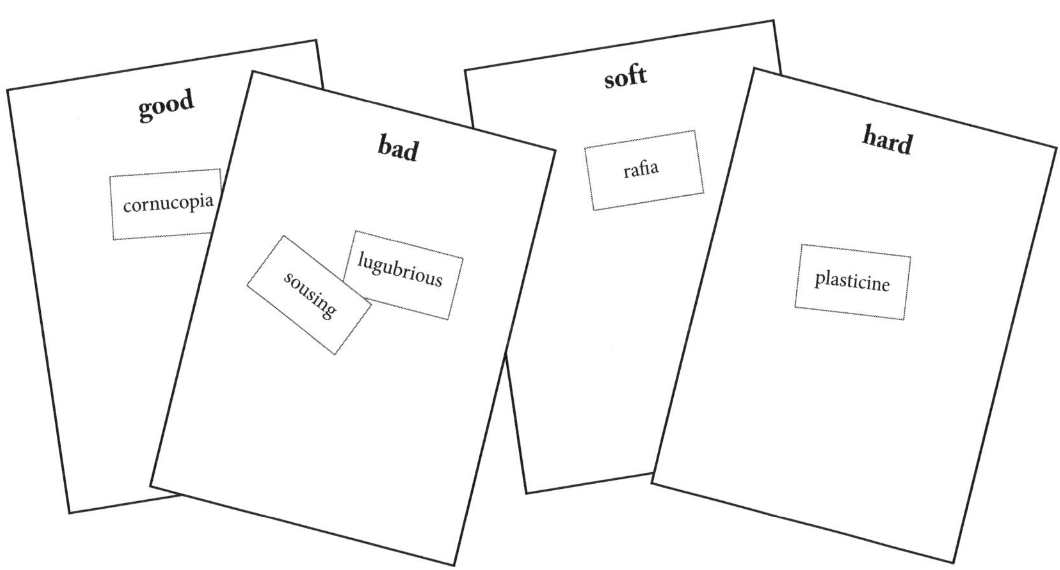

Name:

Date:

Fine Arts: **Biography - Who Am I?**

After doing the **Fine Arts: Music History - Bach** and/or the **Fine Arts: Music History - Tchaikovsky** lesson, research either Bach or Tchaikovsky online or read a book from the library about these famous composers.

Print and paste an image of Johann Sebastian Bach or Peter Ilyich Tchaikovsky into the frame. Write information gathered through your research into the lines below the frames.

Go-Along book recommendations include:

Becoming Bach by Tom Leonard
Johann Sebastian Bach by Mike Venezia
or
Tchaikovsky Discovers America by Esther Kalman
Tchaikovsky by Greta Cencetti
Peter Tchaikovsky by Mike Venezia

Name: ______________________________

Lived: ______________________________

Known for: ______________________________

Connections to story: ______________________________

Name:

Date:

Virtual
FIELD TRIP

Search online for "virtual tour of Paris, France," preview, and then have your student watch. Virtualfieldtrips.org has a fieldtrip titled "Highlights of Paris" (grades 6-9). Specific options you might search online and tour virtually include:

- The Lourve (ties in to Fine Arts: Galleries lesson in this chapter)
- The Eiffel Tower
- Cathédrale Nortre-Dame de Paris
- The Palace of Versailles

Take notes below of information you learn about Paris (or famous landmarks and architecture) while taking the virtual field trip. Print and paste a photo of something you found fascinating about Paris, France in the frame above.

Name:

Date:

Fine Arts: **Orchestras / Peter and the Wolf**

After doing the **Fine Arts: Orchestras** lesson and/or the **Fine Arts: *Peter and the Wolf* by Prokofiev** lesson, introduce your student virtually to a symphony orchestra and the symphonic fairy tale *Peter and the Wolf.*

Search "virtual introduction to orchestra" and "symphony performance of *Peter and the Wolf*" to find videos to watch. For example, the Springfield Symphony Orchestra has a series of videos on YouTube using Peter and the Wolf to introduce the orchestra. Within YouTube you can search, "Springfield Symphony Peter and the Wolf" to find six videos introducing you to the orchestra through Prokofiev's famous symphonic fairy tale. "Maestro Classics Peter and the Wolf" is also an excellent resource that can be found at your library or purchased online.

Print and paste a photo or illustration of your favorite instrument into the frame to the right (or draw it yourself).

Which instrument do you like the sound of the most?

____

Which instrument would you want to learn to play? Why?

____

____

Which instrument do you think best fits its character in *Peter and the Wolf*?

____

____

Name:

Date:

Language Arts: **Creative Writing - Employing New Words**

After doing the **Language Arts: Creative Writing - Employing New Words** lesson, write a short story, play or descriptive paragraph. Include five of the new vocabulary words you've learned during this unit. Use the open spaces below to write the five vocabulary words you've chosen to use in your story/paragraph, and then include them within your writing on the lines below.

Name:

Date:

Science: **Good Nutrition - Yogurt Parfait**

In the **Science: Good Nutrition** lesson, you learned that a varied and balanced diet includes many foods from the basic food groups.

Below you'll find a recipe for granola with many different options that you can mix or match based on your personal preference or your nutritional needs. Typically a recipe is very specific and you wouldn't want to change it too much because it would change the outcome. Granola and yogurt parfaits are able to be created with a huge variety of ingredients and with many variations ... this makes them easy to create and healthy, too; they can include whole grains, nuts, protien-rich yogurt (dairy or non-dairy) and fruit!

Granola Recipe

2 cups oats
1 cup nuts of choice (optional: include an additional cup of oats if omitting nuts)
1/2 cup seeds (pepitas, sunflower)
1/4 cup oil (vegetable, olive, coconut—melted)
1/2 cup sweetener (honey, maple syrup)
1 tsp cinnamon (you can add additional spices to taste, like ginger, nutmeg, cloves, etc.)
1/2 tsp salt
1/2 cup dried fuit (raisons, cherries, cranberries, cut-up dried apricots, cut-up dates, etc.)

Optional: 2 Tbs hemp, chia, sesame seeds

Mix everything except the dried fruit and place on a parchment paper-lined baking sheet. Spread evenly and bake for 20-30 minutes at 300° F. (Granola can burn easily, so check it during baking and stir if needed.) Allow to cool, stirring a few times to break up large chunks. Add dried fruit. Store in an airtight container or resealable bag.

Yogurt Parfait Recipe

1/2 - 3/4 cup yogurt (whole milk, reduced-fat, non-dairy, sweetened, or unsweetened)
1/2 cup fruit (sliced strawberries, blueberries, raspberries, blackberries, etc.)
1/4 cup granola

Simply layer yogurt, fruit and granola in several layers ... enjoy!

Optional: 1 tsp of fruit jam, honey or maple syrup added if using plain yogurt to add a bit of sweetness. Just add it to the yogurt and stir it in before layering the yogurt in the parfait.

Eat a yogurt parfait as a healthy breakfast, an afternoon snack or even as dessert!

The Saturdays - Chapter 6

Name:
Date:
Language Arts: **Biography - Who Am I?**

After doing the **Language Arts: Shakespeare's Plays** lesson, research William Shakespeare and learn more about this famous playwright.

Print and paste an image of William Shakespeare into the frame. Write information gathered through your research into the lines below.

Additional go-along book recommendations include:
Shakespeare's Seasons by Miriam Weiner
A Stage Full of Shakespeare Stories by Angela McAllister

Name: ______________________________

Lived: ______________________________

Known for: ______________________________

____

____

Connections to story: ______________________________

____

____

Name:

Date:

Virtual
FIELD TRIP

Search online for "virtual tour of Venice, Italy," preview, and then have your student watch.

Take notes below of information you learn about Venice (or famous landmarks and architecture) while taking the virtual field trip. Print and paste a photo of something you found fascinating about Venice, Italy in the frame to the right.

The Saturdays - Chapter 8

Name:

Date:

History: **WWII on the Homefront—1941**

To extend the **Social Studies: History - WWII Before America Was Involved** lesson, and learn more about life in America before and during the beginning of World War II, you can request go-along books from your library.

Go-along book recommendations include:

Rosie the Riveter: Women Working on the Home Front in WWII by Penny Colman

World War II for Kids: A History with 21 Activities by Richard Panchyk

Here are a few questions that you might find the answers to while reading additional books, or you could research online to find the answers. Write your answer to one or more questions neatly on lined paper. You can place it with this page or copy this page and attach it to the written answers for documentation.

1. Why did more women begin working outside the home during WWII?

2. What was a Victory Garden?

3a. Why did children (and adults) collect scrap metal?

3b. Read *Hanna's Cold Winter* by Trish Marx (a FIAR Vol. 4 selection). Then answer this question: Think about the townspeople's actions in *Hanna's Cold Winter* and those of American citizens who collected scrap for the war effort. How were their actions similar? How were they different?

Chapter Book

Sample **Lesson Planning Sheet**

Thomas A. Edison: Young Inventor has more suggested lessons per chapter than you will probably want to (or be able to) cover. The sample planning sheets below and on the following pages show ideas that *could* be chosen for the first two weeks of this study. You are free to choose any of the lesson ideas and keep track of your choices by noting them on the reproducible, blank Lesson Planning Sheet (following these pages). For more ideas on making the best use of your Five in a Row curriculum, be sure to read the *Tips and Advice for Five in a Row Chapter Book Studies* section as well as *How to Use Five in a Row Volume 6* earlier in this volume.

Week 1	Monday	Tuesday
Title: *Thomas A. Edison: Young Inventor* **Author:** Sue Guthridge	**Read Chapter 1 together, then:** **Social Studies** Great Lakes lesson <u>and</u> begin the map of Edison's life, using map at end of unit for both (Note: Make sure we have ingredients for Friday's cake)	**Social Studies** Erie Canal lesson, look at pictures online **Fine Arts** Listen to Erie Canal song online

Wednesday	Thursday	Friday
Science Explain (or review) the scientific method, using the activity sheet Fill out for Tom's egg "experiment" **Discussion Question:** Trying to improve something but making things worse, or it didn't work – has this ever happened to you?	**Read Chapter 2 together, then:** **Social Studies** Add to the map of Tom Edison's life **Science** Discuss pitch and waterproofing Go observe things around our yard that have been damaged by water/weather exposure, or would be if we didn't seal them	**Language Arts** Remember the weather the day Tom was born and then tell what the weather was like when [student] was born Tell other information about what happened that day Discuss 5 vocabulary words (read "parlor" description from *Farmer Boy*) and do activity sheet crossword puzzle Write a list of travel options, starting with ones already used, then adding possible ideas for the future **Fine Arts: Cooking** Make Tom's birthday cake! (Store overnight and frost it on Saturday)

Chapter Book

Sample **Lesson Planning Sheet: Week 2**

Week 2

Title:

Thomas A. Edison: Young Inventor

Author:

Sue Guthridge

Monday

Read Chapter 3 together, then:

(**Note:** freeze the block of ice on Sunday for experiment today, and buy an extra carton of eggs this week for Friday)

Social Studies/ Science

Discuss the history of ice skating and do activity sheet

Explain how ice skating works and regelation

Do ice skating experiment with block of ice

Watch a few famous figure skaters (or other ice sports) online while experiment is working

Tuesday

Science

Review/discuss hypothermia and frostbite (remember *The Boxcar Children* lesson from Vol. 5)

Review/discuss homogenized/ non-homogenized milk (remember *The Boxcar Children* lesson again)

Language Arts

Discuss 4 vocabulary words (see dew point lesson if more detail is needed)

Start reading aloud our abridged copy of *Hans Brinker* at lunch

Wednesday	Thursday	Friday
Life Skills Discuss how Tom might have prevented his accident, and obedience **Language Arts** Writing Exercise: Write the conversation Tom might have had with his parents after he got home (review how to use quotation marks, when to start a new paragraph, etc., if needed)	**Read Chapter 4 together, then:** **Fine Arts** Reread about the Edisons' home and then illustrate the chapter using the activity sheet	**Science** Discuss packing breakables Explain egg tossing experiment challenge (involve siblings) Decide whether to toss the eggs across the yard or to drop them off the deck into the grass Write hypothesis/results, etc., using the scientific method sheet Take videos of each toss!

Chapter Book Lesson Planning Sheet:

Week ___	Monday	Tuesday
Title: **Author:**		

Wednesday	Thursday	Friday

Index

Social Studies

Science

Language Arts

Title index

Author index

Fine Arts

Cooking

Music

Life Skills

Supplemental Book List

Thomas A. Edison: Young Inventor

The Erie Canal by Samuel Hopkins Adams
The Amazing Impossible Erie Canal by Cheryl Harness
Locks, Crocs & Skeeters: The Story of the Panama Canal by Nancy Winslow Parker
The Wind in the Willows by Kenneth Grahame
The Erie Canal by Peter Spier
Farmer Boy by Laura Ingalls Wilder
Hans Brinker, or The Silver Skates by Mary Mapes Dodge
Uncle Tom's Cabin by Harriet Beecher Stowe
If You Lived at the Time of the Civil War by Kay Moore
Sojourner Truth: Ain't I a Woman by Patricia C. and Fredrick McKissack
The Hound of the Baskervilles by Sir Arthur Conan Doyle
Gutenberg by Leonard Everette Fischer
Why There's Antifreeze in Your Toothpaste: The Chemistry of Household Ingredients by Simon Quellen Field
Samuel Morse, That's Who!: The Story of the Telegraph and Morse Code by Tracy Nelson Maurer
Song for a Whale by Lynne Kelly

Sarah, Plain and Tall

Little House on the Prairie by Laura Ingalls Wilder
Alice's Adventures in Wonderland by Lewis Carroll

Homer Price

The Iliad by Homer
The Odyssey by Homer
Nancy Drew mysteries by Carolyn Keene
Hardy Boys mysteries by Franklin W. Dixon
The Big Yellow Drawing Book: A Workbook Emphasizing the Basic Principles of Learning, Teaching, and Drawing Through Cartooning by Dan, Marion and Hugh O'Neill
Whatever Happened to Penny Candy? by Richard J. Maybury
Too Many Tamales by Gary Soto
Fireworks, Picnics and Flags by James Cross Giblin
Tales From The Odyssey by Mary Pope Osborne
Argos: The Story of Odysseus as Told by His Loyal Dog by Ralph Hardy
An Egg Is Quiet by Diana Hutts Aston

The Saturdays

Tchaikovsky Discovers America by Esther Kalman
Tales From Shakespeare by Charles and Mary Lamb
Tales From Shakespeare by Marcia Williams
No Fear Shakespeare
The Backyard Birdsong Guide by Donald Kroodsma
Hiawatha by Susan Jeffers
The Four-Story Mistake by Elizabeth Enright
Then There Were Five by Elizabeth Enright
Spiderweb for Two: A Melendy Maze by Elizabeth Enright
Becoming Bach by Tom Leonard
Johann Sebastian Bach by Mike Venezia
Tchaikovsky by Greta Cencetti
Peter Tchaikovsky by Mike Venezia
Shakespeare's Seasons by Miriam Weiner
A Stage Full of Shakespeare's Stories by Angela McAllister
Rosie the Riveter: Women Working on the Homefront in WWII by Penny Colman
World War II for Kids: A History with 21 Activities by Richard Panchyk

Scope of Topics

Thomas A. Edison: Young Inventor

History

Erie Canal
Parlors
Ice skating
American railroad
- Harvey
- Pullman

President Fillmore
President Taylor
Commodore Perry
One-room schoolhouse
Samuel Morse
Telegraph
Guglielmo Marconi
Wireless communication
Steam locomotives
Canada
Underground Railroad
President Buchanan
President Polk
President Lincoln
Pony Express
Railway post office system
Postal service
Golden spike
Johannes Gutenberg
Printing press
Wild West shows
President Hoover
President Coolidge
Great Depression
Skating sports

Geography

Great Lakes
- Lake Superior
- Lake Michigan
- Lake Huron
- Lake Erie
- Lake Ontario

Canada

Career Path

Entrepreneur
News editor
Journalist
Internship

Science

Incubating eggs
Scientific method
Pitch
Speed of light
Speed of sound
Ice skating
Dew point
Frost
Health and saftey
Hypothermia
Frostbite
Non-homogenized milk
Inventing packaging
Pollution
Speed
Tree identification
Measuring distance
Branches of science
Warning symbols
Laboratories
Periodic table of elements
Mecury
Economics
- Market prices

Compound interest
Phosphorus
Human anatomy
  Ear
Electricity
Light bulb
Natural resources
Forms of energy

Language Arts
Writing and discussion questions (every chapter)
Descriptive word choices
Making lists
Autobiography
Biography
Famous sayings
Penmanship
Simile
Metaphor
Sherlock Holmes
Sir Arthur Conan Doyle
Styles of writing
  Personal letter
  Fiction
  News report
Subscriptions
American Sign Language
Idioms

Vocabulary Words
pitch
parlor
light year
biography
autobiography
regelation
dew point
hypothermia
frostbite
cinnabar
entrepreneur

Fine Arts
Music
Cooking
Colored pencils
Color blending
Drawing illustrations
Advertising
Drama
Making your own newspaper
Making your own printing block
Paper dolls
Panoramas
Moving pictures
Movie making

Life Skills
Listening
Obedience
First times
Observation
Being neighborly
Focused attention
Assumptions
Discipline
Being helpful
Organizing your study
Problem solving
Communicating with the deaf
Speaking words of praise
Bravery

Sarah, Plain and Tall

Geography
Maine
Eastern United States
Prairie
North Atlantic sea coast

Science
Human development
Rocks
  Igneous
  Metamorphic

Sedimentary
Fog
Advection
Frontal
Radiation
Upslope
Seals
Whales
Windbreak
Hawk
Rock tumbler
Seashell
Univalve
Bivalve
Buzzard
Vulture
Sand
Dunes
Water sources
Squall

Language Arts

Writing and discussion questions (every chapter)
Letter writing
Postscript
R.S.V.P.
Creative writing
Writing a personal introduction
Cliché
Symbolism
Learning to infer
Plot essentials
Tension
Alliteration
Lewis Carroll
Alice's Adventures in Wonderland
Newbery Medal
Caldecott Medal
Hyperbole
Character compilation
Conclusions

Vocabulary Words

gestation
igneous
metamorphic
sedimentary
symbol
R.S.V.P.
cliché
advection fog
frontal fog
radiation fog
upslope fog
holding capacity
blubber
blow hole
windbreak
bird of prey
talons
falconry
univalve
bivalve
dune
mica
silica
alliteration
Newbery Medal
hyperbole
squall
front
conclusion

Fine Arts

Drawing composition
Illustrating envelopes
Colors of the sea
Thomas Hart Benton
Drawing

Life Skills

Memories
Family activities
Wanting to be liked
Personal traits
Grieving
Making others smile

Homer Price

History
Homer
The Iliad
The Odyssey
Motels of the past
Television
Radio
Music
Telephone operators
Red Cross
County fairs
Political parties
Women's Suffrage

Geography
Highways and roads of America

Career Path
Law enforcement
Landscape architect

Science
Simple machines
- Pulley

Chromium
Horsepower
New technology
Labor saving devices
Economics
- Supply and demand

Bird eggs

Language Arts
Writing and discussion questions (every chapter)
Types of fiction
Headlines
Advertising slogans
Formula fiction
Monogram
Thematic stories
Famous sayings
Washington Irving
- "Rip Van Winkle"

Vocabulary Words
Homer
junction
tourist camp
bungalow
sensationalism
slogan
validate
chromium
horsepower
to coin
foot-pound
monogram
melodrama
disillusionment
suffrage
suburb
urban
rural
receptive
imperative
arbitrate
architect
landscape architect

Fine Arts
Cartooning
Melodrama
Design a sandwich board
Cooking
Illustrating movement
Collections
Art mediums
Making a checkerboard
James Abbott McNeill Whistler
- *Whistler's Mother*

Life Skills
Dealing with disillusionment
Discernment
Frugality
Special occasions
Making a good impression
Making people feel comfortable

The Saturdays

History
Adolf Hitler
Benjamin Franklin
Bifocals
Lucrezia Borgia
Modernization
Christopher Columbus
Circuses
Venice, Italy
1920's America
World War II

Geography
Paris, France
- Eiffel Tower
- Arc de Triomphe
- The Louvre
- Cathédrale Nortre-Dame de Paris
- Palace of Versailles

Venice, Italy

Science
Acid
Neutralization
Amber
Coatimundis
Camels
Snow
Rabies
Olfactory
Static electricity
Nutrition
Algae
Water pollution
Carbon monoxide saftey
Perspiration
Bird songs
Heat and absorption
Tide pools
Sea life

Language Arts
Writing and discussion questions (every chapter)
Narration
Description
Creative writing
- New words

Phone skills
Shakespeare's plays
Consistent characters
"The Song of Hiawatha"
Henry Wadsworth Longfellow

Vocabulary Words
grousing
truck
rubbers
sousing
lugubrious
plasticine
rafia
parcheesi
paltry
kiting
spasm
enigmatic
camphor
resilience
aura
dinghy
launch
albatross
spinster
cornucopia
expostulation
sarcastic
czarina
Apollo
Diana
hurdy-gurdy
alacrity
anvil
grotto
mail
aperture
subterranean

minotaur
labyrinth
rabies
snow crystal
deftly
plaited
incompatible
admonition
heroine
perilous
loathe
bob
Iago
consternation
dexterous
tempest
fervently
hub
perdition
apprehension
portal
baleful
scrutiny
howdah
campaign
adroitly
laboriously
teeming
vanquish
zeal
averted
wigwam
monopolizing
pauper
gondola
surreptitiously
declension
pongee
lapis lazuli
melancholy

Fine Arts

Music history
- Bach
- Tchaikovsky
- Sergei Prokofiev

Pen and ink drawing
Clay art
Art galleries
Cooking
- Petits fours

Orchestra
- Brass
- Woodwinds
- Percusion
- Strings

Peter and the Wolf
Yogurt Parfait

Life Skills

Humility
Conscience
Dealing with difficult people
Dealing with embarrassment

Inspired learning through great books.

Five in a Row is a complete,* well-rounded, literature-based curriculum that takes your child from pre-K through middle school.

For ages 2-4

Before Five in a Row is a rich treasury of creative ideas that help you gently, consistently prepare your children for the lifelong adventure of learning. Now in a revised second edition, this bestselling volume is the foundation for inspired learning through great books and future studies with the entire Five in a Row curriculum.

For ages 3-5

More Before Five in a Row inspires your child's learning through extraordinary children's picture books while nurturing your relationship with them and making memories to last a lifetime! Designed for ages 3 through 5, this preschool and kindergarten curriculum is filled with lessons for you and your child to enjoy together and prepare your child for the lifelong adventure of learning.

For ages 5-12

Five in a Row is an easy-to-follow, highly effective instructional guide for teaching Social Studies, Language Arts, Art, Applied Math and Science using outstanding children's literature as the basis for each weekly unit study. Lessons are designed for children ages 5 through 12, and include discussion guide and questions, teacher answers, hands-on activities and suggestions for further study. Visit www.fiveinarow.com to view suggested age ranges for each volume.

Volumes 7 and 8 Coming Soon!

Five in a Row Supplement (for Vols. 1-4)

The *Five in a Row Bible Supplement 2nd Edition*, provides hundreds of lessons in character development with accompanying Bible references. Each story has numerous lessons to choose from, all in an easy-to-use format.

Made in the USA
Middletown, DE
24 May 2022